FIGHTER COMMAND'S

SERGEANT ACES OF 1940

Ian Blair DFM
113, 501 & 602 Sqdn

Sgt Harold Bennett.
603 Sqdn 1941. Spit V
Hornchurch.

FIGHTER COMMAND'S

SERGEANT ACES
OF
1940

The Story of Six Airmen awarded the
Distinguished Flying Medal during
Britain's Finest Hour

RICHARD C. SMITH

Mitor Publications

Published by
Mitor Publications
20 Theydon Gardens,
Rainham,
Essex RM13 7TU

Copyright © Richard C. Smith 2007

ISBN 978-0-9557180-0-7

Smith, Richard C.
Fighter Command's Sergeant Aces of 1940
The story of six airmen awarded the Distinguished Flying Medal
during Britain's 'Finest Hour'

Typeset by Studio 3, London

Printed and bound in Great Britain by
The Cromwell Press, Trowbridge, Wiltshire

CONTENTS

Acknowledgements   vi

Introduction   viii

Chapter 1   Frederick 'Taffy' Higginson   1
Chapter 2   Peter Morfill   29
Chapter 3   Frederick Barker   47
Chapter 4   George 'Grumpy' Unwin   61
Chapter 5   William 'Gunner' Franklin   89
Chapter 6   Donald Kingaby   107

Appendices
A   Enemy Aircraft Claims of Frederick Higginson   131
B   Enemy Aircraft Claims of Peter Morfill   132
C   Enemy Aircraft Claims of Frederick Barker   133
D   Enemy Aircraft Claims of George Unwin   134
E   Enemy Aircraft Claims of William Franklin   135
F   Enemy Aircraft Claims of Donald Kingaby   136
G   Letter regarding the loss of 'Taffy' Higginson   138
H   Letter from Air Council regarding Higginson   140
I   Letter suspending payment of Service   141
J   Letter informing of Higginson's safety & French Railway ticket   142
K   Caterpiller Club Letter   143
L   William Franklin's Missing in Action Telegram   144
M   DFM's awarded in 1940   145

Bibliography   147

Index   - Personnel   149
       - General - Place Names   152
       - Aircraft   154
       - RAF Airfields, Camps & HQ's   155
       - Squadrons   155
       - Sectors & Flying Training Schools   156

ACKNOWLEDGEMENTS

Without the help and contributions from the people listed below, with personal memories, photographs, and memorabilia, this book would not have been possible. Sadly some of those listed have since passed on. I thank you all.

Mr Frederick Barker DFM
Wing Commander Eric Barwell, DFC
Squadron Leader Peter Brown, AFC
Mr Chris Butler
Mr Jim Davies
Lieutenant General Baron Michael Donnet, CVO, DFC, FR, AE, Retd
Flight Lieutenant William Green, RAF Retd
Mr Paul Higginson
Mr William Higginson
Mrs Shelley Hill
Flight Lieutenant Richard Jones
Mrs Helen Kingaby
Mrs Patricia Kingaby
The late Group Captain Brian Kingcome, DSO, DFC.
Mr Stan Kogel
Mrs Laura Kogel
Air Commodore George Mason, DFC, DFC (US), FBIM, RAF Retd
Mr John Milne
The late Squadron Leader Percy Morfill, DFM
Mr Geoff Nutkins, aviation artist
Squadron Leader Tony Pickering
Group Captain Herbert Pinfold, RAF retd
Mr Fred Roberts
Mr Mark Robinson
Mr Brian Unwin
The late George Unwin, DSO, DFM

Thanks go out also to the following people: Mr Ian Taylor, designer of the excellent book cover and photograph section. Mr Peter Quodt, for formatting design and PDFs, Mr Peter Holloway and all at Cromwell Press for printing production. Mr John Davies, of Grub Street Publications for use of extracts from 'Aces High.' To Tom Eaton & Yvonne Oliver at the Imperial War Museum Sound Archive, Lambeth, London and the National Archive at Kew,

London. Mr Ken Gibson & Peter Malyon of the RAF Hornchurch Association, Arthur Moreton of North Weald Airfield Museum. Special thanks go out to Colin and Rose Smith of Vector Fine Art for their total support and book-launch in this venture. To my wife Kim, who helped greatly in research and production and to my son Robert for his help. Final special big thank you goes to my Mother, Muriel for the financial support in getting this project to fruition

INTRODUCTION

This book tells the story of six airmen during the Second World War and their role during the intense air fighting period during the Battle for France, Dunkirk and the Battle of Britain. During this period they were sergeant pilots and became aces, because of their outstanding skills and courage in the skies against an enemy which had already gained combat experience a few years earlier during the Spanish Civil War. Later during the war, they all rose in rank. Some of them joined the Royal Air Force as a career during the 1920s and early 1930s, some when war against Hitler was inevitable.

After the end of the First World War, the Royal Air Force as it was now called, being the new service, was left with little in the way of expanding its role. When war ended in 1918, many of the young airmen and ground personnel returned to civilian life and the biplanes were destroyed or sold off to individuals who were still enthusiastic on flying as a new mode of transport and fun. By 1919/20, Air Chief Marshal Sir Hugh Trenchard, the leading light and head of the Royal Air Force, was putting forward plans that would expand the service. His policy was that if another war was to come, then air power would become a major player in the defence or attack against the enemy.

A White Paper proposing the expansion of the Royal Air Force was put through Parliament in 1922, which gave further funding for the service and plans were put underway to build new aerodromes and recruit new airmen. For the training of officers, the formation of a college at Cranwell in Lincolnshire had been founded. The building and surrounding grounds had been previously used as a Royal Navy Air Service base during the First War.

Its doors now opened to the mainly higher echelons of society from public schools, colleges and universities. It was here that officer cadets could be trained as future leaders of men. There was also the need to train ground personnel such as riggers, fitters, electricians. For this purpose, a school for apprentices was set up at Halton, near Wendover in Buckinghamshire.

Many young men during the late 1920s and early 1930s were now considering to join the Royal Air Force, which could offer them a chance to learn a skilled profession, and hopefully perhaps eventually the chance of flying and visiting countries abroad. It was to some a great adventure.

Those who became apprentices at RAF Halton, could rise through the ranks from aircraftsmen to the rank of sergeant as regular serviceman, with the chance of becoming a fully qualified pilot. Many of these men formed the backbone of the RAF during the mid thirties and saw service abroad in such places as Iraq, India, Afghanistan and Egypt, where political unrest was never too far away.

As peace in Europe was threatened by Germany's new policy of re-armament under Adolf Hitler, young men rallied the call and learned to fly with the Royal Auxiliary Air Force and the Royal Air Force Volunteer Reserve. The Royal Auxiliary Air Force was first established in 1924 and was solely formed for flying and pilot training. The squadrons were established and given the name of each county, they were based at, for example, No. 501 'County of Gloucester' Squadron. Potential recruits were drawn from their local districts and once accepted, training was carried out on weekends or weekday evenings, and an annual summer camp was undertaken with training alongside regulars from the RAF. Men from all professions and backgrounds who wished to learn to fly, but could not afford the expense, joined the auxiliaries.

The aim of the Royal Air Force Volunteer Reserve, which had been formed in 1937, was to provide and utilize the civil flying clubs and airfields around Britain to produce a reserve of trained pilots in case of war. Again training was mainly at weekends on Tiger Moth biplanes and the like.
It was at the mobilization of the service, when war seemed inevitable in 1938 that many more future airmen joined.

When the call to war did come in September 1939, the part-time flyers responded and were immediately given the rank of sergeant pilot. For those that had spent many years in the service attaining this rank, this seemed to be a slap in the face. However, when the fighting began this was soon put aside.

The class divide within Britain's society was always apparent, and within the Royal Air Force as with the other armed services, this was no different. The separation between the officers and the sergeant pilots was still retained even sometimes, when at their dispersal huts waiting to get into the action. The officers and sergeants each had their own Mess.

But even through this divide, the men were not separated when in combat with the enemy. Many of the squadron's most experienced pilots were in fact sergeants, who had hundreds of flying hours more experience than that of the new pilot officers. During the air campaigns of 1940, some of the experieneced sergeants would lead their flights or sections into battle against the Germans. To the young pilot officers and other sergeant pilots, they were a father figure, someone you could trust if things got 'sticky.'

It was during the Battle of Britain, that the role of the sergeant pilots would be most appreciated. It has always been a myth that the typical public view of those who fought in the Battle was that of dashing young officers with hair brylcreemed back and silk scarfs. It could not be further from the truth; the fact is that one third of those who participated were sergeant pilots.

During the course of 1940, many were to become aces, pilots like Gareth Nowell, who had fought in the Battle of France, 'Titch' Havercroft, possibly the shortest pilot in Fighter Command, Ernest Scott of 222 Natal Squadron who on the day of reaching ace status was listed as missing in action, and from Czechoslovakia continuing the fight against the Nazis, Sergeant Josef Frantisek, who sadly was killed in a landing accident in October 1940. Others became household names as their achievements become known, like James 'Ginger' Lacey' from Wetherby in Yorkshire.

Many would pay the ultimate price during the fighting and to those, this book is dedicated.

Richard C. Smith

August 2007

CHAPTER 1

FREDERICK 'TAFFY' HIGGINSON

Frederick William Higginson was born in Swansea on 17th February 1913. His father, Francis Higginson was born on 3rd October 1879 and his profession was that of police officer in South Glamorgan. His mother, Emily Jane Wyatt was born in June 1880 in West Harpgate Somerset. Soon after his birth the family moved to the village of Gorseinon in Carmarthenshire in south-west Wales. He would later recall one early memory of his father's role as local constable:

> One interesting thing I remember with regard to my father's job was that shortly after he moved from Swansea to Gorseinon, it became the habit there that he and the doctor used to more or less rule the village, in the sense that if the parents found that one of their children misbehaved themselves, then they called my father or the doctor. My father used to give them a clip round the ear, which we also received if we misbehaved ourselves and there was no problem from then on.

He was educated at the local school in Gorseinon, where he won a scholarship to the Gowerton County Intermediate School and at fifteen years was set to take his final examinations. He remembers how he was quite apprehensive about taking them:

> I was there until I was just about 15 years of age. When it came to the point when I knew I would have to take my Welsh matriculation, which was the Welsh examination of the time, I reckoned I would not have much chance of getting through and so I happened to see an advert in a paper for Royal Air Force Halton Apprentices. Unbeknown to the headmaster I applied to the Air Ministry and the examination papers were sent to the headmaster, and I was then given the opportunity of taking the test in 1928 and I passed and was accepted as a Halton Apprentice metal rigger.

He joined the Royal Air Force as an aircraft apprentice at Halton in January 1929; he then spent the next three years learning the skills of metal work and construction design. On completion of the course and passing the necessary exams; he qualified as a metal rigger in December 1931. He recalls:

> In those days one of the courses to take was the metal rigger course as opposed to a wood rigger course. Aeroplanes were beginning to be made out of metal at this time and it seemed the way ahead. I was there for three years and passed out as an Aircraftsman First Class. I was then posted to Worthy Down to

No. 7 Squadron in 1932, where they had Vickers Virginia
aircraft, these were two engine bombers and I became a fitter on
one of the aircraft and sat my Leading Aircraftsman Certificate
and obtained this. I also became the rear gunner on the
aeroplane which I was maintaining.

It was at Worthy Down that the young Higginson would sometimes see a
unique and popular character roaming around:

I remained here and played rugby for the local team, but I didn't
get into the air force team for a little while. I remember distinctly
an Aircraftsman named Shaw who was popular and had been
very active in Saudi Arabia. He used to keep his motorcycle at
Worthy Down and from time to time he used to appear and
when those like myself who knew who he really was, we would
always be on hand to wave him goodbye from the station. It was
Lawrence of Arabia of course. I saw him and stood near him,
but never met him. He was a mysterious sort of character. It was
some time before we knew who he really was. He looked like an
ordinary human being, but I didn't have the opportunity to
judge his pattern of behaviour or anything of that sort.
     I stayed there for about two years and I was posted back to
Halton to take a Fitter 1s course. This meant after I finished that
course, that I could then look after the engines as well as the
airframes. That was a year's course. One interesting thing about
that service was that the bombers we maintained were
presumably meant to bomb the cities in Europe. When the
annual exercise attempt at being at war was conducted, we used
to take off from Worthy Down and fly up the Channel and then
come back and land at Bircham Newton, near Oxford, because
we didn't have enough fuel to get across the Channel, bomb the
city and get back.

He then applied for pilot training and was accepted being sent to start
his first instruction at No. 4 Elementary & Reserve Flying Training
School at Brough on 6th August 1935, then on to FTS Sealand on 2nd
October. On completion of training on 30th June 1936, Higginson was given
his first posting and sent to join No. 19 Squadron at Duxford,
Cambridgeshire on 1st July 1936. The squadron at this time was equipped
with the Gloster Gauntlet biplane fighter. Higginson remembers this period
with the squadron:

There I had some very good instructors including, Bing Cross.
After I'd been at Duxford for possibly a year or less, I was doing
forced landing exercises. Harry Broadhurst was in charge of the
flight and I was practising a forced landing and I was being
watched by a number of people. I failed to notice that there was
sheep grazing in the field, I was coming in low and landing
without an engine, the sheep were getting nearer and nearer to

the edge of the airfield and needless to say at the last attempted forced landing I made, I struck the sheep and everyone had sheep for supper.

It was while on leave that year that Frederick Higginson met the woman he would marry. Her name was Shan Jenkins and she was employed working in a shop at Gorseinon. Born on 6th April 1912, she came from a village named Betws in east Carmarthen about twenty miles from Swansea. They began courting and a year later they were married at her local church

On 20th July, C 'Flight' of No. 19 Squadron left to form the main body of No. 66 Squadron, also based at Duxford, and with it went Frederick Higginson. During his time with 66 Squadron, he undertook anti-aircraft co-operation flights operating from Biggin Hill and Bircham Newton between April to September 1937. What was the role of the squadron? Higginson explains:

> Our purpose was to tow a drogue over the firing ranges on the east coast at Sutton Bridge. The aircraft would come in and fire at the drogue. We then moved down to Boscombe Down, where the unit folded up and I was posted from there to 56 Squadron at North Weald on 20th October 1937.

North Weald aerodrome in the heart of Essex had been established during the First World War as an airfield to combat the threat from the German Zeppelin raids in 1916. It was now part of Fighter Command and its squadrons had been given the new Gloster Gladiator biplane fighter aircraft. He relates his first impression of the aerodrome:

> North Weald had no runways at that time and it had one characteristic which no one liked, on the east side of the aerodrome it had some large pylons, certainly a big obstruction. When you took off you had to make sure that you got to one hundred feet before you reached these obstructions. I was now flying fighters, the latest RAF biplane the Gloster Gladiator. It was a very nice aircraft to fly and it didn't have any vices as far as I can remember. We had a flight commander called Horne and the commanding officer was a chap called Leacocks, who was a Great War pilot. They were both very friendly people and one thing I remember was that No. 56 had an outstanding record in the Great War. I think they had two VC's, McCudden and Albert Ball and in both cases Squadron Leader Leacocks set up a sort of museum in one of the hangars with McCudden or Ball's uniform in a case and the history of the squadron.
>
> When you joined 56 Squadron the first thing they did was to put you into this room to read the history of the squadron and take note of Ball and McCudden and the pilots that fought in the Great War. This helped to create an esprit de corps and although I was only a sergeant pilot, once in the air you were treated as to your ability as a pilot, regardless of whether you

were an officer or an NCO. It was really a very enjoyable period of my service life.

On June 10th 1938, Higginson undertook his first flight in the squadron's new Hawker Hurricane aircraft that had arrived, replacing their old Gloster Gladiator biplanes. His first flight was in L1590 in which he flew for thirty minutes. Fortunately for him and other Hurricane pilots, the arrival of the new aircraft came at just the right time, for three months later, the threat of war loomed again and would become a reality in September 1939. This extra time gave the pilots the opportunity to gain valuable flying hours to get to know the aircraft's performance and vices. Higginson remembers his first flight and also another story from his time at North Weald during this period:

> In 1938, we were re-equipped with the Hawker Hurricane. On 10th June I undertook my first Hurricane flight and my log book shows and certifies that I understood the petrol and coolant systems on a Hurricane I aircraft. I was then authorised to fly the aircraft. By that time I had done 471 single engine hours flying. We were very impressed with the Hurricane, it was a nice aeroplane to fly and its performance was very much better than the Gladiator. It had eight guns and we were very impressed with it indeed.
>
> Another interesting thing I remember was I had a motorcar and later on it became the squadron car. It was an Opel which had been imported from Germany and it landed up on the docks at Southampton. I heard that if one had a small amount of money one could buy one of these much cheaper than a British car, so this is exactly what I did I went down to the docks and for a £100 I got an Opel.
>
> Later on during the Battle of Britain at the end of the day's flying, we quite often used to pile into this car and drive up to the West End of London, spend an evening in a night club and come back for readiness the next day. The other thing I remember about the motorcar was that we had to fit certain devices on the headlights, so instead of them being allowed to show their beam for a long way, they were restricted in distance lighting up objects, so in other words what we found was that when we were travelling long distances by car, we used to get behind a lorry which usually had better lights than we did and stay at the back and follow him.

The Higginson family expanded to three, when his wife Shan gave birth to their first child, a son Paul on 25th September 1938. His birth came on the very day that Prime Minister Neville Chamberlain returned to Croydon by aeroplane from Germany with a slip of paper in his hand, declaring 'peace in our time.' Higginson remembers:

> At the time of the Munich Crisis in autumn 1938, almost every flying trip that I did was concerned with exercises of one sort or

another, formation flying, target for camera gun, reconnaissance, night flying and battle flight climb, air firing ranges. All the flying was concerned with was the probability that a war would arise despite what had taken place at Munich. I felt that war was coming and I had already made arrangements for the family to come back to Wales in the event of hostilities breaking out, or going up to my parents who had retired to Newark in Nottinghamshire.

The threat of war seemed to have been averted in Europe for the time being, but the Royal Air Force continued with its defence exercises throughout the remainder of 1938 and into 1939. The squadron undertook various drills including practice squadron attacks, practice interceptions and air to ground firing. This became the norm until August 1939, when they were put onto a war footing as things began to look bleak once more with Adolf Hitler's increasing desire to expand the Third Reich. On 1st September, German troops crossed over the border and invaded Poland. Immediately France and Great Britain sent envoys to Hitler giving him an ultimatum, asking him to withdraw his armies at once, or risk war with both nations. This was totally rejected and on 3rd September 1939, Britain and France declared war against Germany. For the second time within a space of twenty years, the young men and women of Britain were involved in conflict. Frederick Higginson recalls the day that would change the British way of life for the next six years:

> On the day that war was declared, we carried out camera gun exercises, home defence and air to ground weapon firing. I didn't know anything about the German Air Force and felt quite confident that I could cope with what I thought they might be like. I had no idea, what their tactics were going to be. On 4th September 1939, we undertook our first war operation at 02.50 hours in the morning.

During the next two days, the squadrons at North Weald stood at readiness with their pilots and aircraft dispersed around the aerodrome awaiting orders.

North Weald squadrons were again brought to readiness on the morning of 6th September and during early morning No. 56 Squadron was brought to alert as British Radar picked up an unidentified aircraft plot nearing the east coast of Essex from the North Sea at 6.45 am. The squadron was scrambled and given orders to search and intercept the unknown raider. On the ground radar communications became confused to such a degree that other fighter squadrons were also scrambled. In this confusion, RAF fighters now became unidentified targets as well. Tragedy was to strike, when Spitfires of No. 74 Squadron based at Hornchurch mistook the Hurricanes of B Flight 56 Squadron as enemy aircraft. As a result, two of the Spitfires attacked and shot two of the Hurricane aircraft down, killing nineteen year old Pilot Officer Hulton-Harrop and causing Pilot Officer Thomas Rose to force-land his aircraft wheels-up. As news spread around the aerodrome at North Weald of the terrible circumstances, the two Spitfire pilots involved were placed under open arrest to await an enquiry and possible court-martial.

Hulton-Harrop was laid to rest at St. Andrews church cemetery, Fighter Command's first casualty of the war. This episode has gone down in the annuals of history as 'The Battle of Barking Creek.' Today this would be known as a friendly-fire incident. Both Spitfire pilots were later acquitted and returned to operations.

As Britain waited in anticipation of Hitler's next move, the war entered a phase known as the 'Phoney War.' The RAF fighter squadrons had little to do at this time and carried out in the main, patrols protecting shipping convoys in the English Channel and over the North Sea. This continued well into early 1940 as 'Taffy' Higginson well remembers:

> In January 1940, we were patrolling shipping convoys off the east coast. One interesting thing about the convoy patrols, of which we did very many indeed, was we were invited with a number of other pilots to a convoy patrol briefing, which if I remember rightly took place somewhere in the Thames estuary. The person in charge of the convoy and of the briefing, introduced us to all the skippers of all the ships as being the pilots that would protect them, during their convoy up the east coast. One of the skippers said, he wanted to ask a question and the question was how big is your aeroplane, and how can I distinguish it from a German aircraft. This was an impossible question to answer, but I said, 'you take your box of matches and then if you see the aircraft exceeding the size of a box of matches, then you can assume that it will be a German aircraft.' The answer I got was 'look here pilot if you come anywhere near me, we will bloody well shoot you down'. That was not what they did in practice. Convoy patrolling went on into February, March and April.
>
> This was about the time that activities in Europe were beginning to hot up, and we were sent down to Gravesend aerodrome to operate from and patrol Ostend and Zebrugge, then Blankenburg, Flushing. From Gravesend and Martlesham Heath, we escorted bomber aircraft doing reconnaissance over western Holland. But we made no contact with German aircraft.

The German armies began their advance into Belgium, France and the Low Countries on 10th May 1940. Sweeping through and pushing all Allied opposition aside.

At North Weald orders had arrived that B Flight of 56 Squadron was to go to France. Immediately the pilots and groundcrew prepared the equipment and checked the aircraft thoroughly. Six Hurricanes took off that afternoon and headed first for Manston, their Pilots Flight Lieutenant Ian Soden, Flying Officers' Peter Down and Thomas Rose, Pilot Officer Barry Sutton, Flight Sergeant 'Taffy' Higginson and Sergeant Kim Whitehead. The groundcrew personnel would arrive later, being ferried over to France by Dragon Rapide aircraft.

Their destination in France was to be a grass airfield just outside the village of Vitry en Artois near the town of Douai. Here 56 Squadron B Flight would share the airfield with other detachments from No. 111, 229, 253 and 607 Squadrons

On 17th May the squadron detachment readied themselves for their first day operating from Vitry, Higginson was on the first patrol of the day detailed to patrol east of Brussels. During this patrol the three aircraft of B Flight sighted a German Henschel He.126 reconnaissance aircraft. The aircraft was attacked, but they failed to bring it down. The Hurricanes returned to base without success. He now recalls his first contact with the enemy:

> We did our first patrol east of Brussels. I attacked an Hs126, very much like the Westland Lysander, but very much more mobile. I couldn't understand why I couldn't shoot this thing down, there were no fighters defending it, I was on my own with it and as soon as I got in to fire at it, it had turned around and came facing towards me. It's manoeuvrability and its ability to fly at slow speeds was fantastic. This was my first attack on a German aircraft, which proved unsuccessful.

Higginson later that morning was relaxing at the dispersal at approximately 10.00 am, when suddenly he sighted a flight of three enemy aircraft in the distance south-east towards Douai. He immediately raced for his Hurricane (N2440) and took-off. He reported later:

> I took to the air and climbed underneath five enemy aircraft. Two of them then turned in and fired several bursts at me from the beam at about 150 yards range without hitting me. I was able to slip underneath one and got on his tail. I fired one burst of about 10 seconds from dead astern at 400 yards, closing to 150 yards. The enemy aircraft lurched and started diving downwards with black smoke pouring from its engines. I did not see it hit the ground because at 600 feet, I was attacked by the other enemy aircraft. I broke off the attack and subsequently Pilot Officer Down who had also taken off, but not engaged any aircraft, told me he saw it crash into a field.

The aircraft was later confirmed as a Dornier Do17, not a Dornier 215 as written in Higginson's log-book, which he had attacked at an altitude of 3,000 feet.

Later that day B Flight was again in action. During an offensive patrol east of Cambrai, they encountered a formation of seven Heinkel 111s. Higginson latched on to one of the enemy bombers and set it alight and saw it dive down and crash in a wood.

The following day, 18th May, he was again in the thick of the action. Ordered to conduct an early morning patrol over the airfield at 6.40 am, Higginson accompanied by Flight Lieutenant Soden were airborne and at just six miles south-east of Vitry, they sighted an enemy aircraft heading west from Douai. Higginson was unable to make contact with the enemy, but Flight Lieutenant Soden did. He managed to get on to the tail of the Dornier at a range of about 200 yards at a height of only 600 feet and fired a short burst into it. Higginson reported seeing the Dornier crash into a field and this was later confirmed.

Returning to base, the two pilots reported the news to the squadron intelligence officer Pilot Officer Eric Syson. At around 11.00 am Higginson, Soden and Sergeant Whitehead of B Flight were ordered aloft accompanied by three aircraft of No. 229 Squadron to patrol an area east of Brussels at 10,000 feet. Higginson recalled:

> When we had been on patrol for about ten minutes, I saw about 12 enemy aircraft (Messerschmitt Bf 109s) appear above a patch of cloud. I told Soden by radio and we turned in formation to engage. As we did so, two more large formations of enemy aircraft appeared out of cloud. We were caught in a circle of German aircraft which flew all around us, but did not fire. I saw Soden attack one German who was a little out of formation and it started burning. I turned over and headed downwards. I did not see it hit the ground and Flight Lieutenant Soden told me he did not see the enemy aircraft crash, but was certain it must have. I did not engage, but Soden was hit several times by enemy bullets.

Flight Lieutenant Soden failed to return and was last seen attacking the German fighters. He was listed as missing later that day. Soden was later awarded the Distinguished Service Order posthumously and was mentioned in the Daily Mirror newspaper under the news heading of '*RAF Pilot takes on sixty single handed.*'

The 19th May dawned with B Flight ordered on an offensive patrol, but no enemy activity was observed. On the second sortie of the day the squadron was given the task of escorting bombers, but the Hurricanes were attacked while taking off by fifteen Messerschmitt 109s who flew in at tree top height, strafing the airfield as they went. Unfortunately one pilot was killed, Flying Officer Tommy Rose and Pilot Officer Frank Sutton was wounded, shot through the foot. Things were about to get far worse however, when Higginson and his section who was observing the chaos on the airfield from above, were attacked by twelve Messerschmitt Me110s fighter/bombers. Combat ensued and four of the 110s were shot down, Higginson claiming one of the enemy aircraft.

The airfield had been severely bombed and nine squadron aircraft were destroyed on the ground. The airfield was a complete shambles and the squadron was ordered to evacuate Vitry and move to Norrant Fontes. Higginson remembers the total confusion and chaos during this period of the French campaign:

> The whole external organisation there was hopeless; we had no radar, very little communication with whoever was controlling us. The only messages we got were by telephone, when it was working.
>
> We then had to evacuate to Norrent Fontes. Again there was no organisation to tell us where or when to go. When we got to

Norrent Fontes, I landed and as soon as I got out of my aeroplane, the CO whoever he was, said 'You have got to go back in my car with my driver to Vitry and destroy any aircraft that are serviceable there and any petrol supplies left there.' In those days, petrol was sent to us at Vitry in five gallon drums, they were square drums and they were hidden on one side of the aerodrome. The driver and I went back and on the way there had to drive on the pavement some of the way, because the roads were packed with people and motorcars. It was one of the strangest journeys I have ever taken.

When we got back to the aerodrome, I had my revolver with me and I tried to set two aircraft on fire by firing into the petrol tanks and letting the petrol drip down onto the ground. Then lighting a match and throwing it into the petrol I retired as quickly as I could. In neither case was I successful. We then went to the petrol dump to set that on fire by the same sort of method and that went up in flames. I decided then, as far as I could judge from the noise of the gun firing that the Germans were on the other side of the aerodrome. I wasn't going to take any more chances and I told the driver to return as quickly as he could.

As we were about to fly out from Vitry to Norrent Fontes, Flight Sergeant Spreadborough who was in charge of the maintenance section of B Flight, asked me what he should do, I said 'for God's sake get hold of a bus or any means of transport you can and push off back to the west, go as far as you can to the coast.' It was unbelievable the lack of organisation, it was no wonder we got pushed out of France. When we drove back to Norrent Fontes, I was flying N for Nuts, that was my aircraft N2440. I told my driver where it was and I went across to it and just as I got to it, there was somebody with a parachute on about to climb into the aircraft. I rushed up, got hold of him and said 'where do you think you are going,' he said 'back to England.' I said 'not in my bloody aeroplane,' and I pulled him off and got into the Hurricane and took off and flew back to North Weald.

He arrived back at North Weald one hour and thirty minutes later having that day flown for seven hours and forty minutes. The squadron ground personnel back over in France destroyed whatever equipment they could, in order it did not fall into German hands. They then made their way by truck to the Port of Boulogne and managed to find passage on a ferry steamer on 21st May.

The German advance was breathtaking and their use of Blitzkrieg could not be halted. The French, Belgium and British forces were in mass retreat, heading back towards the coast between Ostend and Dunkirk for possible evacuation.

Arriving back in Britain, 56 Squadron were sent to RAF Digby for a brief rest period, to replenish aircraft lost and new aircrew. Arriving on the squadron as replacement pilots were Pilot Officer Geoffrey Page and Flying Officers Innes Westmacott and Percy Weaver from Chippenham, Wiltshire.

In France, the situation had worsened to such an extent that by the 23rd May plans were put into effect by the British Government and three armed services to evacuate as many troops of the British Expeditionary Force from the port of Dunkirk and surrounding beaches, where a defensive pocket had been established. The Royal Navy under the command of Vice-Admiral Bertram Ramsey now prepared to send as many ships and light craft across the Channel to rescue the troops. The Royal Air Force's role was to provide air cover over the beaches and protect the ships from the Luftwaffe bombers.

The squadron having returned to their home base at North Weald, were now given new orders, as were many of the fighter squadrons located in the south-east of England, to patrol over Dunkirk and protect the evacuation from the beaches.

No. 56 Squadron's aircraft would fly down at first light to operate out of Manston airfield in Kent. During the next few days, they flew patrols covering the area between St Omer, Dunkirk and Calais. 'Taffy' Higginson remembers this time after such a hectic period.

> We then had a few days off flying and my next flight was in a new aeroplane a Hurricane MkII. My next offensive patrol was not until the 23rd May 1940, to Calais and surrounding areas. Then we operated from Manston to St. Omer and Calais. We carried out offensive patrols over Dunkirk sweeping over the St. Omer area and around Dunkirk.

It was not until 27th May, that the squadron claimed a Heinkel 111 destroyed by Squadron Leader E.V. Knowles and two other Heinkels probably destroyed, which were shared by Sergeant R.D. Baker, Flight Lieutenant J.H. Coghlan, Pilot Officer L. Ereminsky and Flying Officer Fisher. In return, Pilot Officer Michael Constable-Maxwell had to force land his aircraft after being hit by Belgian ground fire. He was uninjured and managed to get aboard a ship at Ostend, Flight Lieutenant R.H. 'Dickee' Lee was shot down and forced to ditch into the sea, being rescued one hour later and brought back across the Channel.

The squadron resumed patrols again on the 28th, but with no successes. Again on 29th, the squadron was in action with Sergeant George Smythe claiming a Junkers Ju87 destroyed during an afternoon patrol when 56 and 151 Squadron became airborne from Manston at approximately 2.00 pm. During this patrol 56 Squadron had sighted Messerschmitt 110s flying towards Dunkirk. The Hurricanes made a head-on pass and became embroiled with the enemy. During the engagement Sergeant Smythe sighted Junkers Ju87 Stuka aircraft below attacking naval vessels; he attacked and shot one down into the sea. Sadly the squadron lost two pilots during the encounter, Pilot Officer K.C. Dryden, who crash-landed his aircraft on the beach and later returned safely by ship.

Sergeant Jim Elliot, Higginson's brother-in-law, failed to return in Hurricane L1972. This was a terrible blow to the family and to Higginson personally, who had a good friendship with Elliot. As he recalls:

One unfortunate episode I remember was one of the other pilots in 56 Squadron was my brother-in-law, Jim Elliot, he had met my wife's sister and they had married about six months before this period. They were expecting their first child and he was on patrol with me when I saw him shot down and killed over Dunkirk.

It was not until the early evening of 28th that the enemy was engaged again. At 6.30 pm Higginson and his fellow pilots took off from Manston to patrol at 9,000 feet over Dunkirk. A few minutes later after reaching the beach-head, he sighted twelve enemy aircraft, Messerschmitt 109s. His report states:

> I sighted a broken Vic formation of enemy aircraft over Dunkirk wheeling round to engage our formation. I picked one out and put in a deflection shot and continued firing until I was dead astern. He began to draw away, but suddenly stopped and I overtook him very quickly and he fell in an uncontrollable spin with smoke pouring from him. I saw him fall down striking the ground in flames north of Dunkirk (Note) Enemy aircraft was a lighter colour than others encountered.

During this combat Pilot Officer Leonid Ereminsky claimed a 109 destroyed and Flight Lieutenant John Coghlan put in a claim for two Junkers Ju88s probable destroyed. Sergeant Ronald Baker also claimed a Heinkel He111 as a probable. Higginson's memories of the Dunkirk evacuation and the air fighting, recall the massive undertaking:

> Dunkirk was an extraordinary operation, people leaving by any means available, small boats and big ships. On some occasions there were no aircraft in the sky and other cases the sky seemed as if it was full of aeroplanes. When patrolling Dunkirk, what we did was to fly over to the beach, we did a few circuits around and either got into combat with the enemy or met nothing. At this time the Germans were advancing down through France and to some extent it was far more important for them than the evacuation of Dunkirk. A lot of their aircraft were moving with the front line down to the Somme towards Abbeville and other areas. The RAF had a limited number of aircraft in Britain and the war was still going on in France and my logbook shows later on that we were doing offensive sweeps to Amiens and Rouen, escorting bombers in May and June and there weren't enough aircraft to give them complete protection. I think they did jolly well when you consider that they had as far as I could see, little or no other means of defence and they could put up very little resistance.

For the next ten days from 2nd June, Higginson and 56 Squadron carried out offensive patrols over Amiens and along the French coast to Dieppe and Le Havre including escort to bombers.

After Dunkirk we did offensive patrols over near Amiens. We were at this time operating as a wing with 151 Squadron also at North Weald. No. 151 was commanded by Squadron Leader Teddy Donaldson. He had been leading the wing and we operated with him. In my opinion this was a big mistake because it was alright for those in front, but 'arse end charlies' like myself always got attacked first of all. The best formation which I was keen on was in pairs, then the squadron would have six pairs and the pairs could go off to attack a target, or whatever we met. There was very little air defence activity, mainly offensive operations with bombers around this period and convoy patrols.

On 18th June they undertook escort duty to Cherbourg operating from Tangmere aerodrome before returning back to North Weald. From this period in mid June until 14th July, his log-book shows that he was involved in air-practice flights, testing and some convoy patrols, operating out of Manston, Rochford and Martlesham Heath. The squadron did engage the enemy on 10th July, the official recorded start of the Battle of Britain, when the squadron was ordered to defend a merchant convoy off Dover. A force of fifty plus enemy bombers escorted by 110s and 109s were picked up by radar at 1.30 pm and the squadron was vectored to intercept. During the combat the squadron claimed two aircraft destroyed and several damaged with no loss to themselves.

The German tactics during Phase 1 of the Battle of Britain continued with the bombing of shipping convoys and port installations and military targets during most of July. Higginson added another German aircraft to his score on 15th July, when patrolling over a convoy 10 miles east of Harwich at 2.15 pm at 4,000 feet. As part of Blue Section, they sighted a formation of between nine to twelve Dorniers heading towards the ships. His combat report states:

I was flying No. 3 and suddenly saw the enemy aircraft dive out of clouds to bomb the convoy. I broke formation and fired a preliminary burst from the beam, to try to distract the enemy aircraft attention from the bombing. Most of the enemy broke away except for two or three, the leader of which dropped a bomb directly on a big ship which burst into flames. Two enemy aircraft then broke away to the right in line astern. I got on the tail of the last one. I opened fire at first at about 300 yards with a quarter attack, which must have put his gunner out of action. The enemy aircraft then adopted echelon right formation to give the other German aircraft's gunner a chance to get me. I closed into range again and opened fire at 300 yards from astern. Both enemy aircraft then dived to sea level and I closed in to about 75 to 100 yards, firing continuously. The enemy aircraft then lurched and dived straight into the sea. I was fired at by the rear gunners of both enemy machines, but not hit. Visibility was very bad, with rain and clouds. The rest of the enemy jettisoned their bombs and turned eastwards. I saw no fighter escort.

On return to base, Higginson learned that Flight Lieutenant Gracie had also claimed a Dornier as probably destroyed. Having been operational and in action for nearly three months, Higginson was sent on leave from 15th to 23rd July, for a much needed rest. On his return he received a communiqué announcing his award of the Distinguished Flying Medal for five victories, making him an ace.

The notice of the award printed in the London Gazette of 30th July 1940 read:

> This airman has been right through the operations with No. 56 Squadron and has continually led No.4 Section. He has definitely destroyed five enemy aircraft and had combats with many more, some of which have more than likely been shot down. His cool and courageous leadership has been an example to his squadron and his section throughout. He has shown the greatest determination in the face of the enemy.

Remarks by Air Officer Commanding:

> This N.C.O. pilot has led his section during all operations in No. 56 Squadron. He has destroyed five enemy aircraft and it is probable that he has accounted for others. His cool and courageous leadership in the face of the enemy give me this opportunity of strongly recommending him for immediate award of the Distinguished Flying Medal.

Higginson's next claim came on 12th August, when the squadron encountered an incoming raid at 6.30 pm, ten miles north of Margate. The enemy force consisted of around thirty Dorniers at 15,000 feet with a large fighter escort above at 20,000:

> I was flying as Green 1 and flew on a parallel course with the bombers and attacked from the side, out of the sun. I put my section into line astern and as I came up on the quarter, I put them into echelon right. I opened fire on the extreme left enemy aircraft using short bursts against each engine. I started firing at 300 yards and finished at 150 yards. As I broke away I saw the enemy formation begin turning to the right and black smoke coming from the aircraft I had attacked from the port engine.
>
> This was seen by Pilot Officer Sutton (Green 3). My aircraft was damaged by bullets in windscreen, main-planes, hood and side panel. I noticed that the Dorniers had big yellow roundels on the fuselage, similar in size and position to those of our own aircraft. I could not see what markings were inside the roundels. The Dornier 17 was reported later as damaged and confirmed by Pilot Officer Charles Joubert.

That day the squadron suffered casualties as the Luftwaffe launched its planned attack against the RAF, code-named Adler Tag (Eagle Day). One of

56's casualties was young twenty year old Geoffrey Page, who was shot down in flames, when his Hurricane was hit with a bullet through the petrol tank, which immediately set the aircraft alight. In the process of trying to get out, Page was severely burned, but managed to get out and fortunately his parachute opened. He landed in the sea off Ramsgate and was rescued by boat. He was to spend the next two years undergoing plastic surgery at the pioneering Victoria Hospital at East Grinstead and became a founding member of the Guinea Pig Club for burned servicemen. He eventually returned to flying operations in 1943.

During the early morning of 16th August, Higginson and B Flight flew down to Rochford airfield at 5.15 am and carried out a convoy patrol, which proved to be uneventful. During the second patrol at noon however, one section was attacked by Messerschmitt 109s and one aircraft flown by Pilot Officer L.W. Graham was shot down. Graham fortunately baled out and was only slightly injured. The squadron returned to North Weald and were given instructions at 4.51 pm to patrol over Chatham on their third patrol of the day, this time 56 Squadron had better luck.

At approximately 5.30 pm they encountered a large force of enemy fighters and bombers at 14,000 feet and attacked the formation. Higginson flying Hurricane P3549 coded US-A remembers:

> I was Green 1 in the squadron formation. I was told to take my section and attack the fighters. My section climbed, but we were getting left behind. I then saw a Dornier 17 break away from the formation. I closed in behind to about 300 yards and gave it a burst of about two seconds. He then dived through the clouds and I followed him down and attacked from the quarter. I made another attack from astern and observed the enemy aircraft burning in the fuselage behind the main-plane. I gave a final burst of fire and the aircraft crashed on the beach near Whitstable and burst into flames. I took cine pictures of him blazing to complete my film; just at that moment my aircraft burst into flames and I made an emergency landing south of Whitstable. I was picked up by the London Irish Rifles, who witnessed the attack and confirmed my enemy aircraft crashing and bursting into flames. I must have been hit in the engine, though I did not observe the return fire from the German aircraft. Unfortunately my gun camera film was destroyed.

Over fifty years later, he was able to give more fascinating information regarding this combat:

> On 16th August we engaged a large force of fighters and bombers; I shot down one Dornier in flames over Whitstable Bay. What happened was that I attacked this one from the side and I was firing at it and coming up towards it, and suddenly the area beneath the wing started to glow like a cigar, obviously it had caught fire. It then crashed on the beach at Whitstable. It

so happened that I had one of the very few gun cameras fitted to my aircraft at that time and I thought I would make use of the rest of the film. I went diving down onto this aircraft which was burning and photographed it, when suddenly my own aircraft burst into flames and what had happened was that he had put an incendiary, delayed action bullet into my aircraft. I had to land virtually alongside the burning aircraft on the ground and as I crash landed I broke my nose on the gun-site.

I had a job getting out of the airplane because in trying to get out in a hurry, I had forgotten the fact that my oxygen mask tubes had wound round the back of my body and was still bayonet locked into the aircraft; so as I got out of the aircraft with this pipe still attached I thought the aircraft was going to blow up with me inside it. Suddenly something gave, the tube disengaged itself and I did a backward somersault into a pile of cow dung on the beach. I picked myself up and ran away from the aircraft, and was picked up by the London Irish Rifles; they picked up bits of the Dornier and sent them to me later to keep as a memento. I had a broken nose, but no other injuries apart from bruising. I was back on duty two days later.

Higginson's aircraft had been the only casualty from the engagement, In return 56 Squadron had claimed two Dorniers destroyed, one probable and a further three damaged along with three Me109s claimed as probably destroyed. Quite a satisfactory outcome!

The following morning having been allocated another aircraft Hurricane P3473, Higginson along with the rest of the pilots awaited their call to readiness at North Weald and settled down at dispersal to prepare for whatever the days events would unfold.

At 12.50 pm they received the call to scramble and patrol the line at Canterbury. After patrolling for nearly an hour while flying at 20,000 feet near Ashford, they sighted five Messerschmitt Me110s heading in from the south. The Germans realising they were about to be attacked by the RAF Fighters formed a defensive circle, but this would prove unsuccessful and all five of the enemy were shot down. Higginson did not claim during this combat, but his log-book states that:

Saw Flight shoot five Me110s down in flames. 'Five out of Five'

Later that afternoon, they were ordered to fly down to Rochford and from there to patrol over Manston. At 5.30 pm they received information of a large incoming raid flying north of the Thames Estuary comprising of Heinkel and Dornier bombers with fighter escort, nearly one hundred aircraft in all. The Germans were heading towards their target, 56 Squadron's home base at North Weald. To engage the enemy from the advantage of height the squadron had to in effect pass the enemy formation, turn while climbing and then chase back after the bombers. Higginson leading Green Section went into the attack west of Burnham-on-Crouch and engaged some Dorniers:

> We encountered a large formation of enemy bombers escorted by fighters. I climbed to attack the fighters, but I did not think I should be successful against such odds. I noticed that the leading sections of the squadron were still flying west. I then delivered an attack on a rear section of a large formation of Dorniers. I opened fire at 300 closing to 150 yards and then broke away as I was being attacked by an enemy fighter. I successfully evaded the fighter and saw the bomber which I had attacked fall behind the formation, smoking badly. It dived down and crashed near Burnham-on-Crouch and this was witnessed by Pilot Officer Down and Sergeant Whitehead, who saw him smoking badly and apparently on fire. My aircraft had a few holes in the fuselage after I landed from the engagement and being conscious of the fact that my aircraft had been damaged, I taxied carefully into the dispersal area and as I pulled the stick back, I noticed that it stayed back instead of going forward which it usually did. What had happened was the starboard elevator controls had been badly wrecked and the force of me pulling them back had broken the wire. That was a lucky escape.
>
> Just before my engagement, I saw an enemy machine burst into flames and crash, this must have been the aircraft shot down by Flight Lieutenant Gracie (Blue 1)

The engagement against the raiders had been successful and the Germans did not reach their target, although the weather did play a part in causing them to withdraw, owing to a large build up of cloud cover.

On 26th August at 3.25 pm, flying at 20,000 feet near Colchester, 56 Squadron sighted a formation of twenty enemy bombers with an escort of fifty mixed fighters heading towards North Weald. At 15,000 feet, Higginson with his section broke away after the fighters, climbing and turning as they went to get the sun behind them. He put the section into line astern and saw a formation of ten Messerschmitt 110s form a defensive circle. Going in underneath the German formation, he approached at about 2,000 feet beneath and singled out a 110 and opened fire at 350 yards with a five second burst, closing in to 200 yards. As he broke away from the attack, he noticed black oily smoke belching from the German's port engine and saw it making off towards the east coast. His own aircraft on the starboard side was coated with oil from the enemy machine. By this time the German aircraft was too far away for him to catch, as was all the others. Higginson remained on patrol over North Weald until he was instructed to land. The Messerschmitt 110 was listed as a probable. So what tactics did 'Taffy' Higginson employ when attacking the German bombers?

> The best way to attack a German aircraft (Dornier or Heinkel) was to attack from underneath and climb up opening fire. I preferred to attack from underneath as this limited the ability of the air gunners to defend.
>
> Time and time again we were outnumbered, but it wasn't a question of numbers, so much as they were pursuing their

course, wherever their target was. We attacked them from behind or the side. Quite often we were late in being told to take off or they were too high for us. It wasn't as one imagines, that once you take off, you are put into an ideal position to attack.

At 12.28 pm on the afternoon of 28th August, the pilots at dispersal jumped from their Lloyd Loom chairs and rushed to their aircraft as the scramble bell rang out across the aerodrome. Once airborne, within minutes they received their orders to patrol Rochford airfield near Southend, which during the morning had already been bombed. Now another enemy plot had been picked up by the radar stations; confirming that another enemy raid was also likely to be heading for the airfield. The Germans were sighted at 16,000 feet and engaged. Higginson's combat report states the following action:

> We sighted the enemy aircraft east of us. I broke away and climbed up to the fighters, putting my section into line astern. The enemy fighters crossed over the top of the bombers and dived in open line astern to attack Yellow and Blue Sections, which were going for the bombers. I dived on to the leading enemy fighter and gave him a beam attack using deflection. From 200 yards I gave him a burst of fire for three to four seconds. He straightened out and turned to the right and I opened fire with a quarter attack; giving a burst of six to seven seconds at 200 yards. Pieces fell off the German machine and smoke came from his starboard main-plane and he began to spin down. I pulled out of my dive and saw a big splash in the water.
>
> Hornchurch say that a Spitfire reports seeing a Me109 shot down by a Hurricane at the same time and place. I understand an anti-aircraft battery also report seeing a Me109 go down, the pilot baling out, but his parachute failed to open. The Me109s had orange wing tabs and noses.

The action had taken place off the coast between Whitstable and Herne Bay. No. 56 suffered one aircraft destroyed, that of Pilot Officer Constable-Maxwell who force–landed near Herne Bay and three damaged, those of Sergeants Whitehead and Robinson and Flight Lieutenant Weaver. In return they had claimed three destroyed, four probably destroyed and one damaged.

The squadron continued with interceptions again over the next two days, Higginson's log-book recorded that on 30th August, they intercepted a large raid dropping bombs on the town of Luton and that 56 Squadron claimed five enemy aircraft shot down and that his own aircraft V7532 was shot up.

Early morning of 31st August, radar picked up a mass German raid heading towards North Weald. The squadrons were scrambled immediately at 8.20 am and were vectored on to the incoming enemy formation. The raiders consisted of around fifteen to twenty Dornier bombers escorted by 100 Me110s and 109 fighters.

At 8.40 am between Colchester and Chelmsford battle commenced at a height of 15,000 feet. Higginson leading Green Section dived down on to the bombers delivering a beam attack on the leading section of bombers and opened fire at 400 yards range, closing to 30 yards. He could see no visible effect from his attack and carried on flying between the first and second section of enemy aircraft. As he turned away, he noticed the enemy fighters were just opposite, so he opened fire on a Messerschmitt 109 which climbed away steeply emitting white smoke. He then broke away and saw the 109 he had hit begin to dive down and crash bursting into flames in a field west of the road and railway between Chelmsford and Colchester. Fortunately the pilot had managed to bale out and this was later confirmed by the military authorities.

Sadly, during the fierce encounter with the Germans, the squadron suffered casualties. Flight Lieutenant Percy Weaver who only the day previously had learnt he had been awarded the Distinguished Flying Cross was shot down and killed. Pilot Officer Mounsdon, Flying Officer Westmacott and Sergeant Whitehead were all shot down, but survived. The Squadron Commander, Squadron Leader Manton received orders that day that he was to be posted to take over at RAF Hawkinge. The new commanding officer would be Squadron Leader Herbert Moreton Pinfold.

On 1st September 1940, the squadron were ordered away from North Weald to Boscombe Down Aerodrome in Wiltshire to swap with No. 249 Squadron. Boscombe Down was part of No. 10 Group Sector covering the south-west of England.

For the next two weeks of September, the squadron carried out training exercises with new replacement pilots and aircraft, but continuing to remain operational in case the call came to support squadrons in the front-line of the action. Higginson's log-book states that he carried out a convoy patrol on the 11th September and that on the 12th; his section was called into action, when a single German reconnaissance aircraft, a Junkers Ju88 was sighted, but escaped into cloud.

He had more luck however, on 14th, when following an uneventful morning patrol, he was ordered to take-off with Pilot Officer Constable-Maxwell at 3.44 pm and patrol Bournemouth at 10,000 feet. At 4.00 pm, he sighted a lone Dornier 17 bomber out on a reconnaissance mission above cloud. He attacked and fired a two second deflection shot into the aircraft. A few seconds later the Dornier entered into cloud. Higginson then caught sight of the bomber again and fired. Once more the German flew into cloud for protection. The cat and mouse battle continued and took the two aircraft further out to sea. Finally it appeared once more and he fired an eight second burst from his machine guns and immediately saw smoke begin to pour from both engines. Soon afterwards the enemy crashed into the sea and sank, forty miles from land. He did not witness any survivors. His own log-book entry reads:

> Engaged Do17 who went into cloud. Stalked him for 40 miles out to sea, got him in clear patch and he dived into the 'Drink' 'Whoosh.'

Constable-Maxwell did not witness the action as he had been patrolling separately below cloud during the time of the engagement.

For the next few days, Higginson's log-book shows that he undertook flights from Boscombe Down to North Weald and vice-versa and also practised Fighter Command Attack manoeuvres, no doubt putting some of the less experienced new pilots through their paces and instructing them on fighter tactics. Good news arrived on 24th September, when he received notification that he had been granted a commission and raised in rank to pilot officer.

It was not until 27th September, when a German raid targeted against the Parnell Aircraft Factory near Bristol sent 56 Squadron scrambling to get airborne at 11.05 am. They were given instructions to patrol over Middle Wallop, but missed the enemy formation coming in across the coast. They were then vectored to fly towards the Isle of Wight at 20,000 feet and then finally to Bristol and catch the raiders on their return back to France. At approximately Midday, Higginson leading Blue Section sighted a formation of twenty Messerschmitt Me110s on his starboard side. He turned his section and went into the attack picking out one of the enemy aircraft and firing a burst of five seconds from astern. He immediately saw white smoke billow from the port engine as the Messerschmitt dived and climbed in evasive manoeuvres. He then finished all of his remaining ammunition on the German, who continued to fly into the middle of the formation with white glycol smoke still pouring. As Higginson broke away, he himself was attacked by an Me109, who had obviously been ordered to await the return of his comrades near the coastline. Fortunately his Hurricane N2386 was not damaged. On landing Flight Lieutenant Edwards who was flying as Blue 2, confirmed the combat and Higginson was credited with an enemy aircraft damaged.

At 9.10 am on 29th September, 56 Squadron moved to operate from RAF Warmwell Aerodrome situated in Dorset. The day was uneventful apart from a patrol of two Hurricanes at 2.00 pm being sent off to intercept an unidentified plot, but no interception was made. The squadron returned to their home base at Boscombe Down that evening at 6.40 pm.

The next morning at 9.15, the squadron flew back down to Warmwell and by 10.45 am were given instructions to patrol Warmwell at 22,000 feet. While still climbing for height at 16,000 feet, Higginson leading A Flight sighted an enemy formation of about 70 Me109s and 110s heading in from the south-east at 20 to 30,000 feet above with the sun behind them. His report of the ensuing combat relates:

> I climbed the squadron in to attack head on. I opened fire at the leading enemy aircraft and a dog-fight ensued. I attacked an Me109 from quarter astern from about 400 yards with a burst of fire for six seconds, but observed no results from the fight. Sergeant Smythe, Red 3, saw the Me110 which I then fired on, streaming south, away from the formation with its port engine smoking badly heading back across the Channel.

On returning to base, he claimed the German aircraft as a damaged. His was the only claim from the battle, but two of the squadrons' pilots had been shot down, Flying Officer Ken Marston crashed in Hurricane P2866 at East Knighton suffering from shrapnel wounds, Sergeant Ronald Ray, crash-landed his aircraft, Hurricane P3655, he too was wounded and suffered a broken arm.

The squadron returned home and immediately on landing at dispersal, the ground crews began to ready the aircraft with refuelling and ammunition in preparation for the next call to scramble.

The next call to arms was during the afternoon when at 2.30 pm, the squadron was ordered up to intercept a 50-plus raid reported 10 miles south of Portland. Led by Squadron Leader Pinfold they climbed to 16,000 feet, coming in up sun of the German formation which was higher at 19,000 feet. Above the bombers, circling behind was their escort of Messerschmitt Me110s. Pinfold ordered his pilots into line astern and began the attack on the bombers from quarter astern. Pinfold opened the proceedings with a five second burst on the nearest bomber, but his own aircraft was hit by enemy gunfire causing glycol to stream out. Higginson flying as Yellow 1 reported:

> As Red Section began the attack I saw glycol pouring from Red 2 and thought that the fighters were coming down to attack us and so I went into attack them. I climbed up straight to the circling Me110s and gave one a three to four second burst from underneath. The enemy aircraft broke away from the circle and climbed straight up and I followed. A Spitfire attacked the enemy aircraft from above and I dived and got in behind him and finished all of my ammunition except for 200 rounds. The Me110 poured smoke, flame and glycol from both engines and dived vertically into cloud above the sea.

The Messerschmitt was seen to crash by Spitfire Pilot Officer W.D. Williams of No. 152 (Hydrerabad) Squadron and it was later confirmed as destroyed. Both pilots claiming a half share. Squadron Leader Pinfold successfully nursed his damaged Hurricane fighter (P2910) back to Warmwell and force-landed at 6.05 pm. Following the combat the squadron claimed one Dornier destroyed and another two damaged plus Higginson's shared kill of the Messerschmitt Me110. In return they had lost two Hurricanes destroyed, but both pilots safe; Sergeant Peter Fox had been shot down on his first mission with the squadron, the other was Flight Lieutenant Robert Edwards. Two other aircraft were damaged in forced landings.

In November 1940, they were recovering and re-equipping and practising squadron training at Boscombe Down. In December 1940 there was some activity, formation patrols and mostly training. On 17th December, 56 Squadron was posted back to their original base at North Weald.

As 1940 ended and 1941 began, the preparations for taking the fight back across the Channel to the Germans in occupied Europe had begun with the Fighter and Bomber Command Chiefs setting out their plans for offensive operations against the enemy. At North Weald, No 56 and 249 Squadrons began preparations for the new tactics to be employed, fighter sweeps escorting small bomber forces attacking enemy installations and Luftwaffe airfields. The sweeps would involve squadrons in Wing formations of three or more.

In early January 1941, there was little activity due to the weather and only seven sorties were flown by 56 Squadron. Their first offensive sweep operation was carried out on 10th January, 56 Squadron provided close escort for a small bomber force to the Forest de Guines, but they intercepted nothing. During February, Higginson carried out three offensive sweeps with the squadron on 2nd, 10th and 26th. Most of that month, he undertook convoy patrols and weather tests. This routine carried on throughout the following months until June, when the squadron was involved in greater offensive sweeps as better weather arrived. On 8th April 1941, he attained the rank of flying officer.

It was on 17th June 1941 however, that 'Taffy' Higginson's luck finally ran out, when escorting bombers on a raid to Lille, his aircraft Z 2575 was hit by enemy fire. It has remained uncertain to this day whether he was brought down by an enemy fighter or anti-aircraft ground defences, but the result was the same. Higginson remembers that there was an explosion that cracked the control column apart at the base making it impossible for him to steer the aircraft and that it also tore off his left flying boot and shredded his trousers. Having appraised the situation, he had no alternative but to take to the silk. He jumped and began the slow decent to French soil. On landing unscathed near a wood, he was unfortunately confronted at once by two German soldiers, one officer and a sergeant riding a motor cycle combination, who had seen his parachute descend. Offering no resistance, he was placed in the sidecar, when suddenly a low-flying Messerschmitt 109 zoomed overhead distracting the two German's momentarily. Higginson grabbed the handlebars and pushed with all his strength, tipping over the motor cycle combination and its riders. In seconds, he was off running away from the scene as fast as his legs could carry him. 'Taffy' Higginson recalls his time in occupied France and the amazing assistance he received by members of the escape route organisation to help him escape back home to Britain:

> As dusk approached, I began walking again and found some cottages. I went to the first house I saw and asked the occupants in my schoolboy French, whether they could give me another boot. They gave me a pair of boots and I thanked them. I then walked through the night until I came to a farmhouse, it was early morning then and I wanted to sleep. I suddenly saw a woman in the yard and I asked her if I could sleep down in the hay. She showed me where I could bed down and I did. I imagine she told her husband what I had done and the next minute he said 'hey up, out' so I had to get up and continue my journey.
>
> I carried on walking through the rest of the night until I desperately needed a drink. I got to a T junction in the road and there was a cafe on the left hand side. I went in and asked for a beer and they served me. I then left and proceeded to walk down the road, I had only got as far as 150 yards, when a car pulled up. I asked for a lift and they said 'you're not French are you' and I said 'no I am an English airman can you help,' they said 'yes' and they took me to Abbeville, where eventually a local priest named Abbe Carpentier helped me and took me by car to Lille, and introduced me to a chap called Paul Cole.

At the time I didn't know who he was other than he was an English soldier living with a French woman. It was here that I got my first identity card. It turned out later that Cole had turned traitor and he'd betrayed a lot of people who were shot and killed. He took me then to a house down on the coast. The Germans by then had the country divided into three; there was 'zone interdite', which as it suggests, you are not allowed to move around.

Paul Cole then took me to see a chap who had the means, the stamps and that sort of thing to make French identity cards and he made one for me. We then set off the next day for the frontier exit which the Germans used to man. It was at one end of a bridge and you had to produce an Identity card and present it on the 'zone interdite' side. Once over the bridge you were into 'zone occupe'. We made our way by train to Paris, and stayed the night. We then went to what I would call a brothel, but we didn't book in because no record was kept of anyone that stayed in the building at the time.

In the middle of the night I had to go to the toilet and in this case it was a hole in the floor. I then went back into my room and when the morning arrived and I went to check my money, identity card and my belongings that I was going to take with me. But low and behold I couldn't find any of my papers. I got into a panic and sat down and thought about it and realised I had been to the loo and went back there to check. They had fallen down through the hole and I had to extract them and bring them back and wash them in the sink then put them on the floor to dry. As a result of that we had to delay our departure for some time before eventually we could proceed.

We caught another train and travelled down from Paris to a village in between the occupied zone and free zone, this was St Martin-le-Beau, a village about two miles away from the place where we could cross the frontier, being marked again by a river.

Cole told me that if we called at a post office in this village, we would be told what time the German patrols would pass the point we were making for and we could then proceed. When we went to the post office it was closed, so Paul Cole and I had a discussion and we decided to go, whether or not we knew what time the German patrol was going to be there.

We walked along the road in line astern, eventually coming to the river. Looking across the river on a piece of ground somewhat higher than where we were standing, was a Cafe. Just five minutes or so after we had arrived at this point, we were still deciding whether we should swim or what else we should do, when suddenly a woman appeared from a farm opposite on the left hand side, climbed into a boat and rowed across the river towards us. We asked her for help across the river. We jumped into the boat and she rowed us across - we were so grateful. We then climbed up a little path to join the main road again and just as we got to a junction in the path, suddenly who should appear but a German officer and his sergeant. They had obviously been watching us, which we didn't know at the time.

They started to ask questions and Cole whose French was a little better than mine, was saying 'Oh well you take me to the commandant and I will report you for drinking at my Aunt's Cafe'. The sergeant pointed at me and said 'He is not a Frenchman, he is not talking,' so the officer asked to see my identity card, which I gave him. He showed it to the sergeant, and said 'that's alright' and he gave it back. In the meantime, I had a briefcase under my arm and in this I had a spare pair of socks and pants and some chocolate I had bought. Cole also had a briefcase and a revolver and he had the time schedule of the trains going from Lille to the Russian Front. He asked the Germans if it was now ok to carry on. Once again the sergeant pointed at me and said 'he is not talking, open your brief case.' So I laid it on the ground and opened it, the chocolate had run all over the place and Cole said 'See I told you he was a fool, look at his identity card, he is marked down as a fool.' My false identity card stated I was a French soldier discharged for insanity. The officer looked at it and said 'push off'.

A little time later I walked down the road about a hundred yards around a bend, and hid in a bit of woodland. About five or ten minutes later Cole came walking down the road and I joined him and we went off to get a train.

We then travelled down to Marseilles. There has been some suggestion since then, that Paul Cole was already a traitor at that time, but the fact that he did this and it was done in order that he could appear to be a pretty good, clean honest chap.

When we got down to Marseilles, we were first of all accommodated in a house which was owned by a man called Dr. Georges Rodocanochi and he had an English wife. The two days I was there she was absolutely super and when it was time for lunch or supper, she would give me her arm and we would walk into their dining room. There was severe rationing on and food was in very short supply, what we had to eat was nothing virtually. I was very impressed with both of them. I believe now a street has been named after Dr. Rodocanochi.

While we were there we had a visit from Patrick O'Leary, a Belgian Doctor and apparently he got down to Marseilles and he had taken over what was then an organisation trying to help English people escape which was run by a Scotsman, Ian Garrow. It was at the time when the communication between France and Britain was done by morse code and they communicated with London and obviously Patrick O'Leary's past had been investigated, and they said Patrick could take over from Ian Garrow. Patrick took us from Dr. Rodocanochi to the Port of Marseilles to a house owned by a Rene and Louise Nouveau. He was an author/writer and he had in fact translated

Shakespeare into English, they had a flat overlooking the bay and you could see the sea and I stayed there for a few nights. Patrick decided to move me down to the Spanish frontier and he got a Spanish guide to accompany me.

We got on the train to travel to Marseilles and got off the train at Banyuls sur-mer; here there was a queue to leave the station, which I joined. I was the last in the queue and the Gendarmes who were on the exit looked at my card and said 'what are you doing down here, your card says you are from the Pas de Calais.' I said 'I was looking for my family,' but it didn't satisfy them. I was arrested and ended up in solitary confinement in the Police Station.

After a few days, I was moved to a sewer prison at Perpignan, this was a dreadful place. All I got to eat was one bowl of soup a day and a slice of bread. My fighting weight normally was about eleven and half stone, I went down to seven stone.

After I had been there for a while, three months or so, I was told that Marshal Petain had granted me parole and I was to be released and taken to an internment camp called Saint Hippolyte-du Fort. The Gendarmes arrived and I was put in handcuffs and put on a train with them. They then handcuffed me to the door of the train, while they themselves opened their satchels and pulled out some very attractive food which they proceeded to enjoy, they didn't even throw me a crumb. We reached Saint Hippolyte-du Fort, but I wasn't there for very long.

I imagine what was happening was that politically they were trying to decide what to do with people like myself and others who weren't in a civil prison. They then moved us by train under guard to a French/Italian frontier fortress called Fort de la Revere. It was a fortress above the heights in Nice, the fortress was round with a moat and a drawbridge and very securely guarded. After a short time there, I was introduced to Whitney Straight, who was the senior British Officer in charge, there were about a dozen of us at this time, mostly army, some air force – there were also two New Zealanders.

Shortly after I arrived, we started to get Red Cross parcels and food. We had an arrangement with some of the guards where we would exchange cigarettes for food. Whitney was then transferred to a hospital somewhere in Marseilles and he escaped from there and got back home before me. I was then left as the senior British Officer and I set about getting an escape team together, to see how we could get out of the place. In this team I had Sergeant Nebarra, Higdon, Gary Barnet and Brian Hawkins who was a flight lieutenant.

I noticed one day looking over the wall which separated the end of the rooms from the moat, if you looked down into the moat near the drawbridge, you saw that there was a drain cover. The drawbridge itself was supported by two large vertical round pillars and the drain cover was at the bottom of the first one. Whilst organising our escape, we were able to communicate with Patrick O'Leary through a Polish Priest called Father Myrda who was a go-between. We told Father Myrda on one of his visits what we intended to do and he passed the information onto O'Leary. He agreed to arrange a hide out in Monte Carlo where we could be hidden and if we got to the nearest railway station then he would send someone there to meet us.

We chose a particular day and we organised for the other ranks to have a concert. Every time we had a concert the guards on duty on the drawbridge would wander down and look over to see who was singing or making a noise.

The night arrived and with the concert in full swing, we dropped through the barbed wire into the hole and into the kitchen quite successfully. We then got across to the other side of the moat and got to the drain grille, but it would not shift. We expected some problem of this kind; I had exchanged some of our Red Cross parcel food for a hacksaw. We tried sawing through the grille but eventually managed to kick it out where the concrete had deteriorated and we dropped down into the sewer one by one. We were all covered in excrement.

We proceeded very slowly and got down to the road which ran along the main roadway to Nice and Monte Carlo. We then found the railway line. We had to dress one of us in the best clothes we had, this was Brian Hawkins and he made his way to Monte Carlo and made contact in the principality's Scottish Tea House which was run by a spinster, Miss Eva Trenchard. Hawkins went into the teashop and made himself known. Patrick O'Leary was informed and contact was made. We got onto the railway line and were picked up and taken to Monte Carlo.

We were then taken to a flat and given food and stayed there for two days and supplied with identity cards. It was then suggested that I should travel as a priest with Father Mydra personally escorting me. So I borrowed one of his cloaks and collar and we went to get a train. We travelled to Marseilles, but sitting next to me was a woman who asked me to give her confession, luckily Father Mydra took over. On reaching Marseilles we went to Louise Nouveau's flat and after a few days we were escorted down to Perpignon, on the coast and we spent the night in a hotel.

The next morning we went to the beach at Canet Plage and we were led by Patrick O'Leary, there was about five or six of us. We were told that a boat would arrive and give a light signal; this was in the afternoon/early evening. He would signal back and we would all get aboard the boat. Sure enough two or three hours after lying in the sand, a boat appeared on the water and started to signal and Patrick signalled back. We all ran down to the rowing boat which was run by Polish people and we were taken on board to the other boat which was a Spanish fishing vessel. It had a red sail and a diesel fitted to it. In daylight it travelled by sail and at night would travel by diesel which made it much quicker, as no German would suspect a red sail. We rendezvoused with a naval destroyer and we climbed on board and were delivered to Gibraltar the next day. When we got to Gibraltar, arrangements were made to send us back to the UK but of course we were under arrest until we had been interviewed and debriefed in Scotland and then finally released.

Higginson arrived back in Britain from Gibraltar on 2nd October 1942, after fourteen months of surviving in France either evading captivity or enduring prison.

After his incredible journey back to Britain, all Higginson wanted to do was see his family and to get back into a fighter squadron, which he eventually did being posted back to 56 Squadron on 6th November 1942. They were flying the new Hawker Typhoon fighter/bomber aircraft at this stage of the war. Although he was allowed to fly the new fighter, he was under strict rule not to fly on offensive operations into Europe. Understandably, this was because of the knowledge he had acquired about the operations in occupied France, the Special Operations Executive, the escape organisation contacts and spies etc.

No. 56 Squadron at this time operated from Matlask under the command of Squadron Leader Hugh 'Cocky' Dundas, another veteran of the Battle of Britain who had flown with 616 Squadron. Although arriving back at the squadron in November, Higginson's flying was restricted to the last Hurricane aircraft available on the squadron, AG 196.

His first flight in the new Hawker Typhoon aeroplane came on 9th December 1942, when he carried out a local area flight in Typhoon R7679. From that date to 31st of that month he flew four other Typhoon aircraft, R8827, R8865, R8876 and DN307, conducting air to sea firing, formation practice and local sector reconnaissance. He continued with these duties throughout the remainder of 1942 and visited other airfields like Tangmere, Northolt, Hunsden, Exeter, Hatfield and Bradwell; ferrying pilots to and from the various aerodromes flying Miles Magister aircraft.

On 5th January 1943, Frederick Higginson received notification from the Air Ministry that he was to be posted. Because of his Halton training he was assigned to the Napiers and Son factory. Napiers were the builders of the Typhoon aircraft engine. Once there he was given the job of setting up the Engine Handling School and wrote a prospectus on the subject. Pilots posted to Typhoon Squadrons would come down to Napiers and have a course at the school, a tour around the works in Acton, West London, then back to their squadrons. Good news arrived on 25th January, when he received notification of the award of the Distinguished Flying Cross, to add to his DFM.

For the first year it was interesting at Napiers, but Higginson tired of the job, he wanted to get back flying operationally again. He was finally brought back on flying when Air Commodore Harry Broadhurst asked to see him in late March 1944, as he remembers:

I went to see Harry Broadhurst and he offered me the job to form 83 Group Communications Squadron. This was based first at Redhill and then moved to Thorney Island on 6th August after D-Day. We had two Spitfires, one of these was mine and the other was for the AOCs use. We had a number of Ansons and Austers and a few other strange aeroplanes and a Fiesler Storch which Broadhurst had brought back in a box on his return from the Middle East. My fitters re-assembled the Fiesler Storch, so I could fly this as well.

83 Group's role was to provide the air support for the invasion and close support for the army that went through Europe. Their job was to provide the air communication for the air staff and their counterparts when required; both within the captured part of France and right through until the end of the war. It was to move the top personnel around as quickly as possible. Higginson continues:

It was quite exciting after the D Day operations, when the first airstrip had been made in France; I landed in a Spitfire MkIX 636 on 12th June 1944. The following day I ferried the BBC correspondent Stewart McPherson and four others over in an Anson twin engine aircraft to record a broadcast from the newly completed airbase.

When it was decided to get as many aircraft as we could over to France, I flew the Fiesler Storch followed by four Austers from Thorney Island to Bazenville. It was a very risky thing to do really, flying a German aircraft with no defence whatsoever. We landed at Bazenville after one and a half hours flying.

He continued to fly in this role as commander of 83 Group as the Allied Armies fought their way through France with flights to Amiens, St Andre, to Douai where he had been with 56 Squadron in May 1940 and flights to Brussels, Antwerp and Eindhoven by October 1944. As the war drew to a close, Higginson was posted to Hereford on 5th February 1945, but was only there a month before being posted again to No. 11 Group at Castle Camps on organisation duties; he remained with 11 Group and decided to continue in his career with the Royal Air Force after peace had been declared in August 1945, with the Japanese surrender. He was posted again on 12th June 1947, when he went to work at the Air Ministry, and two months later was promoted to the rank of squadron leader on 1st August 1947. Higginson then undertook a course at the RAF Staff College at Bracknell on 26th January 1948, before going to a post at Headquarters No. 28 Group, again on organisation duties on 18th October that year.

From 1st January 1949, he became personal staff officer to the air officer in command of Training Command, a position he held for one year. In 1951, he attended the Army Staff College at Camberley. In 1952, he was given a position at Air Ministry Operational Requirements Staff and while here was asked to write a paper on the possible use of rotary aircraft. Higginson replied that he could not do this without first getting to know about the new machines and actually flying them, so he was then sent for flying instruction and clocked up flying hours on the Westland helicopter. The family home during this time was at Wimbledon and here his fourth son, William was born in 1956.

That year, Frederick Higginson resigned from the Royal Air Force after twenty-seven years service.

On leaving the Royal Air Force, he immediately joined the Bristol Aircraft Company as their Military Liaison Officer and later became its Guided Weapons Sales and Service Manager at the time when the company was trying to sell the new Bloodhound ground to air missile overseas. The company sale of the new weapon which was chosen in favour of other competitors was due largely to the exemplary work and salesmanship of Frederick Higginson. For this achievement, he was awarded the OBE in 1964. In that year also, he was appointed as a Director to the company.

He finally left Bristol's in February 1967 and became the Managing Director of Rezayat in Europe, a civil engineering construction company. Higginson had met the Kuwait businessman Abdullah Alizera a few years previously and had established Rezayet Services by opening an office in London for him to gain sales from the European market.

Finally retiring from business in 1969, he went and bought a 250-acre farm with a 17th Century house 'Peny-Coed,' in St Clare's, Pembrokeshire, Wales.

Frederick 'Taffy' Higginson sadly passed away on 12th February 2003, after a short illness aged 89 years. He is survived by his four sons.

He was an outstanding fighter pilot and man, who was straight talking and had a decisive attitude to the work he undertook. He was respected by his fellow sergeants and officers in the RAF and by those he worked with during his civilian life in industry. Wales can be proud of having one of the most unique figures who fought within the Royal Air Force, as one of the 'Few.'

CHAPTER 2

'PETER' MORFILL

Percy Frederick Morfill who always preferred to be called 'Peter' was born at
Gosport in Hampshire on 11th December 1914. The son of Ernest Frederick
and Alice Maud Morfill; his father had seen service as a Royal Marine and on
retiring went into the brewery business owning The Coach and Horses Inn,
Salisbury. Peter was educated at the Bishop Wandsworth School in Salisbury
and on completion decided at the age of fifteen to enter into the Royal Air
Force as an apprentice, which he did on 3rd September 1930.

He would later recall his entry into the service:

> I joined the Royal Air Force in 1930 and did my training at RAF
> Halton as an aircraft apprentice, No.564749. I undertook
> training as a metal rigger, one of the first metal riggers in the
> RAF, before that they were known as carpenter riggers, but with
> the new Bristol Bulldog aircraft which was more of a metal
> aircraft, metal rigger was the trade.

After passing out as a fully qualified metal rigger in September 1933, Morfill
was posted to the Fleet Air Arm at Gosport. His stay here was brief
however as he volunteered for pilot training and started his flying instruction
in early January 1936 at No.3 Elementary & Reserve Flying Training School
at Hamble:

> I went to undertake pilot training in 1936 as a LAC from
> Gosport and was sent first to Hamble and then to No.6 Flying
> Training School at Neveravon in March for advanced training.
> The Avro Tutor was the first aircraft I flew, followed by the
> Hawker Hart which was a twin seat job, then the Audax and the
> single seat Fury.

In January 1937, Peter married his fiancée Winifred Phyllis Sartin and they
later had one child, a daughter who they named Nan. In February that year,
he received his first posting to a squadron, No. 65 Fighter Squadron based at
RAF Hornchurch in Essex. He remembers that first day at Hornchurch:

> I arrived at Hornchurch in 1937 and my first impression was
> that the aerodrome was a very smart place with three big Belfast
> hangars, nice modern accommodation whereas previously at
> Neveravon it was literally wooden huts placed on the top of
> a hill.
> I was already then married, so we were for a brief time placed
> in married quarters, then found suitable accommodation and
> lived out from then on.

The Hornchurch squadron establishment consisted at that time of three home-based squadrons, No 54, 65 and 74, and many new pilots had just arrived, some from other parts of the Commonwealth. In 74 Squadron was the South African 'Sailor' Malan, he would later become one of the RAF's greatest wartime fighter leaders. Also in 65 Squadron was the flamboyant character of Robert Stanford Tuck, who had arrived fresh from Cranwell with the Clark Gable style moustache, but he was also an excellent pilot and he would become a top ace.

Other airmen that Peter Morfill would know well were obviously the sergeant pilots he served with, people like Bill Franklin, an ex Halton apprentice whom Morfill was particular good friends with. Others were Philip Tew, Norman Phillips and Stanley Hayes.

The squadron was commanded by Squadron Leader Grace and his two flight commanders, Bicknell and Saunders. The squadron was still equipped with the Gloster Gauntlet biplane during this period, but in 1938 they were to be replaced with the Gloster Gladiator. The new RAF Fighter biplane was the first to have an enclosed cockpit and other new innovations as Morfill remembers when it was time for 65 Squadron to pick up their new aircraft:

> One of the main things I remember about Squadron Leader Grace was that when we went down to Gloster's to collect our Gladiator aircraft, I was flying on his left as his No3 and he brought us back to the aerodrome to do a formation landing. He went to select flaps and began to pump them by hand. This had been the first time we had had an aircraft with flaps on it. The aircraft began to start tipping up, he shouted out 'bugger this new fangled thing,' so he came into land without them. Another thing was that he had always flown in open cockpits and he didn't like the new Gladiator with the new sliding hood; he said it was like sitting in a bloody glass coffin. But otherwise he was a damned nice chap.

No. 65 was the only Hornchurch squadron that had an aerobatic team, which would enter the competitions against rival squadrons and aerodromes within the Royal Air Force. Peter Morfill was a very good flyer and tried his hand at aerobatics and was considered good enough to be chosen to represent the squadron. The other pilots who were in the team included, Flying Officers Leslie Bicknell, Bob Stanford Tuck, Adrian Hope-Boyd and Pilot Officer George Proudman. They would practice their display of aerobatics when time allowed from normal day duties. The three-man display would be seen over the local surrounding areas by the public, performing their loops, turns and rolls preparing for the shows at Empire Air Days and Hendon Pageants. Morfill recalls the preparations they undertook:

> Leslie Bicknell was the flight commander, Flying Officer Tuck was on the right and I was on the left. He was No. 2 and I was No.3 and it was quite interesting. Everyone had a go at this aerobatics, 74 Squadron didn't do very well and neither did 54

Squadron, so 65 were the only aerobatic team at Hornchurch at this time.

Compared with modern day aerobatics we just didn't have the power. Loops were easy, but barrel-rolls were a bit of a job. On a flight formation loop we would come out at around two-hundred feet at the bottom, which was sometimes a little bit frightening at the time.

One incident I remember was we were above cloud, using cloud base as a height and we were bogging along when suddenly in front of us a flight of aircraft came out of the cloud. Bicknell the leader did avoiding action by doing a sharp turn to the left, I pulled up and disappeared somewhere or another, but was just in time to see Bicknell's tailplane hit by Tuck's wing and see the aircraft spinning down. I went down below cloud and found Bicknell coming down on a parachute. He landed right on the edge of the Southend Road and was lucky not to have been hit by one of the motor vehicles driving along the carriage way. He was very lucky having just landed clear of the road on the grass. A car stopped and he was picked up and taken back to the airfield. Tuck in the meantime had managed to steer his damaged biplane back to base.

On the Empire Air Days our flight aerobatic team would go up to places like Castle Bromwich and places like that. We always took a spare pilot with us, invariably it was always a chap named George Proudman who flew up with a spare aircraft in case any thing went wrong, engine trouble etc.

Although the team was together when practising or on the ground discussing the manoeuvres they would be using for the displays, once this was finished the class divide between officers and sergeants regulated that they could not be friends socially. The officers ate, drank and mixed together in the officers' mess and likewise the sergeants did the same in their mess. What was Morfill's opinion on this?

In those days the status between officers and other ranks was clear cut. During the war it broke up a bit, we never did get as bad as the Americans, calling each other Joe and the rest of it. There was a certain class distinction, and looking back it was a good thing, good for discipline.

In September 1938, Hornchurch like other RAF Stations was put on alert as things started to heat up in Europe, when Germany under the leadership of Adolf Hitler threatened peace. Full scale war was averted, when the politicians gave part of the Sudetenland of Czechoslovakia to Germany in return that Hitler would not extend his desire for further German expansion in Europe.

No. 65 and the other home-based squadrons at this time had flown their silver painted biplanes. During the time of the Munich Crisis, they were given instructions to camouflage all of their aircraft, which they hastily did. At one stage, they ran out of the camouflage paint and had to send out parties to scour the local paint shops in order to finish the job. Unfortunately, some of the paint was not of the required colour and the aircraft looked somewhat bizarre. Prime Minster Chamberlain returned from Munich proclaiming that war had been averted and so the major alert was downgraded.

It was fortunate for Britain and the Royal Air Force that war was not declared, for the aircraft the fighter squadrons of the RAF would have gone to war in, stood little chance against the new German monoplanes as they were far superior in speed and armament, the Messerschmitt109s would have cleared the RAF from the skies.

In August of that year, the RAF received its first batch of the revolutionary new fighter monoplane that had been developed by the aircraft designer Reginald J. Mitchell of Schneider Trophy fame. The new aircraft, the Supermarine Spitfire first arrived at RAF Duxford, to No. 19 Squadron where it was evaluated by the pilots. During the next few months other squadrons would receive the new fighter. Hornchurch squadrons first received their Spitfire in February 1939; Morfill remembers his first impressions of the new aircraft:

> We converted to Spitfires in early 1939. Having flown the Spitfire for a few days, some bright spark sent the squadron a Miles Magister to get experience of a monoplane. The first monoplane I actually flew was a Hawker Hurricane with a wooden propeller and that was up at Sutton Bridge on an air-firing instruction course. I thought the Spitfire was nice to handle compared to the Hurricane, which was a bit heavy and clumsy with a fixed-pitch prop, but when they converted to the two-pitched propeller it was alright.

Morfill and the other pilots of the three squadrons spent time getting to know the aircraft and its capabilities. This time was to be a godsend, for the hours they acquired would be put to good use when war was declared later that year.

Over in Europe things worsened and war seemed inevitable. Poland was invaded by German forces on 1st September 1939, and two days later war was declared on Germany by France and Britain. At Hornchurch, the pilots and ground personnel gathered around their radio sets to listen to the Prime Minister's speech at 11.15 am, telling them that Britain was now at war. Soon after the speech had finished, there was the first wail of the air-raid sirens. The overall thought was that immediately hoards of German bombers would fill the English skies and drop their deadly cargo. This was pure fantasy as no aircraft at that time had the range to deliver such an attack. Peter Morfill remembers the squadron's first patrol on that day:

> The day war was declared we had a squadron take-off, the usual panic. We all took-off and flew over Chatham and the naval guns opened up on us and poor old Gerald Saunders the C/O, his aircraft got hit when some shrapnel missed the back of his seat by about six inches and went through his radio.

For the following few months, Morfill and the rest of the squadron continued undertaking monotonous convoy patrols over the east coast and down to the Channel. This period known as the 'Phoney War' continued through the winter months of 1939 into 1940. As spring arrived, the Allies waited in anticipation for the Germans' next move.

On 5th May 1940, after four of the most interesting and happy years of his life at Hornchurch with 65 Squadron, Morfill received notification of posting to No. 501 Squadron 'County of Gloucester' Squadron. He remembers:

> I was posted to join No.501 Squadron from Hornchurch, they also took a Sergeant Davies from 74 Squadron and another chap from 54 Squadron, they also took Hector Proctor from 32 Squadron at Biggin Hill and we all arrived at 501 Auxiliary Squadron at Tangmere, near Chichester on the West Sussex coast.

Tangmere was a well established RAF Station based only a few miles just off the coast from Chichester in West Sussex. On his arrival, Morfill and the rest of the new postings were shown around the drome, the Sergeant's Mess and the aircraft they would be flying, Hawker Hurricane Mk1s. He was introduced to his new commanding officer, Squadron Leader Montague Clube, who had been in charge of the squadron since July 1937, having risen through the ranks from pilot officer.

Morfill, who had been flying Spitfires, adapted to the Hurricane quickly, finding it very manoeuvrable although slightly heavy to handle. On the plus side, its undercarriage was much sturdier than that of the Spitfire and less likely to cause problems on landing on uneven ground. The Hurricane's armament was also deadly, with four Browning machine guns housed together in each wing. The only main disadvantage was the speed, being slower than the Spitfire by around 20 m.p.h.

A few days later, the squadron was ordered to readiness with instructions to prepare for operations in France, as the threat of German invasion into Belgium, Holland and France intensified.

On 10th May 1940, Germany finally unleashed its Blitzkrieg attack, coming through the Ardennes, catching the Allies totally unaware and unprepared for the fast moving Panzer divisions who overran every Allied position barring their way.

At Tangmere, sixteen aircraft of 501 Squadron took off led by their commanding officer Squadron Leader Clube at 2.30 pm, and headed out over the Channel for France and a forward airstrip at Betheniville, North-east of Rheims. Here they would share the site with No. 103 Squadron who flew Fairey Battle fighter-bombers.

The trip took the squadron ninety minutes. On arrival they found the site consisted basically of two Nissen huts, two fuel bowsers and an old van. Immediately various shaped tents were erected to use for accommodation near the local village which was just two miles away and a tent was also set up as a basic Operations Room. The squadron's officers took over a local cafe to use as a billet.

A patrol of two aircraft was ordered up at around 5.30 pm and whilst flying some fifteen miles north-west of Vouziers, Flying Officer Derrick Pickup sighted a lone Dornier 17 bomber on a reconnaissance mission flying slightly below. He attacked and fired a burst of 140 rounds into the German. Pickup noticed smoke appearing from the enemy machine and soon afterwards noticed one crewman bale-out. The aircraft was later confirmed to have crashed.

On Saturday 11th May, the squadron was ordered aloft against the Luftwaffe in an action which saw Sergeant Morfill claiming his first victory in the shooting down of a Messerschmitt Me110 fighter-bomber, between Aiene and Meuse near Toureton. The squadron claimed six enemy aircraft destroyed without loss to themselves that day.

Sergeant R.C Daffron and Flight Lieutenant E.S. Williams claimed a Dornier 17 each, Flying Officer C.E. Malfoy and Sergeant A.D. Payne each a Heinkel 111 and Pilot Officer C.L. Hulse an Me110 destroyed.

During the late afternoon, the remainder of the ground personnel and pilots of the squadron had left Tangmere and were flown in aircraft of the Civil and Service Air Transport. Tragedy was to strike, when one of the three aircraft, a Bristol Bombay L5813, crashed on landing at 5.15 pm killing three airmen, Flying Officer A.C.J. Percy and Sergeants' Whitfield and Barnwell. Six other squadron members and the crew were all admitted to No. 4 Casualty Clearing Station at Epernay with various injuries. One of the pilots injured was Pilot Officer Leonard Byron Duckenfield who had only recently been posted from No.74 Squadron at Hornchurch. The casualties were then sent home to England and the Roehampton Hospital, Middlesex to undergo further treatment.

No. 501 had in the space of a few days felt celebration in action against the enemy and sadness with loss of comrades. Morfill recalled later in an interview those first few days in France:

> We were sent to France at a place called Betheniville which was north-east of Rheims. We had only been there for a day when the bombing started and other sorts of odd things.
>
> The place was a bit of a shambles as we had no ground control as we had in England, when we knew exactly what was happening.

The weather on 12th May again was fine, with visibility up to thirty miles. The squadron was scrambled at dawn, the pilots racing for their machines, when they were alerted as a large enemy force of bombers was sighted overhead. Throughout the day the squadron was in action as the Germans mounted a series of attacks in that area. During the engagement, 501 claimed a further twelve Luftwaffe aircraft shot down. Sergeant Morfill dived down onto a section of Heinkels from astern with Sergeant McKay and fired several bursts before watching both bombers dive into the ground near St. Hubert. Among those claiming that day was Pilot Officer Ken Lee who claimed a Dornier 17, which he despatched near to the Belgium border.

The next day, 13th May, 501 claimed another six enemy machines destroyed, three of these, a Messerschmitt 109, a Heinkel and an Me110 being shot down by new boy, Sergeant James 'Ginger' Lacey near Sedan.

The 15th May was an interesting day for members of the squadron, when they encountered for the first time a captured German airman. Morfill was part of a three aircraft flight patrol over the local area led by Flight Lieutenant Charles Griffiths and Pilot Officer Peter Hairs, when they sighted a formation of Dornier 17s. Going into attack, they set one of the enemy machines alight, Morfill firing short bursts into it as it began to dive to the ground. Only one of its crew managed to bale out before it hit the ground. The German who had managed to bale-out was Corporal Wolfgang Rohde, an air-gunner. On landing, he was luckily picked up five miles west of Bentheniville by Pilot Officer Patrick Hancock who had just been attached to the squadron from No. 1 Squadron and was en-route to 501, when he had sighted the German descending by parachute. Grasped from the clutches of an approaching angry French crowd of civilians, the German was hurriedly driven away. The pilots of the squadron met with the fortunate enemy airman who had survived being shot down and possibly lynched. He was given a meal in the cookhouse, before being taken away.

The following day, British communications relayed the news that German Panzers had broken through and taken the Meuse bridges. It was therefore decided that 501 Squadron would have to pack up and withdraw to Angure, designated as Site 10, some fifty miles back, to help give support to the retreating French and British Expeditionary Armies. Morfill remembers this hectic period, when the squadron received orders to withdraw:

> Out there we had scrambled telephone messages and it was disorganised because we were moving around so quickly, it was like being moved from pillar to post. The Germans were advancing so rapidly. We would stay on one aerodrome for two days perhaps.

While sited at Anglure, the squadron operated their Hurricane aircraft from a forward field at Boos and continued to take a heavy toll on the Germans, shooting down and damaging numerous aircraft, but the retreating Allied forces could not stem the advancing German Blitzkrieg. The Allies now retreated to the area around Dunkirk, where an evacuation had began; to rescue and bring back to Britain as many of the troops as was humanly possible by ship and small boats.

By the afternoon of Sunday 2nd June, the squadron was on the move once again, this time to Le Mans. After a long journey by road that took six hours, they arrived at 9.00 pm that evening and were billeted in the Pits of the famous Grand Prix racing circuit. From this aerodrome 501 provided withdrawal patrols and also escort for RAF bombers in a last ditch attempt to stop the Germans, by attacking railways, troop vehicles and supplies. It was all too late and in vain. Morfill recalls:

> One of the interesting things was we ended up on the Le Mans airfield, where they did the famous motor racing. We were billeted in the forest nearby, in the trees the NAAFI had already moved out and left everything behind. We types, we all had a sandbag full of cigarettes stored on one side of the aircraft and a

bottle of champagne, with the cork taken out and shaken to get
rid of the fizz, because you daren't drink the water. I flew my
Hurricane around with a flat bottle of champagne on one side
and cigarettes on the other.

By the 16th June, 501 was ordered by the commander of the Advanced Air
Strike Force, Air Vice-Marshal Barrett to leave Le Mans and travel to Dinard
by road and air. The road convoy left at 4.00 am that morning and arrived at
its destination towards dusk. Here they found No.17 Squadron who had
received similar orders.
    Orders were finally issued on 18th, for the evacuation of the squadron from
France.
    The main party leaving Dinard for St. Malo at 4.00 am, but the remainder
continued to operate until the late afternoon. The first party arrived by ship
at Southampton the next day, the others flying their aircraft to Jersey in the
Channel Islands, arriving at St. Helier at 6.00 am on 19th June. During the
evacuation all the squadron records were destroyed in case they fell into enemy
hands. Those pilots who flew to St. Helier continued to operate and covered
the withdrawal of the British Expeditionary Force from Cherbourg. Peter
Morfill recalls his attempt to make it back to England:

    During the withdrawal from France I managed to get as far as
    Guernsey, my aircraft had been damaged in the wing tanks by
    enemy fire and I couldn't get back to the mainland, so on
    landing I burnt the aircraft and came back to England on a
    fishing boat with a couple of other chaps left in the same
    position.

The 501 Squadron members who had managed to get passage back by ship,
arrived at Southampton on 20th June on No.1 Train Ferry and on arrival were
transported to RAF Yatesbury and given fresh clothing and a hot meal. Those
who came back by aircraft arrived at Tangmere aerodrome later that night at
9.00 pm.
    During their operations in France, the squadron had claimed a total of
seventy-one enemy aircraft destroyed or probably destroyed. In return they
had lost eight pilots killed and eighteen aircraft. An exceptional figure.
    The following day, they re-assembled at Croydon; the airmen were re-kitted
and granted four days special leave. Having replaced its losses suffered over in
France the squadron was given a new commander, Squadron Leader Henry
Hogan. Morfill remembers this period:

    The squadron reformed at Croydon. It was a bloody awful
    aerodrome to take-off from when flying a Hurricane. We went
    over the houses on the edge of the field about 25 feet above their
    chimney tops, which was a bit dicey when taking off in Vic
    formation. I was very pleased when we left Croydon.

On 2nd July 1940, the squadron was paid a visit by Air Vice-Marshal Barrett,
who had commanded the RAF Forces in France. He thanked them on the

marvellous work they had done during the French campaign and wished them the best for the future. He also congratulated Sergeant James Lacey on his award of the French Croix de Guerre and being Mentioned in Despatches.

No. 501 was declared operational once again on 3rd July 1940 and the following day ordered to operate from Middle Wallop aerodrome near Andover. From here they undertook a few night patrols, but during the day operated out of Warmwell for shipping patrols along the Channel.

During early July, the squadron engaged the Luftwaffe on numerous sorties over the English Channel, when the Germans were targeting the Channel ports and convoys in this first phase of the Battle of Britain. On three separate engagements during this period, 501 lost three pilots killed, Sergeant Fred Dixon on 11th July, Pilot Officer Duncan Hewitt on 12th July and old hand Pilot Officer Sylvester on 20th.

On 25th July, the squadron was moved to the airfield at Gravesend to operate as part of the Biggin Hill Sector and next morning flew down to the forward satellite airfield at Hawkinge near Folkestone. Morfill remembers operating out of Gravesend and encountering Squadron Leader Hogan one morning:

> I was a flight sergeant in the squadron and the commanding officer Squadron Leader Hogan said, 'Morfill you're in charge of all these bloody sergeant pilots, make sure they're out of bed at five o'clock in the morning and not later.' We all lived in a big house at the end of the aerodrome after the sergeant's mess had been destroyed.

The squadron was in action again early on 29th July 1940, when they were sent up to intercept a raid consisting of forty Junker Ju87s with fighter escort, 10 miles east of Dover at a height varying between 2,000 to 6,000 feet. At 7.45 am, the Hurricane aircraft of 501 sighted the enemy. Although completely outnumbered the twelve Hurricanes tore into the enemy formation and each selected a target. Morfill flying in Hurricane P3397 as Green 3 stated in his report:

> The enemy aircraft were seen diving out of the sun, their target being Dover Harbour. The squadron was then flying south, south-east, having just turned around from the opposite course (flying into sun). Due to our position, it was necessary to continue on a southerly course and turn right of the harbour. This was to avoid the anti-aircraft fire over the harbour itself. 501 were detailed for destruction of bombers.
>
> I attacked one Ju87 and on closing to 250 yards range, gave the enemy a good burst. Tracer appeared to strike the enemy aircraft. The aircraft then used violent evasive tactics, turns to both left and right.
>
> I overshot him and fired on a second Ju87. Owing to the close range obtained, I consider that both these enemy machines were damaged.
>
> On breaking away from the second bomber, a 109 was seen to be firing at me from rear quarter. I immediately turned sharp

right, and after more than a couple of turns, I found the enemy
aircraft in front at a range of approximately 100 yards. I fired
using almost full deflection and smoke came from his motor.
The pilot baled out and after a couple of seconds his machine
dived into the sea. On turning a sharp right, I noticed that his
parachute had opened.

On return to base, the pilots were able to report that the engagement had
been very successful, with claims for six enemy aircraft destroyed and six
damaged, Those claiming that day apart from Morfill who claimed the two
Ju87s damaged and the Me109 destroyed, were Flying Officer Ken Lee,
Sergeant Don McKay, Pilot Officer Leonard Duckenfield and New Zealander
Flying Officer John Gibson, who had destroyed two Ju87s. The Junkers Ju87s
claimed were part of II/Stukageschwader1.

The squadron continued to be heavily involved against the enemy raids in
early August, especially on 12th August, when 501 engaged a large force of
Stuka Ju87s and 109s, which were located at 3,000 to 4,000 feet over the
Thames Estuary, attacking a Navy destroyer. Several of the enemy were
claimed shot down and damaged for the loss of one Hurricane and its Polish
pilot, Pilot Officer Kazimierz Lukaszewicz.. During the afternoon of the same
day, the squadron encountered another raid west of Ramsgate. Breaking
formation the squadron aircraft attacked and individually picked out a target
each. The enemy formation consisting of Messerschmitt 110s tried to form a
defensive pattern, but this was to no avail. 'Peter' Morfill was able to position
himself onto one enemy machine and fired his machine guns, sending it
earthwards before it crashed on the Kent Downs. Sergeant James Lacey also
claimed another Me110, and another was credited as damaged by a squadron
pilot.

Sergeant Bill Green, who had joined the squadron in mid July, remembers
Morfill and the impression he had on him during this period of the battle:

I do remember one thing about Morfill which I've never
forgotten was that when we were operating from Gravesend, we
were fed by the army and it was horrible. They use to arrive with
a large steel container filled with what they called 'Stew,' then
they would pour it out on to your metal plate. What Morfill did,
which is to his credit, he went to the CO Squadron Leader
Hogan and he said 'It is no good we can't exist on this food we're
having from the army people, can you do anything about it?
Hogan said 'Right! 'From now on you sergeants will eat in the
officer's mess every night for dinner.' I'd never known this to
happen in the Royal Air Force. There had always been a separate
distinction between the sergeant and the officer's messes. You
could not cross that border line, but due to Morfill standing up
for us with the help from the CO, we ate in the officers' mess for
a period of about three weeks.

I flew alongside him and I can see his face now. Firstly he was
ultra quiet, but whenever he said something it was always worth
hearing. He was already a seasoned and experienced pilot when

I joined 501 and he knew how to keep out of trouble and taught me a great deal about battle flying and perhaps without his advice, I wouldn't be here.

I remember we were homing in on some Junkers 88s over Manston on 24th August 1940 and I looked at him and he looked at me quite clearly reassuringly, as we were flying in a tight formation. Unfortunately soon after that I was shot down by our own anti-aircraft defences. Secondly, he was without perceived fear and was so calm in the face of danger. Thirdly, he was in his quiet unpretentious way, a courageous man, who was certainly a role model to me and I am sure, to others. He had absolutely no time for those given to boasting and making false claims.

On 24th August, the weather was fine and clear. The squadron had flown down from Gravesend for Hawkinge at 9.35 pm that morning, and had patrolled the area without landing. On this patrol, they encountered a German formation consisting of thirty Dornier17s escorted by Me109s, four miles west of Dover. The squadron attacked from a beam position forcing the bombers to break their formation. The Dorniers jettisoned their bomb-loads before turning east, Enemy losses were one Me109 destroyed and one Dornier damaged. Sadly Pilot Officer Zenker, a Pole was reported as missing, believed killed after being attacked by 109s. Following combat the squadron landed at Hawkinge, but were ordered aloft again at 12.45 pm to intercept a force of thirty Junker Ju88s with fighter escort that had just bombed the aerodrome at Manston. The squadron managed to get in amongst the bombers before their fighter escort intervened. No. 501 was able to claim two Ju88s destroyed shot down by the Pole Sergeant Glowacki and two damaged, plus a Messerschmitt 109 also shot down by Glowacki and one further damaged, this fighter was claimed by Morfill.

The only squadron casualties were Pilot Officer Aldridge who was forced to vacate his aircraft (L1865) when it was hit by friendly anti-aircraft fire near Ryarsh. He floated down to land at Pells Farm, West Kingsdown only to land badly and sustain a broken shoulder and arm for his trouble. Also hit was Sergeant Bill Green; his Hurricane had been hit through the engine spraying his front screen with oil. He luckily managed to fly into Hawkinge and carry out a crash-landing successfully without injury to himself, apart from being a little shaken. Bill Green remembers two of those most interesting days in August 1940:

I respected Morfill very much as a person. We shared a room together with Tony Whitehouse who knew him better than I. Morfill had a very dry, quiet wit and a good sense of humour. One instance I can recall was that he lived in the Reading area and I was a Bristolian, and we agreed that if ever we got a day off, that he and I would grab the Magister, which was a two seater training aircraft and used as the squadrons' run about. I would fly and drop him off at White Waltham, which was near Reading and then pick him up the next morning.

On 28th August 1940, the Tannoy announced 'B Flight 'Mandrel' Squadron to stand down until noon tomorrow.' So Morfill and I ran to the Magister, got in it just as we were. I didn't have a tooth brush, I hadn't shaven, I had no gas mask or anything and we looked both the same, two drab looking characters.

When we got back the next day to Gravesend we were immediately on readiness straight away. It was a very bad day on 29th, with very low cloud. I remember sitting down writing a letter to my wife Bertha saying she could breathe easy for a few hours as we were unlikely to leave the ground today, but at six o'clock we were scrambled. The cloud was down to about 200 feet at Gravesend, but we took off and came through the cloud individually and rendezvoused at about 12,000 feet and the controller said 'Mandrel Squadron Red Queen Angels Twenty' which was the code name for Deal. Squadron Leader Hogan said' Come on boys, come to Deal with me,' which I thought was a bit indiscreet really because the Germans used to listen in to all our radio frequencies and they would have immediately heard the name Deal.

Anyway within an hour I was on the end of my parachute, which hadn't opened, wrapped around me like a roller towel and I fell through space from about 17,000 feet down to about 500 feet before it opened. I had also been wounded in the knee by shell splinters. I never saw the chap who shot me down. All I recall was a crash of glass made by a hole going straight through the so-called bullet proof windscreen in front of me about the size of a tennis ball, then feeling the glycol streaming over me giving me a shower. The engine must have been hit on the return pipe after it had gone through the radiator because it was a cool glycol, not a hot glycol. I was picked up in a field in the Eltham Valley and taken to the Woolwich General Hospital for treatment.

The squadron had been bounced by nine Me109s from out of the sun. Apart from Sergeant Green being shot down in Hurricane R4223, Flight Lieutenant John Gibson was forced to bale out of his aircraft (P3102) after being severely damaged in combat. In return 501 claimed three enemy destroyed and two damaged.

When in action against the Messerschmitt 109s, Morfill had a special tactical trick, which he would use if faced with the problem of getting a German fighter off his tail. He would pull his feet up higher above the rudder pedals, and then pull the control stick hard back into his stomach, pushing the aircraft into a vertical climb. This manoeuvre would cause a great deal of G-force, but by not having his feet completely down, this was less likely to cause him to black out. Once he had reached his climb, he would then roll out and hopefully be behind the German aircraft to attack it. It was risky, but it did work.

Two new replacement pilots arrived at the squadron at this time. Posted from No. 32 Squadron at Acklington were Sergeants' Tony Pickering and Tony Whitehouse. Tony Pickering was to be impressed by the standards set by Flight Sergeant Morfill:

> As a flight sergeant, he was responsible for the behaviour of the sergeant pilots; there were a number of us. The squadron was split into two flights with so many officers and so many NCOs. I was only nineteen at that time when I joined him. He was made responsible for us by the commanding officer Henry Hogan. A lot of the young chaps at that time spent a lot of time in the air doing their job, but also spent time in the evening with the girls when off duty. Morfill set an example to us which made me very proud. You could not complain whatsoever about his behaviour, but he was strict with us and it did us good. He was very proud of his RAF upbringing.

Another thing that Tony Pickering remembers:

> When we took off as a squadron, twelve of us; he would invariably be given the job to fly at the back of the formation and act as what was known as a weaver. He used to weave up and down at the back of the squadron to make sure we weren't jumped by the German 109s. They used to come over and try to pick us off. Flying the Hurricane, our job mainly was to go after the bombers. The Hurricane wasn't really fast enough to take on the German fighters; that was really a job for the Spitfires.

The squadron took off from Hawkinge at 9.00 am on the morning of 30th August to carry out standard patrols. At 10.25 am, they engaged a fifty strong force of Heinkel bombers with a large fighter escort, east of Dungeness. Combat was met and Morfill was able to claim another to his score, shooting a Heinkel 111 down into the sea. In all, two bombers were destroyed and two Messerschmitt 110s damaged. They were called back into action again at 4.00 pm, from Gravesend, when they entered combat over Southend at 4.50 pm against a force that consisted of Heinkels, Me110s and 109s. They met the Germans in a head on attack, which caused the left Vic formation of bombers to break up. Two of 501s pilots followed a Heinkel down and witnessed it crash into the estuary. Sergeant Lacey was forced down, when he received hits into his aircraft, Hurricane P8816, shooting off the radiator. The score sheet claimed two Heinkels destroyed and three damaged.

During this day, the Luftwaffe had heavily attacked the RAF airfields in south-east England. The communications with Biggin Hill had broken down owing to the airfield at Biggin being almost put out of action. Hornchurch took over control of Gravesend.

Luftwaffe activity continued against the airfields on 2nd September, when pilots and ground personnel at Gravesend raced for the shelters at 7.50 am, as bombs landed on the edge of the aerodrome. Thankfully no material damage was done, but two soldiers were slightly injured. Hurricane aircraft of 501 had been airborne just 20 minutes earlier and were ordered to patrol Gravesend. They engaged the bombers, but were too late to prevent some of the bombers getting through. A second combat took place during the afternoon in the vicinity around Ashford, Kent

It was during this sortie that Flight Sergeant Morfill damaged a Dornier 17 bomber between Maidstone and Ashford. In all the squadron scored four definitely destroyed, four damaged and four probably destroyed. One pilot was listed as missing believed killed, Pilot Officer Arthur Rose-Price, tragically he had only arrived at the squadron that morning after coming straight from a Fighter Training School. His inexperience as with many young replacement pilots was to be his first and last flight against a ruthless enemy. His brother was the famous actor of many 1950s films including 'Kind Hearts and Coronets,' Dennis Price.

On 10th September, the squadron received instructions from No.11 Group Headquarters to move and operate out of Kenley Aerodrome. The next day on Wednesday 11th September, no action came their way until they were called to scramble at 3.20 pm that afternoon, in company with No.253 (Hyderabad) Squadron, also flying Hurricane aircraft. They were ordered to patrol over Maidstone and then from there to Chatham. They were then instructed to turn south-west towards a point between Biggin Hill and Maidstone. When approximately ten miles south of Biggin Hill the squadron was attacked by four Me109s from a much larger force. This caused the squadron to break and take evasive action. Seven of the squadron managed to reform and three of the pilots including Morfill, sighted and attacked together with three other Spitfire aircraft a Dornier 17 bomber. The enemy machine was a straggler from a formation of twenty that had tried to attack Kenley and turned towards the Thames Estuary. The Dornier was shot down, with Morfill claiming a sixth share in its destruction.

Following the engagement, squadron pilots claimed four Heinkels damaged. Sergeant Tony Pickering was the only casualty. He was forced to bale-out, when his Hurricane P5200 was attacked by enemy fighters and the oil sump shot away. He baled out successfully and landed at the Caterham Guards Barracks.

The weather for the 15th September was fine with good visibility and 7/10ths broken cloud. That morning Morfill and the rest of 501 were called to fifteen minutes availability until 1.00 pm. At 11.00 am they were called to readiness, and at 11.20 am they took off with instructions to patrol Maidstone with No. 253 Squadron. Both squadrons sighted and then attacked a formation of twenty Dorniers, they in turn were then attacked by the German fighter escorts and a series of dogfights ensued over the Kent countryside. Morfill flying Hurricane P5193 was able during this time to pursue one of the bombers and send it plummeting to earth near Ramsgate.

Squadron Leader Harry Hogan's aircraft V7433 was hit through the radiator during this combat, but he successfully force-landed at Sundridge without injury. Not so fortunate was Pilot Officer Albert van de Hove d' Erstenrijck, a Belgian who had arrived the previous day from 43 Squadron. He was killed struggling to control his badly damaged aeroplane P7260, when it exploded over Chilham at East Stour Farm.

Eight squadron aircraft took off again at 2.00 pm to patrol over base at 8,000 feet, accompanied by Hurricanes of No. 605 Squadron from Croydon. Over Heathfield, they intercepted an incoming raid of Dornier and Heinkel aircraft at 5,000 feet with 109 escorts above. No. 501 was attacked by the enemy fighters and in the following melee two of the enemy were destroyed without a squadron loss. Ace 'Ginger' Lacey claimed the final coups de gras at 7.00 pm by shooting down a Heinkel 111 and a Me109.

By days end, the squadron was able to claim on that most important of days, six enemy aircraft destroyed. The Dornier 17, Morfill claimed was to be the last enemy aircraft, he would shoot down during the war. The squadron would continue to score against the enemy well into October and by the end of the Battle of Britain had been credited with 43$\frac{1}{2}$ enemy aircraft destroyed. In return the squadron had lost eighteen pilots killed.

Morfill's recognition as an exemplary pilot and skilled fighter came on 22nd October 1940, when the notice of the Distinguished Flying Medal was printed in the London Gazette:

> Flight Sergeant Morfill has served with the squadron since 5th May 1940, and has taken part in most patrols. He has shown skill and calmness in combat ability to seize the best opportunity to strike at the enemy (7 destroyed, 2 probably destroyed or damaged). His general steadiness and flying ability has been praiseworthy.

Remarks by Air Officer Commanding:

> His calm ability and skill has enabled him to seize the best opportunity to engage the enemy successfully, thereby he has shot down 7 enemy aircraft and probably several others. I strongly recommend him for an immediate award of the Distinguished Flying Medal.

On the day that he received his Distinguished Flying Medal from the King at Buckingham Palace. 'Peter' Morfill remembers an amusing story that took place at the award ceremony:

> Before we stepped forward to receive our gongs from the King, each of those present who was to receive an award had a small clip hook put on to their uniforms, which the King would hang the medal. I was with a group which consisted of a naval officer, an army officer and a officer from the Royal Air Force. We each were presented to King George, shook his hand and received our awards. Once the ceremony was over each of us would give our medals to the King's equerry in another room. The naval officer was given his award in a nice box as was the other two officers in turn. When asked to collect my award, I was given it back in a brown paper envelope. Again the class system was evident.

As bad weather returned during the latter part of 1940 and the German daylight raids began to peter out, the Luftwaffe continued with its night offensive against the capital in London and other cities of Britain. On 17th December, the squadron was posted back to their original base at Filton and here for the next few weeks the pilots were able to recuperate from the intense action they had seen over the last six months. The squadron however, sent a detachment of their pilots and aircraft to Charmy Down near Bath in January 1941, to be used on night patrols to try and locate enemy bombers on raids over that area. It seemed a hopeless task at that time, as no RAF single-engine fighter was equipped with radar to pick-up the raiders and intercept them. On one of these nights, Peter Morfill was at readiness in case the call came for him to become airborne. He recalls the night in question:

> I was sitting at readiness, when the call came that an enemy aircraft had been picked up by the searchlights and the anti-aircraft guns had started to open up on it, but had lost it. I immediately got airborne and was vectored by the ground control chaps over my radio to the nearest and last location that the German raider had been sighted. The anti-aircraft had stopped and the searchlights had been turned off and I was looking for the tell-tale glow of aircraft exhaust which would give away his position. It was a fairly clear night, but cold. I then suddenly sighted the white contrail from an aircraft engine and thought at last my luck had changed. I climbed up and began to follow the trail, which would bring me in behind the German. After a few minutes, it became clear I was acting the complete idiot. I was actually following the contrail the wrong way as it began to break up and disappear in the distance. No luck that time.

The squadron continued with some night operations, but by February their main role was protection of convoys over the Bristol Channel. This continued until April, when 501 was moved to Colerne, where they began to take part in offensive sweeps over Northern France in escorting light-bombers in attacks on ports and enemy installations. On 24th April 1941, their trusty Hurricane aircraft were replaced with Spitfires.

Peter Morfill's time with 501 County of Gloucester Squadron finally ended that June, when he was posted away to No. 58 Operational Training Unit at Grangemouth as an instructor; he was also promoted to the rank of warrant officer. He had fought and shared the hardships of the squadron for over a year, and had witnessed the loss of many colleagues during the fighting in France, and the Battle of Britain.

Following a short period at Grangemouth, he was sent to the Central Flying School at Upavon to undertake another course as an instructor. On completion, he returned to 58 OTU to carry on instructing. He was then sent to No.61 OTU at Heston in October that year.

On 15th January 1942, he was commissioned to pilot officer while instructing back at CFS. He was promoted in rank again on 1st January 1943 to that of flying officer and was sent to instruct at 3 Flying Training School at Hullavington in Wiltshire. He remained here until he was made flight lieutenant on 15th January 1944, when his next posting took him to instruct at the Central Flying School at Norton in Southern Rhodesia, training new pilots on Miles Master, Harvard and Avro Anson aircraft, and here he remained until the end of the war.

He decided to remain in the service after the war and was given a permanent commission in 1946 and served at the Air Ministry for a year before being posted in 1947 to the Ministry of Aircraft Production on Bomber Research and Development. After receiving a further extension to his commission, he then went to CFS at RAF Little Rissington in Gloucesterhire, where he became the chief instructor on jet aeroplanes such as the Vampire. He followed this with the position of chief flying instructor at the University Air Squadron of St. Andrews based at Leuchers in Scotland, then to Headquarters 63 Group at Hawarden where he completed a gliding course and attained the rank of squadron leader on 1st July 1953.

For the next two and a half years, he worked at the Radio Engineering Unit at Henlow, before accepting the post of Officer Commanding the Station Flight at RAF Tangmere, which was then being used as a master diversion airfield. This was to be his final posting before retirement. He finally left the Royal Air Force on 4th February 1958 with the rank of squadron leader.

Following his retirement, he bought a bungalow in the village of Singleton and found work with the company, Wingards. The bungalow had a huge garden, and as he was a keen gardener it thrived. The garden had over one hundred fruit trees and many vegetables. He had a garden shed which housed his work bench and tools. He did all the DIY decorating and painting and along with his wife were well organised. Sadly his wife Winifred died of cancer in 1966.

While working at Wingards, he met and fell in love again with Janet Robinson in 1967. The following year they were married at the Chichester Register Office on 12th October 1968 and spent his final years at their house in Spring Bank, Chichester. He was a very private man especially regarding his experiences and achievements. He did however spend enjoyable occasions, when he met up with his fellow wartime colleagues at 501 Squadron reunions or special anniversary events. One event that stands out was when he and his wife Janet were invited to the Guildhall in London to commemorate the Battle of Britain and meet the Queen Mother. The happy moment for each man was to have a handshake with the Queen Mother herself. The admiration that he had for Her Majesty and the late King George VI was still quite resolute after all those years.

Squadron Leader Percy 'Peter' Morfill sadly passed away at home on 2nd April 2004 at the age of 89 years. His funeral was held at the Chichester Crematorium on Friday 16th April. Attended by family and friends and many tributes were paid. Two written tributes to him came from former wartime colleagues, Wing Commander Ken Mackenzie of No. 501 Association, who said:

> 'Morf as we called him was a superb pilot in 501 and well worth his DFM. He was a man amongst men, a good disciplinarian and a great character. He will be greatly missed by his many friends and ex-501 Squadron survivors.

Bill Green also added:

> I liked and admired Peter and it follows that, although I had seen
> little of him in recent years, I feel, with all those who knew him,
> the poorer without him.

CHAPTER 3

FREDERICK BARKER

Frederick James Barker was born in the East End of London in the area known as Bow on 16th March 1918. He was educated at Old Palace School and then Coopers Company School. Fred Barker joined the Royal Air Force Volunteer Reserve in April 1939 as an airman under training wireless operator/air gunner, his number being 747751. He remembers:

> I was actually a reserve, called up before war was declared and posted to Sutton Bridge and from there went to Pwllheli in north-west Wales for the air-gunners course. Here we did basic instruction in the class-room and then the air experience on flying in Demon biplanes, which had a fixed bead gun-site on the rear firing machine gun. You would be suspended by a chain which was secured to the floor of the aircraft.

On completion of training he was called to service on 1st September 1939 joining No. 264 Squadron on its reformation at Sutton Bridge on 30th October. No. 264 had been formed during the last year of the First World War in April 1918, as a coastal reconnaissance flight using Short seaplanes in the Mediterranean Sea. The squadron was disbanded on 1st March 1919. On 1st November, Squadron Leader Stephen Hardy reported his arrival at 264 Squadron from Headquarters Fighter Command at Stanmore.

It was here at Sutton Bridge that Barker was to team up with Sergeant Edward Roland Thorn, a native of Portsmouth, who had joined the Royal Air Force as an aircraft apprentice in September 1928 and later applied for pilot training. Barker recalls his colleague:

> Ted Thorn was an ex-boy apprentice at RAF Halton. He went through the complete course; he was an air-gunner, then an observer and wireless operator, then a pilot. He had a thorough understanding of the air force and the actual routine. Regarding the aircraft itself, any problems he was well aware of anything he could do, he had the whole training. He was a man of few words, but the confidence I had in him was outstanding and other people respected him. He was a man who would not boast at all, a thoroughly decent type.

The new squadron was to be equipped with the Boulton-Paul Defiant aircraft. The Defiant's design and concept was of a single-engine fighter that had a rotating turret in the rear, which could deliver a massive amount of firepower to shoot down bombers. The prototype had made its first flight on 11th August 1937 and was powered by a Rolls Royce Merlin I engine achieving a speed of 302 mph. As for its performance in the air, it was a very stable and manoeuvrable aircraft and on landing its wide undercarriage proved very sturdy. Its armament consisted of a Boulton-Paul MkIID turret in which four belt-fed 0.303 Browning machine guns were housed. Each gun had 600 rounds of ammunition. By March 1937, eighty-seven of the aircraft had been ordered and a further three hundred and sixty-three by 1938. No. 141 and 264 Squadrons were both designated to receive the new aircraft, but had to wait until late 1939. In the interim, 264 Squadron had moved to Martlesham Heath in Suffolk. Barker recalls those early days on the squadron.

> When we got to the aerodrome the Boulton-Paul Defiants had not yet arrived, so the pilots did their training in the Miles Magister aircraft, which we got a bit of air experience in too.

When the aircraft finally arrived, the pilots and air-gunners spent many hours practising co-ordination and communication between themselves in the air and preparing tactics to use against the enemy. Both Thorn and Barker were happy with the new fighter as Barker remembers:

> The pilots themselves, they obviously had no experience on that type of aircraft, so they were a bit new to it, but everything seemed to mould together and once we were assigned to our pilots, the confidence grew more and more. The co-ordination between the pilot and gunner was through headphone communication. The pilot was responsible for getting you in a good attacking position, but if I called for him to dive or climb, his response was immediate and fully co-operative and understanding.
>
> Operating the gun-turret was remarkably easy, you only had one main control which was like a joy-stick with the normal method of pushing it back and forward, it was a smooth operation in fact better in my opinion than the old Frazier Nash turret. There was also a small lever which if you released it you could move the turret around by hand.
>
> On the aircraft you had a cut-out, which avoided you hitting any part of the aeroplane when firing the guns. The only thing wrong with it if anything was you couldn't carry enough ammunition. Only six hundred rounds on each one.
>
> The gunners all wore a special type of parachute, which was more or less like an overcoat. It was the best type to use in that sort of turret and there were two ways of escaping. Either putting the turret to one side, opening the door and jumping out that way or supposedly releasing the bottom seat you sat on, crawl through the aircraft, release the bottom hatch and fall through that. Jumping out the side, one of the biggest problems was not hitting the tail. The confidence was mainly revolved around the pilot and from my point of view I was perfectly happy with the Defiant and had no problems at all.

The squadron moved to Duxford in early May and by 11th May, had one section at readiness from 4.30 am. Red Section, Squadron Leader Philip

Hunter and Pilot Officer Michael Young conducted a convoy patrol that evening over the Happisburgh lightship, before returning after dark.

The following day, the 12th, A Flight proceeded to Horesham St. Faith, where they refuelled and linked up with six Spitfires of B Flight of 66 Squadron. They then flew direct to the Dutch coast to patrol near the Hague. Red Section consisted of Squadron Leader Hunter and his gunner LAC Fred King, Red 1 was Pilot Officer Whitehouse and Sergeant Smalley, Red 2 consisted of Pilot Officer Young and LAC Johnson. Yellow Section comprised of Flight Lieutenant Nicholas Cooke, Corporal Lippett, Pilot Officer Eric Barwell and Sergeant Qinnie and Pilot Officer Whitley with his gunner LAC Turner.

The Flight took off from Horsham at 1.10 pm and commenced to patrol over the Hague at 1. 55 pm, each section was flying behind a section of Spitfires. An aircraft afterwards recognised as a Junkers Ju88, was seen approaching and dropped one bomb near three naval destroyers at 2.50 pm. Red Section cut him off as he turned to port inland; he dived down to ground level. An overtaking attack commenced, and then each Defiant made a cross-over attack in turn. Tracer bullets could be seen entering the Junkers, then smoke began to pour from its port engine. It crashed in the middle of a field which was full of cows and surrounded by dykes. Meanwhile, Yellow Section accompanied by a section of Spitfires had sighted a Heinkel 111 bomber at 3,000 feet; this promptly dived to ground level. The three Spitfires attacked from behind and Yellow 1 carried out a cross-over attack from the starboard side. Smoke immediately issued forth from both of the German bombers engines. Yellow 2 was about to make a second cross-over attack on the German from the port side, when the bomber crashed into a field, ending up against a hedge.

After delivering their respective attacks, no other enemy aircraft were observed, so each section returned to Duxford landing between 3.25 and 3.35 pm. There were no injuries sustained by any personnel or aircraft.

The following day on the 12th, B Flight were sent out on a similar patrol from Martlesham Heath. Over Holland they encountered German aircraft and claimed five shot down, but in return only one of the six Defiants returned. Eric Barwell, who was a pilot officer with the squadron and remembers this action:

> They took off that day early morning and when over Holland they ran into Me109s and Me110s. We heard nothing from them until the afternoon, when a lone aircraft landed, flown by a chap named Kay. His Defiant was full of bullet holes. The other five were shot down. Several were killed and others became prisoners of war, while a couple managed to escape and get home.

On the 14th May, the squadron received the news that two of their pilots had arrived back from Holland after being shot down in action. Pilot Officer Thomas and Pilot Officer Hatfield had met at Sleewyk in Holland and were both arrested as German spies and were nearly shot out of hand, when their Dutch captor was found to be a Nazi. Hatfield reported that he was fired at when descending by parachute. The following message was received from the officer commanding No. 12 Group stating:

> I want to congratulate No. 264 Squadron most heartedly on the success of their operation over Holland, which has proved the success of the Defiant as a fighter. I much regret the loss that 'B' flight suffered in the second operation. The courage and determination displayed were of the highest order and create for No. 264 Squadron a tradition that any Squadron might well be proud of.

This was signed by Air Vice Marshal Trafford Leigh Mallory, Commanding, No. 12 Group.

Also received was the following:

> Following message which has been suitably acknowledged has been received from C.A.S. You have done magnificent work during the last 48 hours in Holland and Belgium and fully justify the confidence placed in you. Keep it up.

The squadron continued to undertake patrols over the east coast during most of May, until events over in France suddenly took a turn for the worse as the Germans pushed through France and the Low Countries and pushed all before them, causing the Allies a crushing blow, which they could not recover from. The Allies were in total disarray as they were pushed back across Belgium and France towards the Channel. Finally the British and French reached the Channel port of Dunkirk and an evacuation was put into action, to rescue the troops. No. 264 was given instructions to patrol and cover the beaches around Dunkirk and Calais. This would be their first blooding.

After flying down south from Duxford, the squadron's first patrol over to Dunkirk took place on the morning of Tuesday 28th May 1940. At 11.35 am, ten Defiant aircraft under the command of Squadron Leader Phillip Hunter headed across the Channel from Manston bound for the Port of Dunkirk and surrounding area. Only minutes into their patrol they encountered a force of thirty Messerschmitt Me109s ten miles from the French coast. 264 Squadron immediately adopted a defensive circle formation as the 109s began their attack. One German fighter was shot down by a burst of lethal fire from Fred King, Phillip Hunter's turret-gunner. Another was seen to burst into flames, the victim of Pilot Officer Michael Young's aircraft.

Fred Barker and Edward Thorn were flying as Blue 3 during this patrol and state in their combat report for that day:

> The CO ordered us into line astern. We then circled and the enemy aircraft, which were not in formation dived and the attack developed. The leading enemy aircraft caught up the squadron and commenced to fire from astern. The squadron then became broken up, leaving myself as the last aircraft in the circle. We received hits in the main-plane and tail. Two of the

enemy aircraft hit caught fire for sure. One fell away apparently
out of coolant. The aircraft were not seen to hit ground because
the action was fought above 8/10ths cloud.

Barker continued the report:

> When firing at the enemy, my pilot put the machine in left bank
> and I fired over left of rudder. I fired 400 rounds, no stoppages.
> 100 rounds each gun.
>   The enemy machines thought that we were either Hurricanes
> or Spitfires. A red flare was observed during the action and the
> CO ordered reform. Red and Blue Sections reformed and
> proceeded on course of 290 degrees to Manston.

On return to Manston aerodrome, it was learnt that they had suffered the loss
of six aircrew, Flight Lieutenant E.A. Whitehouse and Pilot Officer H. Scott
in Defiant L6959, Pilot Officer A. McLeod and Pilot Officer J.E. Hatfield in
L7007 and Sergeant L.C.W. Daisley and Leading Aircraftsman H. Revill in
L6953. The German losses were five Me109s destroyed, three claimed by
Barker and Thorn and two by Squadron Leader Hunter and his gunner
Leading Aircraftsman Fred King.

This had been the squadron's first blooding in action. Over the next few
days, the squadron would have further successes, but suffer some sad losses
as well.

On the afternoon of Wednesday 29th May, 264 Squadron were detailed to
patrol Dunkirk and engage any German bombers attacking the beaches. They
took off from Manston at 2.45 pm and were accompanied by Hurricane
fighters of 56, 151 and 213 Squadrons flying at various altitudes above.
German aircraft were sighted consisting of Messerschmitt 109s and 110s and
Junkers Ju87 dive-bombers. Squadron Leader Philip Hunter shouted his
instructions over the R/T for the Defiants to form line astern.

Whether the Germans had mistaken the Defiant aircraft as Hurricanes in
the quickness of battle is unsure, but they paid a heavy price during the
engagement. Nine Messerschmitt 109s were claimed by the squadron as
destroyed, seven Me110s and one Junkers Ju87 Stuka. Thorn and Barker
claiming the Stuka and a Messerschmitt 110.

The squadron's only casualty had been Leading Aircraftsman E.J. Jones,
who had baled out when his aircraft flown by Pilot Officer Desmond Kay had
been hit. Kay had landed back at base not knowing his gunner had vacated the
aircraft. Jones's body was washed ashore on the French coast days later.

After returning to Manston at 4.30 pm, it was to be another two and half
hours before the squadron was ordered on their second patrol. Taking off at
7.00 pm with an escort of aircraft from 56 and 151 Squadrons they again
headed for the port of Dunkirk and on arrival found the sky full of enemy
aircraft preparing to or already attacking the shipping below. It was at this
precise moment that Squadron Leader Hunter sighted a large formation of
Stuka dive-bombers heading for the harbour.

Ted Thorn and Fed Barker were flying as 'Blue 3' at 8,000 feet in section
line astern. The commanding officer then commenced to attack, turning

steeply to starboard to engage one Me110. During the attack the squadron went into cloud. Thorn manoeuvred his aircraft into an attacking position on a JU87, which Barker shot down in flames. They returned to 8,000 feet and began a cross over attack on two Ju87's – these were certainly damaged, but not seen to crash. At this point, Thorn was warned by Barker that six Me109s were on their tail. The port tank was hit and leaking and the gun turret received damage, but Barker was not wounded. Thorn put the aircraft into a vertical dive coming out at 150 feet. He then set course for Manston and landed with only one wheel down.

The rest of the squadron had been equally successful and had completely decimated the Stuka formations during their attack, accounting for eighteen destroyed and four probably destroyed or damaged. A further Junkers Ju88 was also destroyed and one damaged. With no loss to themselves, this was an outstanding achievement for the squadron. By days end, No. 264 had claimed an astonishing thirty-five enemy aircraft destroyed and three probables. Fred Barker recalls 264 Squadron's first combat operations:

> The first operation I had was at Dunkirk. That was the most outstanding effort by the Royal Air Force in helping to cover the evacuation of the troops stranded on the beaches.
>
> We flew in the standard Vic formations on our way out to Dunkirk and once over there we tried to protect the troops, which seemed pretty hopeless when you saw the bombing going on and the ships on fire, which was a terrible thing to see, the smoke and everything else. We broke formation and then went on the attack and then sorted out an enemy aircraft to attack. But once we were attacked, we adopted the formation of line astern and headed down as low as possible to the deck. This meant that any attack on us would have to come from above and we were in position to fire upwards. The official records show we were successful at the beginning as the Germans thought we were Hawker Hurricane aircraft.

It was not until Friday 31st May that Barker would be in action again. The previous day had seen little air activity over France due to bad weather, but this had improved and by early morning of the 31st it had turned to cloudy, but fair.

There was still little enemy activity during the morning, but by early afternoon RAF Squadrons were once more on the alert. No. 264 went on their first patrol at 2.00 pm reaching the French coast at 2.20 pm at 10,000 feet with Hurricanes from 213 Squadron above at 15,000 and a Spitfire top cover provided by No. 609 Spitfire Squadron at 20,000 feet. Immediately, a formation of up to seventy Messerschmitt 109 fighters were sighted, with twenty Heinkel bombers below arriving from the south-east.

On seeing such huge numbers of enemy fighters, Philip Hunter gave instructions for the squadron to form a defensive circle. As the 109s dived to attack, the Defiant gunners opened up with their Browning machine guns and claimed two of the enemy in an instant. Unfortunately, one Defiant aircraft (L6980), flying too close to another, collided, causing the other machine to disintegrate immediately. Fortunately Pilot Officer Michael Young and his gunner Leading Aircraftsman Johnson were able to bale-out. The other Defiant (L6961) flown by Pilot Officer Whitley and his gunner Leading Aircraftsman Turner had no option but to force-land their damaged aircraft near Dunkirk.

Sadly they lost Pilot Officer G.L. Hickman and his gunner Leading Aircraftsman A. Fidler, (L6968) when they were shot down. Both men were seen to bale out, but were killed. During this combat 264 claimed three Me109s and one probable.

The second sortie of the day took place at 6.40 pm with No. 111 Hurricane Squadron acting as cover along with Spitfires of No. 609. A few miles north of Dunkirk, the RAF Squadrons sighted a large formation of Heinkel 111s with fighter escort. Phillip Hunter radioed his pilots to form battle formation. Ted Thorn recalls in his report:

> We went into line astern and attacked one Heinkel 111 watching it crash in flames. Three other Defiants attacked at the same time. We reformed with Red Section and attacked two sections of three Heinkels. The leader of the enemy formation fell away in flames as we commenced overtaking and attacked the second formation. Some were seen to fall away but we were so close that a certain amount of damage must have been done. The CO ordered us to reform and we returned to base.

Following this combat Barker and Thorn were credited with one Heinkel destroyed and a further two as damaged. The rest of the squadron claimed three Heinkels destroyed and three damaged. Two Defiants had been shot down. The aircraft flown by Pilot Officer Barwell, (L6972) was forced to ditch in the Channel, but both airmen were rescued by a Royal Naval Destroyer. Flight Lieutenant Nicolas Cooke and his gunner Corporal Albert Lippett were both listed as missing in action after they failed to return.

Pilot Officer Richard Stokes aircraft had been badly shot up, but he managed to crash-land back at Manston, after ordering his wounded gunner Leading Aircraftsman Fairbrother to bale out. Fred Barker remembers the tactics employed by the squadron during this period:

> Our most effective method of attacking the German bombers was if possible to the side and slightly underneath, where hopefully they could not see you. During Dunkirk when we went after the enemy bombers who were inflicting the damage, there were so many fighters around that our main effort at the time was self preservation, which defeated the object of going there in one respect.
>
> The operations were successful in one respect, but after a week of this activity and back to Duxford, one was aware of the loss of crews, because we did lose a few of the chaps. I always stress this and believe it was down to pure luck. People got killed without knowing what killed them. Although one was successful in doing these operations and shooting aircraft down, it was still pure luck

that one still survived. There was no heroism and that sort of thing, just luck.

On 14th June 1940, the London Gazette gave notice that Barker and Thorn had both been awarded the Distinguished Flying Medal with immediate effect. The notice of the awards read:

> These airmen have shown considerable determination and skill when engaging the enemy. On one occasion when three Defiants behind them had been shot down, leaving their aircraft the last in line, three Me109s, which were concentrating their efforts on the rear of the squadron, were shot down due to the skill of Sergeant Thorn and the good shooting of Leading Aircraftsman Barker, forcing the remaining enemy aircraft to break off the engagement. Sergeant Thorn and LAC Barker have up to date accounted for six enemy aircraft.

Following the Dunkirk evacuation, the squadron was sent to Fowlmere to undertake training for night operations. Following Dunkirk, although they had collectively claimed over forty of the enemy's aircraft, they had also lost nine of their own destroyed. The powers that be in Fighter Command were already re-evaluating the role in which the Defiant could be used.

As the Battle of Britain began in July 1940, the squadron remained out of the action.

On 22nd July, the Air Officer Commanding No. 12 Group, Air Vice Marshal Trafford Leigh Mallory visited Duxford to present decorations. Pilot Officer King and Sergeant Edward Thorn and Fred Barker each received the Distinguished Flying Medal for their actions over Dunkirk. The following day the Squadron moved to RAF Kirton-in-Lindsey in Lincolnshire.

The next two weeks the Squadron undertook more convoy patrols over the Lincolnshire coast and around the Wash. A night patrol was carried out on the 15th August by Pilot Officer Whitley and he intercepted a Heinkel 111. During the chase, he was sighted by the Heinkel when closing to attack and the german bomber opened fire. In return his gunner fired two bursts into the enemy aircraft before it escaped into cloud. Whitley was unable to report on the damage caused to the Heinkel, but his Air Gunner, Sergeant Turner reported that the tracer was blinding and between bursts, the pilot was able to see the enemy, but the gunner could see nothing. Following this, it was suggested that only ball and armour piercing ammunition be used at night. This was the Squadron's first engagement by night.

Finally, they received the call to move down to 11 Group on 22nd August, to Hornchurch. Barker recalls:

> We were sent to operate from Hornchurch in August and on arrival undertook sorties on the same day. We were billeted in the sergeant's mess, but we didn't spend much time there being put on thirty minutes readiness and so on. The aerodrome there had a grass flight-path, but this did not cause any problems with

landing the aircraft as the Defiant had a wide undercarriage which helped its stability.

Red Section on arriving at Hornchurch that day were sent down to patrol Manston during the afternoon and in the evening the Squadron made a patrol of Manston.   Pilot Officer Jones landed at Eastchurch because of engine trouble, but no enemy aircraft were sighted during the day.   Although 264 suffered mounting casualties during this period of the Battle of Britain, the aircrew continued to undertake operations as Fred Barker explains:

> Funnily enough you didn't think about it, I know it sounds strange, but you had a bit of a twitter on the ground, once you were airborne it didn't cross your mind at all because you were too busy concentrating. I suppose the biggest tragedy was when you saw like I did over Dunkirk, one Defiant collide with another and see the turret drop away. Those are the things that momentarily shake you, but you forget it until later on.

On 24th the Squadron took off from Hornchurch at 5.10 a.m.   Red, Yellow and Green Sections landed to refuel at Manston in preparation for dawn readiness.   Blue Section remained aloft on guard and landed at 7.00 a.m. During the refuelling operations, the three sections scrambled to orbit the base at 10,000 feet and were recalled after 25 minutes. At 8.30 a.m., the Squadron was again ordered to patrol base.   Flight Lieutenant Campbell Colquhoun had difficulty in starting his engine and was late in taking off.   Once airborne, he sighted two aircraft in the distance, which he took to be members of his section.   They were, however, Messerschmitt 109s and they immediately attacked and his aircraft was hit just behind the turret by an explosive shell which ignited the verey cartridges.   He took evasive action and returned without further damage to Manston.   During the patrol, other Me109s had dived to bomb the Squadron but none of the aircraft were damaged.   The Squadron then returned to Hornchurch at 11.30 p.m.

At around 12.45 pm, when enemy aircraft had been sighted in the nearby vicinity. A force of 20 Junkers Ju88s with escort was sighted over Ramsgate at an altitude of 13,000 feet. Thorn and Barker were flying as Red 2, when they attacked the German formation. Thorn reported:

> Just after taking off from Manston, I met a flight of Ju88s diving on the aerodrome. I dived and attacked from the front, my gunner firing 180 rounds from 100 yards range in two second bursts. I saw the aircraft burst into flames and dive into Ramsgate harbour. I noticed no enemy fire

The next day, seven new machines arrived at the squadron.   The aircraft however, had many modifications left undone and it would take another 48 hours in which to make them operationally serviceable.   Some had no self-sealing tanks.   Many had the wrong spark plugs.   The guns were not harmonised and many other details had to be carried out by the Maintenance Section.   The work continued throughout the night but was seriously hampered by air raids during which no light was allowed in the hangars. At 7.00 p.m. that evening, ten Defiants took off to patrol Dover under cloud base when enemy seaplanes were reported in the vicinity together with fighter escort, but none were seen. The squadron went down to sea level to investigate an apparent attack on a ship half way across the Channel, but it turned out to be a friendly fighter.

On 26th August, the squadron having taken off and ordered to patrol over the Dover area, when approaching the vector at 11,000 feet flying in Vic formation in line astern, they sighted twelve Dornier 17 bombers also in line astern formation coming inland over Herne Bay. At 12.20 pm, 264 Squadron attacked the bombers over Manston. Sergeant Pilot Ted Thorn's account of what happened next reads:

> Red Section took up position and started a No.1 attack, my gunner opened fire on one of the leading German section and observed fire coming from its starboard engine and then the machine fell in flames. He then opened fire on the second machine and its engine also caught fire. The enemy aircraft fell away, burning hard. On returning for a further attack, I observed the enemy aircraft well split up and two of them diving out to sea. We commenced to chase them when a Me109 hit us in the radiator.
>
> I spun down taking evasive action. When at 500 feet, we were again attacked by the Me109, who set us on fire. My gunner fired back and after crash-landing, the military informed us that the 109 had also crashed. Barker had opened fire at 200 yards closing to 150 yards on the first Dornier and 150 yards to 100 yards on the second. The Me109 was hit at point blank range. The majority of our bursts were for one or two seconds and we used approximately 1,500 rounds. I observed tracer from Red 1, Flight Lieutenant Banham hitting the Dornier 17, which caught fire and went diving in flames. My machine is Category 3 (total write-off).

When interviewed by the author, Fred Barker recalled the engagement:

> Basically what happened was we were doing our job, fighting away, when all of a sudden out of the blue this Messerschmitt appeared coming towards us firing. My instant reaction was to shout 'Dive' to Ted Thorn, dive, dive panic stations and he immediately did that. As we were going down the German came around again and I looked around to see if everything on our side was ok and returned fire. Unfortunately we had been damaged and Thorn was able to crash-land the aircraft, but on coming down I thought I had also seen the German in trouble. Again it was a momentary thing which happened in seconds. The same time our aircraft crashed on landing into a tree, we had to get away from it pretty promptly because the aircraft was smoking a bit. We then got arrested by the Home Guard, which

was another problem, but we convinced them who we were and then we had to make our way back to Hornchurch. Carrying our parachutes, we finally arrived in London journeying by train and there we met another pilot who had also been shot down, so we all came back together.

Barker and Thorn had been flying Defiant L7005, had crash-landed at Marshside, Chislet, Kent. They were credited with two Dorniers and a Messerschmitt 109 destroyed.

The squadron lost two other aircraft during this action. Defiant L6985 was shot down and crashed into the sea off Herne Bay, pilot Flight Lieutenant Arthur Banham baled out and was rescued, but the gunner Sergeant Barrie Baker was listed as missing. The same fate befell Defiant L7025, shot down by 109s. Pilot, Flying Officer Ian Stephenson baled out injured, but was rescued by boat; Sergeant Walter Maxwell sadly was lost.

The 28th August, was the last day that 264 would play a part in the Battle of Britain. The German raids that day started to appear over Cap Gris Nez at about 8.30 am; one formation of twenty-seven bombers was heading for Rochford airfield. That morning 264 were operating from Rochford and took off to intercept the raiders.

The Defiants were again outclassed by the German fighters and paid severely. Two Defiants, N1574 and L7026 were both shot down by Me109s at 8.55 a.m; their crews, Pilot Officer D. Whitley and Sergeant R.C. Turner, Pilot Officer P. L. Kenner and Pilot Officer. C.E. Johnson, were all killed. Defiant N1576 was badly damaged, hit by return fire from a Heinkel 111 over Dover at 9 a.m; Pilot Officer W.F. Carnaby and Pilot Officer, C.C. Ellery returned to base, both unhurt. Defiant L6957 was hit in the petrol tank while in combat over Folkestone at about the same time; the crew, Sergeant A.J. Launder and Sergeant V.R. Chapman were both unhurt and got back to base.

Squadron Leader G.D. Garvin and Flight Lieutenant Ash were not so fortunate; their aircraft L7021 was shot down in flames by German Ace Adolf Galland near Faversham. Squadron Leader Garvin bailed out and survived, but Flight Lieutenant Ash was killed when his parachute failed to open.

This day was another disastrous episode for the squadron. At day's end, the squadron received communication from headquarters of Fighter Command that because of the severe casualties they had suffered over the last several days, they were to be withdrawn from the day fighting. It was decided they should be sent to rest and perhaps used in the role of night fighting.

The squadron was relieved from Hornchurch on the 29th August and sent back up to Kirton-in-Lindsey in Lincolnshire. The squadron remained here at Kirton to rest and recuperate and make good the loss in pilots and aircraft for the next few months.

Sadly on the 4th September, Flying Officer D. K. C. O'Malley and Sergeant L.A.W. Rasmussen were both killed when their Defiant N1628 crashed on take off during a routine patrol. One of the squadron flights was sent to operate on night patrols from Luton aerodrome. Luton had only a small take-off area in an east-west direction, the runway only being six hundred yards in length, so one had to be pretty accurate in landing there. If you overshot the runway, you would be in trouble. This is exactly what happened on Monday October 7th when Defiant N1578 crashed on take-off, flown by Pilot Officer G. Hackwood and Flying Officer A O'Connell, both airmen were injured and admitted to hospital. The aircraft was a complete write off. The squadron continued to undertake night operations until the end of 1940.

At this stage of the war, the facilities and equipment for operating against enemy aircraft at night were primitive and the chances of encountering German bombers and shooting them down was extremely rare. The RAF night fighters were basically controlled by ground radar which vectored the night fighter as near to the target as possible, once in the position given by radar, the night fighter pilot had to basically scan the night sky looking for the tell-tale glow from the German bombers exhaust stubs or if he was lucky, the silhouette of the enemy aircraft against the night sky.

Fred Barker remembers the early night-fighter methods employed during the late months of 1940 and early 1941.

> We did a bit of training on night-fighting to get used to it and get co-ordination with the ground wireless and radar people. At that time it was basically hit or miss, we didn't have good aircraft radar interception sets installed. We did some practice runs with Havoc aircraft, the idea being to put a search-light on the enemy aircraft, while we would go in and shoot it down, but unfortunately it was not very effective.

On 11th February 1941, Edward Thorn and Fred Barker received the news that they had been awarded a Bar to their Distinguished Flying Medal for their actions during August 1940. The London Gazette notice read:

> Flight Sergeant Thorn and Sergeant Barker have constantly operated together as pilot and air gunner in Defiant aircraft and were awarded the D.F.M after shooting down six enemy aircraft. As a team, they have now accounted for six further enemy aircraft. Subsequently on 31st May 1940, operating with their squadron from Duxford over the beaches at Dunkirk, they destroyed two Heinkel 111s. On 24th August, they took off from Manston to patrol the coast and encountered 20 Ju88s escorted by Me109s and He113s (109s) and destroyed one Ju88. On 26th August, operating from Hornchurch they patrolled Dover with their squadron and made combat with a formation of 12 Dornier 17s escorted by Me109s and succeeded in destroying two Dorniers and one Me109. The Defiant took fire and the pilot dived down, so as to put out the flames. On coming out of the dive, the air gunner, Sergeant Barker, found an Me109 on his tail and with the aircraft still on fire, they manoeuvred so as to engage the enemy and assist a Hurricane which came to do combat with the Messerschmitt. It was not until the Hurricane had shot down the Me109 that they abandoned their machine, making successful parachute drops.

Altogether Flight Sergeant Thorn and Sergeant Barker have destroyed 12 enemy aircraft, 6 of these being subsequent to their receiving the D.F.M. They are strongly recommended for immediate awards of a Bar to the Distinguished Flying Medal.

One can take note that the above report in the London Gazette regarding the action of 26th August 1940 differs to Fred Barker's own account of that action and that they force-landed and did not parachute to safety or any mention of a Hurricane aircraft. If another RAF Fighter aircraft was involved in the action, neither Barker or Thorn could have been aware at the time with the pressing matter of trying to fly a damaged aircraft in a combat situation.

On the night of 9th April 1941, Flight Lieutenant Thorne and Sergeant Barker were called to action at Biggin Hill at 10.50 pm. Their aircraft call-sign was Plater 22.

Under the guidance of Kenley Ground Interception Control, they were vectored to Beachy Head, where they orbited at 15, 000 feet. The weather that night was very clear above the cloud base of 10/10ths at 7,000 feet. They were instructed on to an enemy aircraft plot and after many attempts to locate the aircraft, they finally sighted it over Brooklands in Surrey at 11.45 pm. From 1,000 yards astern and 200 feet below, flying on the same course at 18,000 feet, Thorn closed the Bolton-Paul Defiant to 100 yards, on the enemy's starboard side and Barker fired a two second burst into the fuselage; the ammunition being seen to burst down the middle of the enemy machine. At this stage there was no return fire from the German rear-gunner.

Thorn then manoeuvred the Defiant under to the port side of the German and Barker gave another good two second burst of fire at which point the port engine was seen to glow. The bomber then started to lose height and turned away to starboard. Crossing over the top of it, Barker was able to get a good burst at the cockpit. A final burst was put into the fuselage. There then appeared to be return fire from the German's forward gun with tracer appearing as they crossed over once more. Thorn now asked ground control for his position; their reply stated that he was now over Brooklands.

The enemy aircraft, a Heinkel 111 of 5/KG55 was now losing height rapidly with the Defiant following it down to 9,000 feet. The bomber dived steeply into cloud, emitting white smoke from both engines and fuselage. It was last seen heading due south, before crashing at Burbridge near Godalming in Surrey. Thorn and Barker landed back at Biggin Hill at 12.16 am on 10th April, having been airborne one hour and twenty six minutes.

This action was the last enemy aircraft claimed by this outstanding two man team who had survived Dunkirk and the Battle of Britain.

Fred Barker recalls this period of defending Britain's night skies against the German raiders:

We did get vectored on to various aircraft by ground-control who would give us information to steer a course of so many degrees and height etc. We only sighted one enemy aircraft during this period, but we did bring one down over Surrey later on. Desmond Hughes and Sergeant Fred Gash had been

successful in bringing down a Heinkel 111 somewhere near
Brentwood in Essex during the Battle of Britain.

We used to do intruder patrols over to France at night. What
shook me once on one patrol was you could see London burning
during the Blitz being lit up and being seen from that distance
was unbelievable in my mind.

Barker remained with 264 Squadron until he was posted away and sent to
Dulcross in Scotland. He was there for a couple of months, before being sent
to RAF Manston where a new type of gun-sight was being tested. He
undertook instruction on the new sight, and then went on an Air-Gunner
Instructors Course. On completion, he was posted back to Dulcross. He
remained there until the end of 1942, before being posted to Egypt as an air-
gunner instructor, training gunners about to go out to the Far East. The
courses lasted five weeks and during that time, he had to instruct the recruits
on basic gunnery and the workings of machine guns, and then take them up
to air gunnery firing ranges, to see if they were up to standard. Barker was
commissioned as a pilot officer on 25th April 1944, and ten months later on
the same date in October was promoted to flying officer.

Edward Thorn was posted to No. 32 Squadron at Angle, Wales in October
1941 and made a pilot officer on 11th October, becoming commander of the
squadron in April 1942. The squadron's role was mainly convoy protection in
the western approaches, still flying Hurricane Mk1s. He remained here until
that September, and on 22nd September was awarded the Distinguished
Flying Cross. He then went on to serve with No. 169 Night-fighter Squadron
as a flight commander, flying De-Havilland Mosquito MkIV aircraft, and was
with them when he was awarded a bar to his DFC. He remained in the RAF
after the war, but sadly, was killed in a flying accident on 12th February 1946,
while flying a Meteor jet fighter. The aircraft crashing at Rectory Farm in
Cambridgeshire.

Fred Barker left the Royal Air Force in 1946 and returned to civilian life.
He set up home in Essex with his wife Doreen and is now 89 years old. Barker
and Thorn were the most successful pilot and gunner Defiant team of the war.
Their final total of enemy aircraft claimed stands at twelve and one shared
destroyed and two damaged.

CHAPTER 4

GEORGE 'GRUMPY' UNWIN

George Cecil Unwin was born on 18th January 1913 at Bolton-on-Dearne in Yorkshire, approximately eight miles from the town of Doncaster. His father was George Henry Unwin, whose occupation was that of a coal miner, who worked at the collieries of Banbury and Hickleton. His mother Lydia Royle nee Dickinson was one of five daughters and five sons born to Thomas and Matilda. George was the eldest of four children, Sidney was the second eldest followed by daughter Phyllis and then the youngest son, Brian. The family lived at Derwent Cottages. George was educated at Wath-on-Dearne school, where he excelled academically and was especially good in sport, and was seen to be a very gifted footballer. He passed his Northern Universities matriculation exam at sixteen before leaving school in 1929.

Not wishing to follow in his father's profession, he looked for another avenue of employment. Whilst scouring the newspapers for any interesting work vacancies, he noticed an advertisement pamphlet offering apprenticeship placements in the Royal Air Force. He replied to the advertisement immediately and a few weeks later went to be interviewed and accepted into the RAF as an apprentice clerk (RAF No. 590289) at the RAF Records Offices at Ruislip. His family gave him their full support in this new venture. His father had always wanted better for his children and had told George 'I don't want you going down the Pit.' His father had told him tales of working on his knees in water with a pick doing twelve hour shifts, six days a week.

He was promoted to leading aircraftsman and served as administrative clerk general duties at the Headquarters Fighting Area at RAF Uxbridge from 24th April 1931 until November 1935, whereupon soon afterwards with help from his commanding officer, who was instrumental in him applying for flying duties. He was rejected twice and on the third attempt, he found out that the examining officer; Air Vice-Marshal J.E.A. Baldwin was a keen equestrian. When he came up in front of the officer, Unwin was asked 'what are your interests' Unwin replied 'I'm keen on horse riding,' 'Oh are you' replied the air vice-marshal. Of course, the only horses he had ridden were the pit ponies whose backs he had jumped on to ride in the local fields.

This third attempt was successful and he was selected to undertake pilot training. On the 25th of that month, he began his ab-initio course at the Elementary & Reserve Flying Training School at Woodley. Following flying instruction on Avro 504 and Tiger Moth biplanes, George was sent to No. 11 Flying Training School at Wittering on 17th February 1936. On completion of his training and receiving his wings brevet, he now awaited to find out which squadron he would be sent to. George was overjoyed when he received the news that he was to go to No. 19 Fighter Squadron based at RAF Duxford in Cambridgeshire as a sergeant pilot. No. 19 were one of the Royal Air Forces top fighter squadrons and had seen many famous names within their ranks including Squadron Leader Philip Babington MC, DFC and Squadron Leader L.H. Slatter OBE, DSO, DFC. Other notables included Flight Lieutenant Harry Broadhurst who had led the squadron's excellent aerobatic team on numerous occasions, especially at the Hendon Air Pageant.   Pilot Officer Johnny Kent was another who would later became a famous fighter leader during WW2 and finally attained the rank of group captain.

Unwin arrived at Duxford in August 1936 and after a few weeks began to feel at ease with fitting into the everyday workings of squadron life. He teamed up and became good friends with another sergeant pilot, Harry Steere who came from Wallasey. Unwin remembers those early days soon after arriving at Duxford:

> No.19 Squadron was supposed to be the best fighter squadron in the Royal Air Force.   My flight commander at the time was Harry Broadhurst who was the best shot in the RAF and that is where I learned to shoot. Broadhurst emphasized the key to shooting was to get close, the closer you got the more chance you had of hitting the target.   One of the weaknesses of all fighter pilots at the start of the war was that no one had been taught how to shoot properly. Estimation of range was the biggest weakness, as I found out when I became a gunnery instructor. Estimation of range was hopeless unless you were close enough; you were not going to hit anything.   All we fired at during this period was a drogue being towed along at 100 miles an hour. Broadhurst explained the size of the drogue in the gun sight, thus giving you the range. Nobody at that time thought there was going to be a war anyway in the mid thirties; the Royal Air Force was just a happy flying club.
>
> The squadron won many trophies and there were many trophies to be won in those days. Fight attack competitions, map reading, shooting and 19 Squadron seemed to win everything. They were the first to get new aircraft like the Bristol Bulldog and Gloster Gauntlets and later on the Spitfire in 1938.

In 1937, romance bloomed after meeting a local girl Edna May Cornwall who was always called 'Jimmie' at a dance in Cambridge and they later married in 1939.

Life at Duxford during the later part of the 1930s was an exciting, yet civilised form of service. Depending on the weather, on most days there would be flying and the squadron's aerobatic team would be preparing for the annual air displays that they would attend around Britain. Duxford would hold its Empire Air Day as well as attending the massive Hendon Air Pageant. On other days, some pilots would borrow a squadron aircraft and fly to other RAF aerodromes to visit colleagues. George Unwin remembers:

> In those days we would borrow the squadron hack and go and visit pilot friends at other airfields. Sometimes I would fly down to Hornchurch or North Weald, spend a pleasant afternoon chatting, have a drink and fly back before it got dark.

As the final years of the 1930s began to close, the threat of war with Germany under the leadership of Adolf Hitler and his Nazi regime seemed to draw nearer. In 1938, the squadrons of the Royal Air Force had been put on a war footing as politicians from many nations tried to halt Hitler's attempts to enlarge the German empire by occupying land in Czechoslovakia.

As Neville Chamberlain, Britain's Prime Minister travelled to Munich in an attempt to halt war, the RAF continued its preparations. Many squadrons had already practiced Home Defence Exercises over the previous months in case of such an emergency and No. 19 Squadron was no different. Fortunately for them, they had received a month earlier, the RAF's latest monoplane fighter, the Vickers-Supermarine Spitfire. The new fighter first arrived at 19 Squadron flown in from the Supermarine factory at Woolston, Hampshire on 4th August 1938 by the squadron's commanding officer Squadron Leader Henry Cozens. Unwin remembers this period of conversion on the new revolutionary fighter.

> We all took a turn at sitting in the cockpit and were shown the controls. We then had to mentally rehearse in order the various controls and starting procedures etc. Then shortly afterwards you were on your own. I took to the air and was immediately impressed with the Spitfire. Flying the Spitfire in comparison to any other fighter aircraft I had known was like driving a Ford 8 or an MG, it was a super aircraft, so sensitive on the controls. There was no heaving, pulling, pushing or kicking, you just breathed on it. If you wanted to turn, you just moved your hands slowly and she went. She really was the perfect flying machine. I would say that the Spitfire Mark II was the perfect ratio of power to weight, she hadn't got a vice at all, she would only spin if you made her and she would come straight out of it as soon as you applied opposite rudder and pushed the stick forward, she came straight up. I've never flown anything sweeter.
>
> Another thing was that No.111 Squadron was the first Hurricane Squadron and as soon as they could muster twelve aircraft, the first thing they did was come over to beat us up at Duxford, because we were the number one fighter squadron of the Royal Air Force. But of course, when we received our Spitfires and when we had twelve available, we went straight down to Northolt and beat hell out of them. It was just a very healthy rivalry with all the squadrons.

George Unwin was a keen real ale enthusiast and visited the local pubs around Duxford, but some of the pubs were strictly off limit to the sergeants and only frequented by the officers:

> Every time I was off duty I was back off to my wife who lived in a little village Cumberton which was five miles west of Cambridge. We use to frequent the Pub at Whittlesford, the Red Lion which was only a mile or so from the aerodrome.

Oddly enough without any orders being given, this was regarded as the officers' pub, although we were allowed in, there was no question of forbidding us, we just quietly kept away. We could always go to one of two pubs in Cambridge, the Criterion or the Prince of Wales, give a secret knock, three times on the door and ask for Nelly and you were in.

It was at Duxford, that Unwin was photographed with the early Spitfire aircraft and in one particular photograph he was pictured with his pet Alsatian dog named 'Flash.' George Unwin's brother Brian remembers the dog well:

He would bring the dog home on leave to South Yorkshire; they would go off together to a place called Bromfleet with cardboard boxes to pick mushrooms. The dog on one occasion got soaking wet and they set off back home with George at the wheel of the car and the dog tottering behind, trying to get him dry. When he went on sorties 'Flash' would be left in the sergeants' mess, not in the living quarters, because he was friendly with all the pilots. There were large French style windows in the mess and when he had to force-land once in the Battle of Britain near Brentwood, the pilots back at Duxford said, that the dog sensed something and raced straight through the open windows and was gone. 'Flash' was gone for days and finally returned with bleeding paws, obviously looking for his master.

On 9th March 1939, Unwin was flying Spitfire K9797, when suddenly the aircraft began to splutter and overheat. The engine then partially seized. Unwin had no option but to try and force-land the aircraft. He was at this time over Sudbury in Suffolk and looking for a suitable place to put the aircraft down. He noticed a large playing field adjacent to a school and decided to land there. As he dropped the undercarriage and prepared to land, he noticed the small figures of school children. They had seen the Spitfire and started running towards where he was about to land.

With only a hundred feet left to go before he would touch down, he banked slightly and landed in a thick hedge on the edge of the playing field, thus avoiding the school children. On hitting the ground, Unwin's Sutton harness snapped and he was shot forward hitting his forehead on the gun-site which gashed his right eyebrow, apart from this he was unhurt. On inspection of the Merlin engine it was found that the coolant pipe had broken and had punctured the engine casing, causing the engine to seize. As a result of his quick thinking in difficult circumstances and avoiding possible casualties on the ground, he was awarded a commendation.

The squadron continued to fly and practice Fighter Command manoeuvres that were mainly based on out of date tactical thinking. It was always envisaged that the fighter would only have to deal with bombers. In reality, there were no tactics to deal with fighters.

By mid-August 1939, Britain was put on a war footing as the dark cloud of Nazism seemed bent on conflict. After Poland was invaded on the first day of September, France and Britain declared war on Germany on 3rd September 1939.

It had been expected that the Germans would launch attacks against the rest of the European countries immediately, but after the first few weeks of war, Britain settled down to a routine of apathy, when everything seemed to go on as normal apart from the blackout which claimed more lives due to car accidents and pedestrians being knocked down than any action against the enemy. The Phoney War continued through to winter of 1939 and beyond into early 1940. The only successes had been at sea, where the Royal Navy had scored a victory against the German pocket-battleship the Graf-Spee at Montevideo in Uruguay at the Battle of the River Plate in December.

A new pilot arrived at 19 Squadron on 7th February 1940; it was Flying Officer Douglas Bader, who gaited into the officers' mess on his tin legs after returning to operational flying. He had previously undertaken a refresher course at the Central Flying School at Upavon, having been out of the RAF for quite a few years due to his flying accident in which he lost both legs. Many of the pilots who were in the mess probably wondered what use would a man with artificial legs be once the real fighting began? Bader was of course later to prove them all wrong.

At a Conservative meeting held on 4th April, Prime Minster Neville Chamberlain told members that Adolf Hitler had failed miserably to take advantage of his military superiority in September the previous year and that, 'he had missed the bus.' Five days later on 9th April, German troops invaded Norway. The real war had just begun.

On 19th April, 19 Squadron sent a section to operate from the airfield of Horsham St. Faith, near Norwich, Norfolk. It was while here that George Unwin remembers Bader and an accident that he was involved in:

> I first knew of Douglas Bader when he was convalescing from his accident at the RAF hospital at Uxbridge, after he had lost his legs. I was then a young clerk at Hillingdon House at Uxbridge and handled the papers for the court of enquiry associated with the accident, and that's when I first came across him. We used to see him every morning going pass our huts being pushed around in his wheelchair and we used to say good morning to him. I never saw him again until February 1940, when suddenly Flying Officer Bader arrived on 19 Squadron, stomping around. He actually flew as my No.2 on a few occasions on convoy patrol, getting the feel of things again and procedures back again. He then flew with us over Dunkirk as a flight lieutenant with 222 Squadron which didn't last very long because soon afterwards he was made a squadron leader and sent to command 242 Squadron at Coltishall, and then he came back to Duxford and as commanding officer led the Duxford Wing, the first of the Big Wing boys.
>
> He was the man who gave me my nickname of 'Grumpy.' On one of those visits to the east coast to patrol the convoys, I went up there with him and I said to him if the balloon goes up this time you can lead, and I'll fly as your No.2.

We took off from Horsham St. Faith one day and we had a very short area to take off. Off we went and Bader forgot to put his aircraft into fine-pitch for take-off, never got airborne and crashed. As a result, he damaged his tin legs and had to get replacements, he wasn't hurt but the aircraft was a write-off. He got a new pair of legs and of course they were not machine made, so they had to be adjusted. We had a little hut at the aerodrome where you could get your head down for a sleep and I was trying to do this at half past three in the morning, while Bader was trying to adjust one of his legs with a screwdriver and a tin of oil. He was going scrape, scrape, scrape and then he strapped it on and walked around the room, then the leg started squeaking and you can image the noise; eventually I said to him 'for God's sake if you must do that, go outside.' The film with Snow White and the Seven Dwarfs was on locally, he said 'oh shut up Grumpy' and from then I retained this nickname.

Bader left soon after and was promoted to the rank of flight lieutenant with No.222 Squadron also based at Duxford during this period. The squadron continued throughout April and the beginning of May carrying on with patrols around the 12 Group area of the Midlands and North-East Anglia coast.

On 10th May, the long awaited German offensive began as the lightening Blitzkrieg pushed its way through the Ardennes and swept into Holland, Belgium and France. Within ten days of fighting the Allies had been pushed back by the hammer blows dealt to them by the Panzer divisions and the continuous bombing from the dreaded Stuka dive bombers.

No. 19 claimed its first victory of the war on 11th May, when a Junkers Ju88 bomber was intercepted by Spitfires of Blue Section flown by Flight Lieutenant Wilfred Clouston, Flying Officer John Petre and Flight Sergeant Harry Steere. They all attacked it and sent the German plunging into the sea.

In France the British Expeditionary force fell aback in retreat and by the 13th Sedan had fallen, it seemed a hopeless task to stop the German advance. By the 20th, Amiens had been taken, the British were now ordered to withdraw towards the port town of Dunkirk.

Back in Britain, frantic plans were now being put into motion by the heads of all the armed services to evacuate the stricken armies in France. Under the leadership of Vice-Admiral Bertram Ramsey, Operation 'Dynamo' was launched.

As the preparations for the evacuation got underway, the RAF fighter squadrons were briefed on their role, to fly over to the French coast and protect the naval vessels that would pick up the Allied troops from the port of Dunkirk and its beaches. At Duxford, they too were called to get ready to send No. 19 Squadron south, to operate from the Essex aerodrome at Hornchurch. George Unwin recalls the squadrons call to arms:

We shot off down to Hornchurch on 25th May and flew our first operation the next day, the second day of the operation, and we stayed there and covered the whole period up to the 5th June.

That was the first time we ever saw anything to shoot at. The Spitfires were not allowed to go to France, but once it fell, a lot of Spitfire Squadrons went to Dunkirk. We arrived at Hornchurch and took the place of 92 Squadron who after 36 hours had only got three aircraft left. We also flew as a wing at one stage from the aerodrome with the other home based squadrons.

On the opening day of operations for No. 19 Squadron, the pilots were up early and had breakfast before going to take up position at dispersal for their first flight of the day.

At just after 7.30 am, they received instructions to take off and patrol over Calais. Twelve Spitfires led by Squadron Leader Geoffrey Stephenson, taxied out on to the grass flight path and in seconds were airborne. Twenty minutes later they had arrived over their patrol area at an altitude of 18,000 feet. Suddenly while undertaking a turn, the squadron sighted an enemy formation of twenty plus Junker Ju87 dive-bombers 'Stukas' heading seaward from Calais. The German aircraft seemed unaware of the RAF fighters in their vicinity and flew on in formation. Stephenson gave the order to engage the Stukas, but then became aware over the radio, that above was a formation of thirty or more Messerschmitt 109s who were probably acting as escort to the dive-bombers. The squadron split, some to attack the Stukas the rest to engage the 109s. Combat was met with the sky full of diving and twisting aircraft trying to better the other. George Unwin recalled that the sky seemed to be full of Messerschmitts and that one could not easily take in the situation.

A Messerschmitt 109 attacked me and I just froze for a few seconds, watching his guns as they spouted bright sparks along the wing edges. I was instantly brought back to reality, when my aircraft received two bullet hits just behind the cockpit. Shaken into action, I immediately broke away and headed for home, lucky to have survived my first combat sortie. Many didn't.

During this action, the squadron had suffered losses, Squadron Leader Stephenson's aircraft was damaged and he was forced to land in France, becoming a prisoner of war. Pilot Officer Peter Watson was attacked by 109s and seen to bale out of his Spitfire, but was later reported as missing and Flying Officer Eric Ball was wounded in combat, but managed to return to Hornchurch, his aircraft coming to a halt in the middle of the flight path. Ball had survived a close call, when a bullet had shaved his helmet and hair leaving a small wound. In return the enemy had suffered the loss of three Me109s destroyed and one damaged with another six Junker 87s claimed destroyed and one probably destroyed.

On return to Hornchurch, the pilots recounted in detail their first experiences of combat with the intelligence officer and with fellow pilots. Unwin would later recall that first day:

On the very first trip over Dunkirk we followed the book, in other words, there were three fighter command attacks, but they were all in formation, more suited for a Hendon air display. You went in formation in threes in line astern, picked off your targets, which were only supposed to be bombers.

The powers that be had worked it out that no escort fighter would get over to this country from Germany, which was true, there would only be bombers. You attacked a formation of bombers which flew straight and level and didn't try and evade you. This was the plan and of course the first lot we saw were a load of Junkers JU 87's dive bombers, very slow aircraft.

We went in Fighter Command Attack No.1 in threes and we were going about twice the speed, and were rapidly overhauling them, throttling back and trying to get a bead on them, forgetting about the fact that there might be escorts. Then suddenly the escort fighters came down and clobbered us. The front three, the C.O. and his two wingmen were shot down and one was killed. The CO spent the rest of the war in a prisoner of war camp and the other, Michael Lyons, who eventually became an air-vice marshal, he'd got a bullet through the knee and that was the end of 1940 for him.

From then on Fighter Command attacks disappeared, we never received any instructions on what to do, we devised our own tactics from then on and those were to get in and out quickly. No loitering around and then returning for another attack. Eventually we copied the Germans, they flew in two's and the number two's job was to look after number one.

During the afternoon, the squadron now led by Flight Lieutenant Brian 'Sandy' Lane in absence of Squadron Leader Stephenson, whose fate was unknown, were sent off again at 2.30 pm. Coming in at 8,000 feet over the French coast, they patrolled for thirty minutes before they were attacked from astern and above by 109 fighters. Fortunately, in time, Flying Officer Gordon Sinclair shouted a warning to break as the Germans dived down. A dogfight ensued with both sides taking casualties. The Germans lost one Messerschmitt destroyed, shot down by Lane and two further probably destroyed or damaged by Flying Officers' John Petre and Gordon Sinclair. On the minus side, sadly Sergeant C.A Irwin was killed and Pilot Officer Michael Lyne was wounded in the knee, but managed to fly back across the Channel before having to force-land his Spitfire near Deal in Kent. So concluded 19 Squadrons opening day of operations over the French Coast.

The next morning of the 27th May, the squadron was at readiness to await the call to take off across the Channel to patrol over Dunkirk. They finally got the call at 11.00 am and proceeded with instructions to patrol a line between Calais and Dunkirk. Led by their commanding officer Flight Lieutenant Brian Lane, the squadron sighted a lone Heinkel 111 and attacked it near Gravelines. Lane chased the enemy who headed for cloud to avoid the encounter. The CO expended most of his ammunition into the aircraft, but could not claim any visible damage to the German, although the rear gunners return fire had stopped.

Unwin, who had been flying as Lane's No.2, had unfortunately become separated from his leader and while Lane had been dealing with the Heinkel, Unwin had attracted the attention of three Messerschmitt Me110s. Fortunately Unwin had managed to evade the enemy machines and head back to Hornchurch unscathed.

Later that day, 19 Squadron were ordered back across to France on an evening patrol at 7.00 pm. At around 8.00 pm, they sighted aircraft in the distance and went to investigate. Dorniers were recognised and attacked by Sergeant Bernard Jennings and Wilfred Clouston who attacked his enemy from astern and with the sun behind, a perfect tactical manoeuvre. Both aircraft were claimed destroyed. In the meantime, Flight Lieutenant Lane, George Unwin and Sergeant Frank Brinsden had observed a German reconnaissance aircraft at low-level, a Henschel Hs126, flying at 1,000 feet. Both Lane and Brinsden attacked the small craft, but failed due to the German pilot's exceptional flying skills and aircraft's manoeuvrability.

After following it inland for many miles, both Lane and Brinsden broke off their chase and headed back towards Dunkirk. Unwin however, had continued to observe the enemy aircraft from a higher position up sun as it continued inland heading into Belgium, as far as Ypres. Thinking that the danger had passed, the German pilot began to fly straight and level unaware of the solitary Spitfire still stalking him. George Unwin's report states:

> I gave chase and the enemy aircraft began to evade my attack by stalling, followed by a spiral dive. I got him in my sights and fired one very short burst and got him on my first pass. He then burst into flames and fell into a field.

On his return back to Hornchurch, Unwin was able to claim his first victory of the war.

The very next day, because of the increased enemy air activity over the Dunkirk beaches, it was decided that the Hornchurch Squadrons would fly in Wing formations of three. No. 19, 54 and 65 Squadrons took off on the early patrol at 4.30 am, but only 54 and 65 Squadrons saw any action during that flight. No. 19 returned from their uneventful mission and was told to expect to undertake a further patrol at 9.00 am accompanied by 65 and 616 Squadrons.

At 10.00 am, the squadron now over the French Coast, was confronted with a large formation of fifty enemy fighters at an altitude of 16,000 feet and a mighty combat ensued, with aircraft all over the sky, diving and climbing for position. During the engagement Unwin attached himself to one Messerschmitt 109, attacking it from the beam with a full deflection shot from 250 yards, firing one second bursts. He then came astern of the German closing to 150 yards and fired more rounds into the enemy. It was last seen spinning towards the ground from 8,000 to 3,000 feet, before Unwin had to break away to head back. On his return, he claimed the Me109 destroyed, using only seventy rounds from each machine gun.

The next two days were uneventful with regards to claims by the squadron over on patrol in France, but they received a new commanding officer in the form of Squadron Leader Phillip Pinkham. Unfortunately, Pinkham had no previous combat experience having been an instructor at Sutton Bridge, before going to the 11 Group Pool at Andover in 1939, then acting squadron leader in January 1940. Due to his inexperience it fell upon Flight Lieutenant Lane to continue to lead in the air.

Saturday 1st June 1940, was to be a particularly interesting day of operations for 19 Squadron flying from Hornchurch. They took off for the early morning patrol at 5.00 am with 41, 222 and 616 Squadrons' and headed across to Dunkirk. Two to three miles east of Dunkirk they sighted twelve enemy aircraft at 4,000 feet. George Unwin flying that day as Red 3 takes up the story:

> We formed in line astern and engaged the enemy. They formed line astern and used evasive action by turning. The aircraft looked like Me Jaguars (Me110s). I climbed underneath one and gave a burst of approximately five seconds at 150 to 100 yards range. The aircraft blew up over my head. I then chased another who turned and climbed as I got within range. I gave him a long burst and his starboard engine then stopped and threw out oil and smoke. I carried on firing until about 100 yards, and then dived under him to avoid collision. I looked around for a while for more aircraft, but could only see Spitfires. Being almost out of ammunition I returned home. Practically no return fire was experienced. The German aircraft were fast and I had to use 12 Boost to catch them.

He claimed one Messerschmitt 110 destroyed and the other as a probable. The rest of the squadron had fared very well and had claimed a further five Me110s destroyed and three damaged as well as a further three Messerschmitt 109s. The only casualty being Sergeant Jack Potter, who ditched his aircraft Spitfire K9836, in the sea 15 miles from the English coast, he was fortunately picked up by a nearby passing boat. Unwin remembers Potter's unexpected swim in the Channel:

> A friend of mine, Sergeant Jack Potter, had a rather unique experience, he got a shell through the wing which he knew had hit something that mattered but couldn't remember which side the oil cooler was on. It had hit the oil cooler and on the way home the engine stopped. He mistakenly decided to stay with the aircraft and belly landed in the sea not knowing what would happen. The Spitfire immediately began to sink, he did manage to get out and eventually came to the surface, he was picked up by a French fishing vessel and gave him a fisherman's dry sweater and trousers, filled him full of wine and took him all the way back to Dunkirk. This vessel came back with him on board and 200 soldiers, that was quite a story. The most valuable thing about Dunkirk from everybody's point of view, was the amount of experience you gained in that very short spell of about ten days. It was invaluable to us, the survivors of 1940, I am sure that was a major factor with the experienced hands

surviving, because it is incredible how many experienced pilots survived in 1940.

After being refuelled and rearmed after the early patrol, Brian Lane led 19 Squadron back into the air once more at 8.25 am. With them again were 41, 222 and 616 Squadrons totalling thirty-seven aircraft. They were given instructions over the R/T to patrol from Nieuport in Belgium down to Dunkirk, but no activity was sighted until 10.00 am, when Lane's attention was directed to what he thought was a bomb being seen to burst near three ships off Dunkirk. Unwin's report of the following action relates:

> We formed in line astern and I felt a blow on the leg. I turned the aircraft round thinking enemy fighters were behind me and then discovered that the radiator handle had shot forward. By this time the other two Spitfires from my section had disappeared. I climbed above the clouds and found numerous anti-aircraft bursts and a few lone Spitfires.
>
> Suddenly I saw two large twin engine aircraft, which were Heinkel 111s. I gave chase and was joined by some aircraft of 222 Squadron. One Heinkel 111 went through the cloud. The other tried to hide in them, but as they were only a few feet thick, the aircraft was clearly discernable. I gave a burst of about five seconds from 400 yards with return fire coming back from the German. I must have then got the rear-gunner as no more return fire was experienced. I therefore closed to 100 yards and with slight deflection shot, gave him the rest of my ammunition. His starboard engine stopped and I then left him to the fellow of 222, having no more ammunition. If he went down, it would have been four to eight miles inland from Dunkirk in a north-easterly direction.

Unwin claimed the aircraft as probably destroyed. Only Sergeant Harry Steere would claim a confirmed victory from that patrol, with another Heinkel. Two further Heinkels were claimed as probable or damaged by Pilot Officer Leonard Haine and Pilot Officer Gordon Sinclair and a Dornier 215 by Sergeant Jennings.

The squadron continued to carry out patrols on 2nd, 3rd and 4th June, but during three days they made no contact with the Luftwaffe. On 5th June, 19 Squadron were ordered to return back to their home base at Duxford. George Unwin's memory of those final flights over Dunkirk, were still vivid many years later:

> The view we had of the beaches at Dunkirk, especially on the last day was incredible. There were no German aircraft, we flew up and down the coast and there was the most awful sight of waste, debris, trucks, you name it. I've never seen so much war material, so derelict and there wasn't a soul around. The oil tanks were burning all the time, you didn't need a compass to get to Dunkirk. You took off from Hornchurch and the prevailing

wind was from the south east and the smoke from Dunkirk
drifted over the Channel to London, you just flew down the
smoke and you were there. The oil tanks were still burning weeks
afterwards, it really was absolute desolation.

Back at Duxford after the operations over the French coast, the squadron had
a brief rest period. It was 19 Squadron who was chosen that month in June to
be given the task of carrying out trials and evaluation on the first cannon-
armed Spitfires. The first aircraft that arrived at Duxford was R6261, others
soon followed. Unwin remembers the cannon Spitfires and some of the
problems they accounted with the new armament.

From the end of the Dunkirk period to the beginning of the
Battle of Britain, we received the first cannon Spitfires,
exchanging our eight gun Spitfires for the new 20mm cannon
aircraft. The reason for that was obvious, you got a bigger
hitting power, but you needed it, because they were armour-
plating the German aircraft; the old 0.303 ammunition wasn't
getting through so often.
    Unfortunately, they hadn't got the secret of belt feed
mechanism and so we had a small magazine which only carried
sixty rounds per gun, this only allowed six seconds of total fire
power. We only had two cannons, nothing else and if you
applied any G force the magazine feed stopped. This was due to
the bullet failing to go into the breach properly and jamming the
gun. The aircraft had these special wings with a huge blister on
top where the magazine fitted.
    We went through quite a large part of the Battle of Britain
until the beginning of September, trying to shoot with these
cannons and suffered quite a few casualties through getting into
scraps with the enemy and not being able to hit back. There was
nothing more infuriating than getting yourself into a scrap,
especially outnumbered and when you pressed the cannon to fire
nothing happened. We were losing people through this and we
kept protesting because these things should never have been
issued in that state, they should have been tested at Boscombe
Down. How the hell they ever got through without being tested
I don't know. We were just furious that we should be issued with
equipment that had obviously never been tested in the middle of
a war.
    We had them a long time, quite a few weeks with these
damned aeroplanes. They were especially made, you couldn't
put them in an ordinary Spitfire, They only made eighteen of
them to start with and we were given them and they were
absolutely useless. You could only fire absolutely straight and
level as soon as you put any more than 1-G on, or turned and
your guns would stop.
    It was only during this period that our morale did falter and
eventually 'Stuffy' Dowding had to come and see us personally

and find out why we were so bloody minded and I must say he finished up by saying 'I won't teach chickens how to suck eggs, you shall have your eight gun Spitfires back by tomorrow morning' and thank God we did. Eventually they got the belt feed mechanism secret from France and there was a film made about that, supposed to be fiction, it was called 'The Foreman went to France'. With the belt feed mechanism you could carry a lot more ammunition and it worked, subsequently all fighters had the 20mm.

The trials on the new cannons continued well into July, the pilots spending most of their time trying out new tactics for firing the weapon, while the ground personnel carried on trying to sort out the problems connected with the magazine feed

On Tuesday 9th July, while taxiing out to take off on a patrol; George Unwin's aircraft K9853 was suddenly struck by Spitfire K9799 piloted by Pilot Officer Peter Howard- Williams. There was the terrific sound of buckling metal as the two aircraft met. Fortunately neither pilot was injured but for the aircraft it was a complete mess. Unwin's aircraft fuselage was completely crushed with the stern frame chewed up. The other Spitfire's airscrew was beyond repair, the undercarriage had collapsed with both main planes and stern frame buckled. One can only imagine the choice words that George Unwin would have spoke at the time. Taxiing accidents were not uncommon as the Spitfire with its long front section made it difficult for pilots to see ahead and they had to basically zigzag their way to the take off point. In a hurried scramble with other aircraft, there was always the possibility of running into another aircraft if not careful.

. On 24th July, 'A' Flight moved from Duxford and took up position a few miles down the road at the satellite airfield at Fowlmere. This airfield had been built during the First World War as a landing ground for Home Defence Squadrons to combat the Zeppelin airship menace in 1916/17. It had remained open until 1922, when the land was handed back to the landowner. It was now opened again for operational use. Accommodation at Fowlmere consisted only of six Nissen huts and a large barn which they converted into a Mess.

John Milne was a flight rigger with the squadron in 1940; he arrived at Duxford on 3rd March 1940. He was responsible for the upkeep and repairs on the Spitfires airframe, and worked for many long hours doing this, especially during the battle. He recalls his time spent at Fowlmere and Duxford:

When we first moved to Fowlmere, there was no permanent accommodation. We slept in bell tents with out feet pointed to the central pole. A mobile cookhouse accompanied us and one day it caught fire. We had to dig latrine trenches and spent most of our time out of doors. Nobody seemed to mind. Fowlmere later had Nissen huts, never popular, as the condensation dripped down from the underside of the cold steel roof onto one's bedding and oneself.

The airfield was far from level and dipped down considerably in the corner nearest to Duxford. Parts of it were laid with metal mesh decking to improve the surface. I will always remember the sound of the Merlin engines starting, taxiing and the Spitfires flying low over the airfield; the smell of glycol coolant leaking onto hot metal and the smell of the one hundred octane fuel and the staining from its green dye.

Of course I remember George Unwin, as I worked on his aircraft numerous times; and the time he and Howard-Williams collided on the ground. He wasn't very happy and the words he uttered are pretty unprintable.

During this period the Battle of Britain had begun in earnest, officially recorded as starting on July 10th 1940. While the squadrons based down south in 11 Group were heavily immersed in action against the increasing raids by the Luftwaffe, those in No. 12 Group waited around for the call that would send them against the Germans.

In that month, former 19 Squadron Flying Officer Bader had been promoted since his time with them and 222 Squadron. Now made an acting squadron leader, he was given command of No. 242 'Canadian' Squadron, who were suffering from low morale. They were now based at Coltishall and Bader was sent to sort out the problem and bring the squadron back to operational standing, which he did. He was also getting extremely frustrated at not being able to get into the battle and made this quite clear to the commander of 12 Group Air Vice-Marshal Trafford Leigh Mallory.

Action in the battle for 19 Squadron finally came on 16th August 1940, after they had flown into Coltishall that day. Following an earlier patrol that afternoon, with no enemy activity encountered, the squadron prepared to fly back to Fowlmere that evening. At 5.15 pm, A Flight was ordered up to investigate an X-Raid. Brian Lane led seven Spitfires flown by Sergeants' Unwin, Potter, Roden and Jennings and officer pilots Brinsden and Cunningham. At 5.35 pm, thirty-five miles east of Harwich off the Essex coast, the flight sighted the incoming enemy raid. Unwin's report of that patrol reads:

> I was Red 3 with Flight Lieutenant Lane and Sergeant Roden. We left Coltishall at 5.15 pm and we were ordered to vector at 15,000 feet. After vectoring for about twenty minutes a large formation of enemy aircraft was sighted ahead and slightly above. They were escorted by a large number of Me110s, and above them was an escort of Me109s. We tried to reach the bombers unobserved, but were sighted by the Me110s (about 30), we immediately engaged and I gave a 110 a short burst at close range, he half rolled and went vertically down. I was immediately attacked by another 110, but managed to get rid of him by turning. I found myself presented with a perfect target at about 100 yards. I fired all my rounds into him and he fell over on his side with bits falling off. He dived steeply and his tail came off. I followed him down and on coming through the

clouds I saw the end of a splash, where he had gone in. I returned to base at 6.30 pm. During the combat my starboard cannon had a stoppage.

During the combat nearly all the Spitfires' cannons had malfunctioned and the pilots reported on landing that the guns had jammed. Unwin reported his claims as one Me110 destroyed and another as probably destroyed.

> At the start of the Battle, we were not in the thick of it, we were at Duxford, which was forty miles as the crow flies from the heart of London We were in 12 Group, not 11 Group and there was a lot of rivalry between the two group commanders. It was only when we got permission to fly the Big Wing, the five squadrons together, three Hurricane and two Spitfire Squadrons that we really did take a big part in the battle and that wasn't until later on.
>
> Most of our operations were patrolling the 11 Group aerodromes whilst they were on the ground re-fuelling and re-arming. We would sit up there like stuffed Turkeys and have no fun. This was aggravating because in retrospect, I know that it must have been due to the rivalry. I have spoken many times with the Biggin Hill, North Weald and Hornchurch boys and they were flying four to five times a day. This was ridiculous. We would be sat at Duxford with five squadrons and probably do nothing all day long. Day after day this used to happen.

Unwin's next enemy claim was to come on 3rd September, when he was leading Red Section on a standing patrol over their base. At 10.35 am he sighted smoke bursts towards the south, coming from the anti-aircraft guns. The Spitfires headed towards the bursts to investigate and south-west of Colchester they saw a formation of fifty enemy bombers with a massive fighter cover of between one hundred to one hundred and fifty aircraft flying east. The Spitfires formed into line astern and climbed into the sun in front of the bombers, intending to take on the fighters.

The commanding officer Squadron Leader Pinkham, then turned to attack and that's when Unwin saw an Me110 turn towards his Spitfire. This machine was two to three miles ahead of the main enemy formation apparently a look out. On sighting me, he turned away and he gave a very short deflection burst, but missed. However the enemy machine then flew straight and Unwin closed to a hundred yards and blew the enemy's port engine out. The 110 continued to fly on and there was no return fire observed. He gave the 110 another burst from his port gun as his starboard gun had stopped firing. This time the enemy's starboard engine fell out and the pilot baled out. The aircraft crashed south of Maldon, near Battlesbridge at the inland point to one of the rivers.

This aircraft was later identified as crashing at Edwins Hall, Stowmaries in Essex at approximately 11.00 am. Its two crewmen Oberleutnant Messner and Unteroffizier Santoni both baled out and were captured.

Squadrons of the Duxford Wing were called into action during the late afternoon of 7th September. At 4.45 pm, the Wing was given instructions

over the R/T by the Sector Group Controller to patrol 15 miles north of the
Thames Estuary. 19 Squadron consisting of eight aircraft led by 'Sandy' Lane,
were sent to cover the area around North Weald.

Unwin's report of the patrol states:

> We were sent to patrol North Weald at 10,000 feet and saw anti-
> aircraft bursts and a number of enemy aircraft, about fifty in all.
> Squadron Leader Lane suddenly saw Me110s diving down in
> front of him. We attacked and one crashed in flames. I had dived
> down to 4,000 feet by this time and lost my section. I climbed
> back up to 25,000 feet and saw a Hurricane Squadron going
> somewhere in a hurry, so I trailed them and suddenly saw three
> separate formations of about thirty enemy bombers each with
> escorts of about thirty fighters. The Hurricanes attacked the
> bombers and I found myself surrounded by Me109s. The usual
> fight ensued, during which I definitely hit at least five of them,
> but only two were definitely shot down, both in flames. I then
> climbed for a breather and shadowed the third formation, when
> I sighted a fourth new one arriving. By this time two of the three
> other formations had turned north and the other went straight
> over North Weald. The leading formation then turned east and
> was at 25,000 feet above. As there didn't seem to be any fighters
> left, I dived down on the rear Vic of bombers and used the rest
> of my ammo, about fifty incendiaries at about 400 to 50 yards
> range. The aircraft wobbled, but carried on and I returned to
> base

On 11th September, the squadron was called to action during late afternoon
when enemy aircraft were picked up and plotted heading for London. Spitfires
of No. 74 and 611 Squadrons joined with 19 Squadron to form a three
squadron wing to intercept the raiders.

At 4.15 pm, the enemy was picked up flying north of Gravesend at 20,000
feet, consisting of Dorniers, Heinkels and Me110s. The RAF squadrons went
into the attack and pilots picked out their targets. Unwin recalls:

> I suddenly saw this lone Dornier. How he was on his own I'll
> never know, but he was off on his way home. So I went after
> him. The drill against the Dornier was that he had a dustbin rear
> gunner hanging down below the fuselage and you had to fix him
> first and then close in for the aircraft. This I did, I could see him
> shooting at me and I closed in and gave him a burst and shut
> him up, least thought I had. I'll never know to this day whether
> I did or didn't or whether someone took his place.
>
> As I closed in on him and started shooting, I suddenly saw his
> rear gunner shooting back at me with little red sparks you can
> see. I didn't pay much attention to it; I just thought a quick burst
> of the guns would silence him. Suddenly I was covered in smoke.
> To my horror a hole appeared. I was leaning forward of course as
> one did to view the gun-site which was fortunately protected by

a screen of bullet resistant glass, about an inch and a half thick, some six inches across a hole appeared in front of my face. I thought 'good god I must be dead' or something, no blood, no nothing but I'm covered in smoke, I thought I was on fire. I whipped the hood back, undid my straps and started to get out.

By this time I'd broken away and was going down hill, I was halfway out of the cockpit when suddenly I saw that smoke was coming from the top of the engine, through the engine cowling which is where the glycol pipe is, the coolant pipe. It was really brown in colour, it wasn't black smoke and I could smell it too, it was glycol.

I got back into the cockpit and strapped myself in again, leaving the canopy hood open. I continued down in case someone was following me and started looking for a field to land in. In those days you were not to, or ordered to land with your undercarriage up as you were supposed to in any forced landing, you were supposed to get it down without hurting the aircraft. So I waited until I'd found a field and got down to about 1,000 feet, dropped the undercarriage and did a forced landing in a field which had a few cows in it. It was quite a big field and I had no trouble at all in landing.

I hadn't even got out of the cockpit before an army jeep with a young subaltern and two soldiers with fixed bayonets came roaring through the gate. As soon as they saw it was 'one of ours,' they changed their attitude. I got a screwdriver from one of the soldiers and we took off the cowling and found a bullet had gone through the glycol pipe.

Unwin was driven to North Weald aerodrome, which was close by, leaving one of the army chaps to guard the aircraft. Arriving at North Weald, he found that the aerodrome had suffered heavy bombing recently, but was still operational. He duly arranged for an engine fitter to patch up the damaged Spitfire the next day and then flew it back to Fowlmere on the 13th. The aircraft P9546 was then sent away to a Maintenance Unit for further repair.

At Fowlmere on the morning of Sunday 15th September 1940, the pilots were at readiness waiting for instructions to get airborne. The weather was ideal with clear visibility that early morning. No large enemy formations had been picked up by 10.00 am and Fighter Command wondered what the Germans were planning next.

However, news was relayed to Sector Stations from Headquarters Fighter Command at 11.33 am, that radar stations had picked up German aircraft gathering over south-east of Boulogne, turning out across the Channel heading for the English coast between Dover and Folkestone. Fighter squadrons from No. 11 Group were immediately scrambled to intercept the threat. The Duxford Wing was called into action soon afterwards and instructed by control to patrol over the Gravesend to Canterbury line. The Wing led by Squadron Leader Bader of 242 Squadron consisted of two Spitfire squadrons, 19 and 611 and three Hurricane squadrons, 242, 302 and 310.

At 12.10 pm, the squadron sighted twenty enemy bombers with an escort of around thirty Me109s at a height of 20,000 feet near Westerham in Kent. Brian Lane ordered his pilots into the attack although they were disadvantaged with the German fighters above.

> I was 'Red 3' with Flight Lieutenant Lawson. We sighted the enemy aircraft, who were in Vics of three. The escorts dived swiftly on us and I engaged one of them (an ME109) with a yellow nose. I gave one burst of six seconds and the enemy aircraft burst into flames. The Pilot baled out and the enemy aircraft crashed approximately between Redhill and Westerham. I searched around for half an hour, but could not find any other aircraft so I returned and landed back at base.

Once the pilots had landed, the ground crews sprang into action, re-fueling, re-arming and preparing the Spitfires for the next sortie, which could come at any moment.

The RAF fighters had severely mauled and shocked the Luftwaffe aircrews back to reality, as they were confronted by not only 11 Group fighters, but also a sixty strong fighter wing from 12 Group. How was it that the Luftwaffe High Command had told them that the Royal Air Force was a spent force and had only a few squadrons left to defend London and the south-east? The morning combat had sent the raiders back across the Channel with their tails firmly tucked between their legs.

The next German assault came between 2.10 and 2.30 pm, when radar screens showed aircraft massing over the Pas de Calais area. Once more, squadrons from 12 Group were called and the Duxford Wing took off, this time heading for London.

Unable to gain the height necessary to have the advantage over the enemy, the Wing had to climb and in doing so was attacked by German fighters. The Wing was ordered to break quickly; it was every man for himself. A massive dogfight then ensued.

Unwin was flying as 'Red 3' with Squadron Leader Lane, when they had sighted a large formation of enemy bombers flying in Vics of three in line astern and heading west. Above there seemed to be a large number of ME109's. Unwin engaged one and gave the German a three second burst at close range. The enemy machine immediately half rolled and dived steeply into the clouds. Unwin followed the aircraft down, but his windscreen began to freeze up and he lost him. He then climbed up to 25,000 feet and observed two 109's overhead flying south south-east. He chased them as far as Lydd, the 109's still flying in formation, he fired at one which burst into flames and it went down, the second 109 also received a burst from Unwin's guns and this too crashed into the sea.

While Unwin and the rest of his flight had been engaged with fighters, 'B' Flight had intercepted six Dornier 17s claiming three destroyed. One aircraft, being brought down by Unwin's good friend Sergeant Steere.

As the retreating Germans headed back to France during the late afternoon, the pilots of Fighter Command realised they had dealt a serious blow against the enemy and their plans for invasion. Initial claims for that day stated that

185 German aircraft had been destroyed. This was an incredible moral boost for the nation especially the people in the east end of London, who had suffered the bombing. Sadly the figures in reality were much less. Later, records confirmed that only fifty-six enemy aircraft were destroyed for the loss of twenty-seven from Fighter Command. No. 19 Squadron's score for that day was twelve destroyed, four probably destroyed, one damaged and three shared.

Over the next two days, the weather turned unfavourable with cloud and rain during the day, but during the night, London, Bristol and Merseyside were bombed.

On Tuesday 17th September, the squadron received notification that George Unwin was to be awarded the Distinguished Flying Medal. In the squadron's operations book it states:

> Flight Sergeant Unwin was today awarded the D.F.M. Good Show! Ten Huns to his credit.

The next day, 17th September, the squadron resumed the fight, when they were called at 4.30 pm to carry out a patrol over Hornchurch with the rest of the Duxford Wing. At 5.25 pm, the Wing sighted an enemy formation of thirty aircraft consisting of Junkers and Heinkel bombers with an escort of Messerschmitt Me110s.

The Hurricane squadrons went into the attack against the bombers, while the escort fighters would be dealt with by 19 Squadron and 611 Squadron who were flying as top cover. As combat was met Unwin picked out a target over the Isle of Sheppey at 15,000 feet. He reported in his combat report:

> I was flying as 'Blue 3' with Flight Lieutenant Clouston when we were detailed to keep off the enemy fighters. At about 5.20 p.m., we sighted a small number of enemy aircraft below. The Hurricanes attacked and we kept above looking for enemy fighters. However, the German fighters were below and I dived on a Me110 who tried turning as evasion. No rear fire was encountered, so I closed to 50 yards and gave a burst of about 4 seconds. Immediately, his starboard engine caught fire and the pilot baled out. The aircraft crashed near Eastchurch and I climbed back up to 15,000 feet but could not find any more aircraft. I landed at 5.55 p.m. An aircraft of No. 66 Squadron confirmed the victory.

For the next several days, the Duxford Wing carried out numerous patrols, but these all proved uneventful. Good news arrived on 25th September, when a new batch of Mk IIa Spitfires arrived at the squadron to be exchanged for their well worn Mk1s. The new aircraft had been fitted with a Merlin XII engine giving 1,175 horse-power which drove a Dowty Rotol constant speed propeller. This gave the Spitfire Mk II a speed of 357 mph compared to 346 mph of the early Mk1s. The ceiling height of the aircraft was also improved and starting the aircraft's engine could be done by the use of a Coffman cartridge rather than plugging in the electrical trolley accumulator.

The German Air Force resumed its operations on London and southern England on Friday 27th September by launching three large raids. The first raid consisted of one hundred Messerschmitt 109s and 110s and eighty mixed bombers. 11 Group fighter aircraft were sent up to meet the threat and stop the enemy's advance towards London.

The main clash came over the Maidstone area of Kent, where once engaged the bombers broke formation and headed for home. The German fighter pilots could not stay and fight for long, having to keep an eye on their fuel warning light, telling them it was time to go back, hopefully with enough fuel to make it back to the mainland of France or otherwise an unpleasant ditching into the cold waters of the Channel.

Taking off from Fowlmere at 11.30 am, 19 Squadron had been instructed to patrol London. At noon, a second German raid was picked up, a formation of three hundred aircraft heading towards the Canterbury area. The squadron was informed over the R/T and given the appropriate instructions to fly south and intercept the incoming Luftwaffe bombers and fighters.

George Unwin was leading 'Yellow' section in the squadron when they sighted anti-aircraft bursts south of the Thames Estuary and went to investigate. They suddenly sighted about twenty bombers with an escort of thirty fighters below them and another twenty flying on the same level as the squadron. All of the escort were Me109's with the usual yellow noses. They attacked 19 Squadron and Unwin led 'Yellow' section against a pair of 109's. The Spitfires were then attacked and forced to split up, He then latched on to the tail of one of the Me109's and after about 10 minutes of aerobatics, during which the enemy manoeuvred nearer to the French coast and began to fly straight and level. Unwin closed to fifty yards and gave him a seven second burst without result. He fired another long burst, but no result. Finally he moved to the side and fired the remainder of his ammunition with a thirty degree deflection shot. The enemy aircraft stalled and spun into the sea. Unwin concluded in his combat report that obviously the 109's were now heavily armoured.

On return to Fowlmere, the pilots claimed for seven of the enemy destroyed. In return Pilot Officer Eric Burgoyne was lost having been shot down in Spitfire X4352, who crashed at Coldred. Fortunately Sergeant David Cox was to fare better; he was wounded in the right leg, when his aircraft X4237 was set upon by four Me109s. Forced to bale out, he landed in a ploughed field at Walsford near Ashford in Kent. He was sent to the hospital to undergo treatment and was taken off operations until the end of 1940.

On 1st October 1940, the award of the Distinguished Flying Medal to George Unwin was printed in the London Gazette, it read:

> This airman has displayed great courage in his attacks against the enemy and has destroyed ten of their aircraft. On a recent occasion when returning from an engagement alone, he intercepted a formation of enemy bombers escorted by about 30 fighters and destroyed two of these fighters. He has displayed skill and courage of the highest order.

Throughout October, the Duxford Wing squadrons flew a total of fifteen patrols, but no interceptions against the enemy were made. It was also during this month that the infamous meeting took place at Duxford between Air Chief Marshal Sir Hugh Dowding, Head of Fighter Command, and other Group Commanders regarding the tactics he had employed and the use of the 12 Group 'Duxford Big Wing.'

Much criticism was launched against Dowding and his 11 Group commander Air Vice-Marshal Keith Park by other high ranking officers including the commander of No. 12 Group, Air Vice-Marshal Trafford Leigh-Mallory. Mallory who had introduced the 'Big Wing' into the battle with the help of Squadron Leader Douglas Bader, who felt that Dowding had kept them out of the battle, when they could have been called earlier.

Dowding and Park's tactics of sending either single or pairs of squadrons to attack the incoming German raids was proven quicker to intercept the enemy bombers on their way in, rather than wait for three to five squadrons to get airborne and then form a Wing formation before heading out to attack the Germans. Unfortunately for Dowding and Park, the high-ranking air staff officers at the meeting, some unfriendly towards Dowding anyway, seemed to have made their minds up on the final decision, to remove both Dowding and Park from their positions. For the last sixty years, many people have aired their views on this meeting and the dismissal of Dowding, after the victory over the Luftwaffe in the Battle of Britain. George Unwin had his own views regarding the use of the Big Wing.

> We didn't take a very intensive part in it, but when we did later on, and then we really did make a big difference, because apart from the number of aircraft we shot down, the effect on the morale of the German pilots was tremendous. They had been told the RAF hadn't really got many aircraft left now and it is going to get easier and then suddenly they came across sixty aircraft in one gaggle coming to meet them and it was very noticeable that the standard of their younger pilots was appalling. The Messerschmitts didn't need any excuse to go scuttling back home. It was our job to keep the Messerschmitts away from the Hurricanes whose job it was to attack the bombers. Bader, who was leading the wing and the Hurricane Squadrons were attacking the bombers virtually unmolested, which was perfect, they could go back into the old Vic of three formation line astern, it really did work.
>
> The argument between Park and Leigh Mallory about the value or otherwise of the 'Big Wing' was completely nonsense. It couldn't be done in 11 Group, you couldn't get five squadrons together in the air just like that, it takes time. We were perfectly situated; we had Duxford and to the west, Fowlmere. The take off was always to the west from these two aerodromes, so we would line up to take off at Fowlmere. The Hurricanes took off from Duxford and as they went past us we then took off. All you had to do was a ninety degree turn to the left and you were on course for London and we were in a perfect position. You

couldn't do it in 11 Group because you were in the fighting area immediately, so why the air officers commanding argued and fought over this I will never know. The Big Wing would work if you could get it there and it did work, we proved it.

The number of times we weren't alerted soon enough was fantastic. Whether it was due to the rivalry I don't know, but North Weald should never have been hammered like it was. We arrived at North Weald as the last German aircraft was dropping its bombs. Sixty of us, now we could have stopped an awful lot of that happening, if we had been sent off in time. North Weald was badly hit, I know because I was shot down that day and made my way there and it was devastated, there wasn't a telephone in working order. Had we been there ten minutes earlier we might have stopped all that. It seems so silly in the middle of the war, if what we are told was true about the disagreement between Keith Park and Leigh Mallory.

For us, the Battle of Britain wasn't tiring at all, because we didn't do enough flying, this was our big grumble. It was annoying to have five squadrons absolutely panting to get off day after day. We would go two or three days without flying at all. When you think of Biggin and North Weald flying four to five trips a day with sometimes only eight aircraft when we had a full complement always. Why they didn't switch the squadrons around, let these chaps have a week off or something and send us down there, I never could understand that. There was no strain on us whatsoever. In fact I used to run the roster, we had a week's leave once every ten weeks and once a week we had a day off and you would be surprised the number of blokes that wouldn't go away on their day off in case there was a bit of flying. If you went up flying on the day they were off they were very upset and jealous, there was no question of lack of morale we just weren't flying enough and it was criminal, it must have been if the Biggin Hill boys were doing four or five trips a day.

Unwin's next enemy victory was to come on 5th November 1940. The squadron was called to take off with the rest of the Duxford Wing to patrol over the Thames Estuary. At 9.35 am and for the next hour, German fighters were flying sweeps across from France, coming in at Dungeness and heading for Biggin Hill. The squadron observed ten German aircraft and proceeded to catch them, claiming two destroyed, Unwin was unable to pick a target during that engagement, however he would have better luck during the afternoon.

Radar picked up a formation of German raiders during the afternoon and once again the Duxford Wing was asked to fly south and patrol between Canterbury and Dover. At 4.20 pm, the Wing was bounced by a formation of between twenty to thirty Messerschmitt 109s, who attacked the Hurricane aircraft of No. 310 Czech Squadron, causing two pilots to bale out and damaging three other aircraft. The Wing broke formation and combat ensued. No. 19 Squadron pilots went into attack against the 109s; a furious dogfight then proceeded in the skies over the Kent countryside. Unwin recalled:

I was 'Red 3' in the leading section. I sighted a number of enemy aircraft above. Flight Lieutenant Lawson instructed me to carry on and lead. I climbed to 28,000 feet and commenced to attack. I saw a Me113 on the tail of a Spitfire. Before I could catch him he had shot the Spitfire down near London. I caught the enemy aircraft just south of Dover and gave a long burst of seven to ten seconds. He crashed into the sea in flames. By this time I was well over the Channel (which I thought was the Estuary). I was attacked by numerous Me109's but evaded them successfully, as far as I was concerned, but not as far as the aircraft is concerned.

During this action, his aircraft P7427 had come under heavy attack by German fighters and was heavily damaged, luckily without injury to himself. After evading the 109s, he nursed the Spitfire back to base. The squadron claimed five of the German aircraft destroyed, but lost one pilot killed, Czech Pilot Officer Frantisek Hradil, who crashed into the sea off Southend in Spitfire P7545. His body was recovered and he was buried at Sutton Cemetery at Southend.

19 Squadron were detailed to patrol a convoy off Felixstowe on 15th November. They were at 12,000 feet and Unwin was leading 'Yellow' Section when they sighted two planes at 27,000 feet about 15 miles apart flying west. 'A' Flight pursued the first aircraft and 'B' Flight the second. They climbed but did not gain on the first enemy aircraft. Unwin then saw that he had a good chance of cutting off the rear one and asked permission to do so. Squadron Leader Lane gave permission and he climbed to meet the second aircraft. At 27,000 feet the enemy aircraft passed over Unwin and spotted him. The Me110 dived steeply and Unwin followed. He closed and gave a long burst which stopped one engine. He carried on and 'Yellow 2' fired at him. One wing fell off the enemy aircraft. Unwin broke away and saw the Me110 crash into the sea. He noted that two Spitfires of 'B' Flight also engaged the enemy aircraft. Unwin shared the claim with other squadron pilots.

George Unwin's final enemy claim came on 28th November 1940, when the squadron was carrying out a convoy patrol some twenty to thirty miles south-east off Southend. At approximately 3.20 pm, while leading Yellow Section, he was informed over the R/T by the 'Search Section' who was flying above, of enemy aircraft diving down. He turned the section and saw six Me109s with black fuselages and yellow noses. His report continues:

I put Yellow Section into line astern and we chased two of the Me109s heading south-east. They dived and turned and I closed from 200 to 100 yards. I gave a long burst of fire as did Sergeant Fulford. I then delivered another attack on the same aircraft which dived away steeply. I followed him and shortly afterwards, he dived straight into the sea. Sergeant Jennings was Yellow 2 and he chased away the other 109 who tried to attack me. I landed at 4.20 hours.

During the combat Unwin's good friend Harry Steere, who was leading Green Section, destroyed one of the 109s, as did Flying Officer Leonard Haine's. Unwin's Me109 was shared with Sergeant Fulford who was flying as Yellow 3.

His outstanding airmanship and courage was recognised when he received the news of the award of a Bar to his Distinguished Flying Medal, which was printed in the London Gazette of 6th December 1940: It read:

> This N.C.O. has consistently shown the greatest keenness, courage and determination to engage the enemy. He has destroyed 13 enemy aircraft, shared in the destruction of another and probably four more. He is an outstanding type of fighter pilot.

With 1940 coming to a close, what was the morale of the RAF fighter like at this stage in the war? And what about those who could not take the stress and strain of constant battle, named at the time as 'Lack of moral fibre.' George Unwin would reflect sixty years later:

> The morale in the squadron had never dropped, it is one of the peculiarities nowadays, having read the facts of what we were up against, and we all agree that we were probably mad, but no one every thought that we could be beaten, no question of it, certainly in a Spitfire Squadron and the Hurricane boys the morale was just as high. In view of the facts we now know, the Germans used the wrong tactics.
>
> I never came across lack of moral fibre in a fighter squadron, in fact quite the opposite. I knew one chap, Sergeant Roden who was scared stiff most of the time, he really hated it, but he never gave in. He should have genuinely been taken off operations, but he flatly refused to go and sadly was killed that November. I think that was courage of another kind altogether that he managed to carry on. We knew in the sergeants' mess, but the officers never found out.

On 29th December, after serving for five years through peace and war, George Unwin was posted away from 19 Squadron to undertake an instructor's course at the No.2 Central Flying School at Cranwell. Following completion of this course, he was then sent to No. 16 Elementary Flying Training School at Derby on 23rd February 1941, to begin instructing. While here, he was promoted in rank from warrant officer to that of pilot officer on 31st July 1941 and on 1st December, was promoted to flying officer.

He remained at Derby until he received a new posting to the No. 2 Flying Training School at Montrose on 3rd March 1942, becoming a flight lieutenant. He continued here until 19th October 1943, when his next posting sent him to No. 12 Pilots Advanced Flying Unit at Grantham to undertake a conversion course on to Mosquito aircraft. He then spent a short period at 60 Operational Training Unit at High Ercall before he returned to operational flying, being posted to No. 613 Squadron on 5th April 1944, based at Lasham.

The squadron was involved with undertaking night intruder operations against German targets prior to the planned invasion of France in June that year. As preparations for the D-Day landings at Normandy got underway, George Unwin and his navigator Flying Officer K.A. Hackett flew on these missions.

On 1st May, the two men flying Mosquito B-HP 927 took off at 11.07 pm. They were detailed to bomb the Rosines airfield. The target was located and bombed at 12.18 am. They made two passes over the target and hangars which were to the south-west, and the dispersal areas were also attacked with two 500Ib bombs with eleven second delays. Big flashes and terrific red glows were seen on each occasion and a large fire as they departed. Fortunately, they experienced no enemy anti-aircraft fire. They landed back at Lasham at 1.34 am that morning.

Unwin's next mission took place on 16th May, this time he was accompanied by three other Mosquito aircraft in what was termed a 'Rhubarb' operation. On this occasion, Unwin was flying Mosquito B/HP 930. The four aircraft took off at 9.08 pm and headed for their target, a navigation beam station at Sortosville-en-Beaumont. Once over the target, they dropped ten 500Ib bombs from a height of three to five hundred feet, but results were inconclusive. They then attacked the station using cannon and good strikes were obtained on the building and the base of the mast. On return, at 11.00 pm. they were able to view the damage from the cameras that had been fitted to the aircraft.

After the successful landings at Normandy on 6th June 1944, Unwin's squadron's role was to attack and prevent the German transportation system bringing fresh supplies of troops and materials to the battlefront. On 6th July, Unwin flying Mosquito MM408 took off at 1.35 am accompanied by twelve other aircraft to carry out the raid. Each Mosquito carried four 500Ib eleven second time delay bombs. Unfortunately, the weather was not in their favour and very little enemy movement was observed. The weather remained poor for their next mission on the night of 10th July, when they were scheduled to attack targets at Chartres, Dreux, Laigle and Doufront in support of the army.

Unwin and Hacket were flying MM408 again and took off for the mission at 10. 34 pm. This mission was successful, but due to the bad weather back in Britain, several of the Mosquito's on their return were diverted to the aerodrome at Dunsfold. One Mosquito was lost, that flown by Flying Officer Cohen and Flight Sergeant Deaves.

George Unwin's last recorded mission with 613 came on the night of 16th August 1944, when the squadron attacked several targets, mostly railways at Arras, Amiens, Rouen, Abbeville and Bourget. Again the weather turned poor, so many aircraft bombed using Gee to locate the target. They suffered no losses and Unwin landed back without incident at 2.20am that morning. He was posted away from the squadron in October that year after completing over fifty operational sorties.

His next posting was to instruct at the Central Gunnery School at Catfoss on 30th October, and while here he was promoted to flight lieutenant on 1st September 1945. He remained here until war's end. His total number of operational hours during wartime stood at 600+ hours. He continued instructing and was then sent to the gunnery school at Leaconfield on 18th November 1945, where he continued until 12th June 1946.

With the Royal Air Force Auxiliary being resurrected in 1946, Unwin was sent as chief instructor for No. 608 North Riding Auxiliary Squadron based at Thorney Island on 12th June 1946, he held this position for thirteen months before accepting a staff job at Headquarters 23 Group on 23rd September1947. Unwin had also been promoted, made a squadron leader on 1st August that year. He was again on the move, when he was posted to the staff of Headquarters No. 12 Group on 11th January 1949.

He was then put back on operations in August that year and given command of No. 84 Squadron on 9th September. 84 Squadron was at that time based at RAF Habbaniya in Iraq, flying Bristol Brigand aeroplanes.

During that year, conflict broke out in the Far East country of Malaya as the British tried to stop the insurgents who were using guerrilla warfare against their opposition. As the emergency increased, No. 84 was transferred to Singapore, where they were to fly from Tengah airfield in ground support role. Most of the clashes between the Malayan rebels and the British and commonwealth troops were fought in the hills and jungle, so it was essential to be able to call up air support, when needed.

Unfortunately, the squadron did suffer some casualties during their time there. Some were the result of failures in the Brigand aircraft's design and armament. One fault was the premature explosion of the Aden cannon rounds, the gun being mounted just beneath the aircraft's fuel tanks. When they exploded you stood no chance. Unwin had noticed this failure and presented the facts to those above, and it was rectified. During his time out in Malaya, he led the squadron on over one hundred and eighty attacks, firing rockets and dropping bombs against the enemy positions.

He was unfortunate enough to break his leg on 24th August 1951, whilst off duty, playing football in the squadron team. This was enough to have him flown back to Britain to recuperate and be promoted to the rank of wing commander with a desk job. During the following year, he received news of the award of the Distinguished Service Order on 21st March 1952, for his outstanding work on operations flying the Brigand aircraft against the terrorists out in Malaya.

Once recovered his next posting was that of Wing Commander Administration at RAF Kirkham near Blackpool. He returned once more to Singapore in 1955 as chief administrator for RAF Tengah and was able to get to fly the jet aircraft stationed there. The post lasted for three years and on his return to Britain, he was appointed as Permanent President of Court Martial. Following his time in this position he later joked that; *I presided over three hundred court martials and not one chap was found guilty of low flying.'* This was George Unwin's last role within the Royal Air Force, on the 18th January 1961; he retired from the service as wing commander.

He set up home in the county of Dorset with his wife and became involved with another passion, golf. He also enjoyed the role as the Controller of Spastics Appeals within the southern counties which raised countless money for the charity. He continued to play golf at his local club, the Ferndown, sometimes seven days a week, and served as a committee member. In his last years, he cut down his playing, but continued till he reached the age of ninety. Brian Unwin recalls his brother's golfing talents:

...fficers and sergeant pilots of No.56 Squadron pictured at North Weald in front ...their Gloster Gladiator biplanes in 1937/38: Sergeant Frederick 'Taffy' Higginson ...standing second from right. Author via Higginson Family Collection

...e wedding of Frederick Higginson to Shan ...nkins, which took place at the Betws local ...urch in 1937. The other airman present was ...n Elliot, who was the best man. He was later ...led flying operations over Dunkirk in May ...40. Author via Higginson Family Collection

Pictured with fellow pilots at the squadron dispersal at North Weald in 1939.

Author via Higginson Family Collection

Hurricane aircraft of 56 Squadron in the air and on the ground at North Wea
Aerodrome in early 1939. Author via Higginson Family Collection

Taking time off to relax at North
Weald. Left to right: unknown,
Higginson and on his right
Sergeant Jim Elliot.
Author via Higginson Family Collection

N for Nut's: 'Taffy' with his Hawker Hurricane US-
This photograph was taken at Martlesham Hea
in early 1940. Author via Higginson Family Collection

Pilots of 56 Squadron photographed inside their dispersal hut during the Battle of Britain. 'Taffy' Higginson seated next to the oil fire.   Author via Higginson Family

Group photo of 56 Squadron pilots in February 1941. By this time Higginson had been made a pilot officer. From left to right: Sgt P. Robinson, Sgt P. Hillwood, F/O J. Himr, F/O B. Wicks, F/O I. Westmacott, Sgt Mayall, F/Lt E. Gracie, F/O G. Bailey, P/O T. Guest, F/O R. Malengreau and P/O Higginson.

Courtesy of the North Weald Airfield Museum

The pencil portrait drawn by famous wartime artist Sir Cuthbert Orde in 1940.
Author via Higginson Family Collection

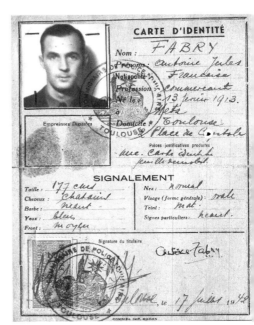

Higginson's forged identity card and photograph that he used during his escape and travels through occupied France in 1942.
Author via Higginson Family Collection

Forced into Touch! A rugby match between Richmond and Llanely held on 4th November 1950. Higginson playing for Richmond is pictured with the ball being tackled by Cyril Higgins. Author via Higginson Family

Frederick William Higginson OBE. This photograph was taken when he was the Sales & Service Director of Guided Weapons Division at BAC in 1963.
Author via Higginson Family

Young 'Peter' Morfill, pictured at Aldergrove, Northern Ireland, during 65 Squadron's air-gunnery summer camp in 1937.
Courtesy of Stan Kogel

Photographed at Hornchurch at the time of the last Empire Air Display in May 1939. Sergeant Pilots of 54*, 65 and 74 Squadron pose for a relaxed shot: Left to right: Peter Morfill, Sgt Bushell of 74 Squadron, Norman Phillips, Phillip Tew* and Bill Franklin.
Sgt P. Hayes

Pictured in the cockpit of his Spitfire, seen having a lark.
Author via Morfill

An early Hawker Hurricane Mk1 is seen being worked on by ground crew. Note the early identification colours on the aircrafts underside, painted black and white. At this stage, the Hurricane had only the two bladed propeller. Authors Collection

Pilots of 501 pose for the camera: Left to right back row standing: P/O Dicky Hulse
F/Lt Derrick Pickup, F/O Michael Smith. Kneeling: P/O Ken Lee and P/O Peter Hairs
Seated: Sgt James 'Ginger' Lacey, F/Sgt Payne, Sgt Paul Farnes, Sgt Peter Morfill
Sgt Don McKay and Sgt Bob Daffron. Author via Morfill

Ground crew use a trolly accumulator to start a Hurricane aircraft of 501 Squadro
at Betheniville. Courtesy of IWM Ref C1682

Pilots of 501 pictured at Filton in December 1940 with the tail-rudder of a German aircraft they had shot down. Left to right, back row: F/Sgt Peter Morfill, F/O Denys Jones, Sgt Anton Glowacki and P/O Robert Daffron. Front: P/O Stanislaw Skalski, Sgt Wilf Holroyd, F/Lt V. Morello, F/Lt Ken Mackenzie, Sgt Konrad Muchowski and P/O Tony Whitehouse. Courtesy of F. Roberts

As an instructor at No.61 Operational Training Unit, RAF Heston in October 1941. Back row: W/O Harrison, W/O Morfill DFM, Sgt Godderham. Front Row: P/O F.S. Perkin, F/Lt W. H. Hopkin DFC, F/Lt M.P. Brown and S/Ldr A.G. 'Sailor' Malan DSO, DFC. Courtesy of S/Ldr M.P. Brown AFC

'Peter' Morfill in his garden at home in Chichester in 1994.

Authors Collection

Pilots and air-gunners of No. 264 Squadron photographed at Duxford before th
Dunkirk evacuation in May 1940. Seated on chairs; left to right: F/Lt Nicolas Cook
S/Ldr Philip Hunter, P/O Michael Young, P/O Richard Stokes, Sgt Ted Thorn an
LAC Fred Barker.   Authors Collection

Above: Defiant aircraft of 264 Squadro
at Hornchurch, August 1940.

Courtesy of RAF Hornchurch Association

Left: An air-gunner of 264 Squadro
prepares to board his aircraft. He i
seen wearing a GQ Parasuit whic
incorporates a parachute harness an
life jacket within the smock overalls.

Courtesy of IWM Ref CH824

Sergeant Edward Thorn and his air-gunner Fred Barker seated in the Defiant's gun turret during the Battle of Britain.

Courtesy of RAF Hornchurch Association

ergeants Ted Thorn and Fred arker pictured outside Buckingham alace after each of them were warded the Distinguished Flying fedal in May 1940.

ourtesy of RAF Hornchurch Association

red Barker, with former 264 Squadron pilots and gunners, at a RAF Hornchurch attle of Britain Exhibition in 1992. Left to right: W/Cdr Eric Barwell DFC, Sgt red Gash DFM, Fred Barker DFM, and F/Lt John Launder.   Author via D. Ringrow

George Cecil Unwin aged 17 years. Seen here feeling proud in his Royal Air Force uniform during his time as an apprentice clerk at Ruislip in 1930. *Courtesy of Mr Brian Unwin*

That's funny? George and RAF friend Bi Nunnerley having fun on leave at Hillingdor Uxbridge in 1932. *Courtesy of Mr Brian Unwin*

Pleased as punch. George Unwin dressed in his Sidcot suit after going solo and earning his 'wings' in 1936.
Courtesy of Mr Brian Unwin

Pictured with members of No.19 Squadro before the outbreak of war.
Courtesy of Mr Brian Unwin

...win with his pet Alsatian 'Flash' at ...xford standing with Spitfire K9798 late 1938.   Author via George Unwin

Keeping a look out. 'Flash' seated on George's Spitfire in 1940.

Courtesy of Mr Brian Unwin

...lots of the squadron gather at Manor Farm, Fowlmere after a sortie. Those ...entified are 4th from left, S/Ldr Brian Lane, Sgt Harry Steere, Sgt George Unwin, ...O Hradil - bending over, Sgt Lloyd behind and Sgt Bernard Jennings with leather ...ing jacket with 'Flash' the Alsatian.   Courtesy of IWM Ref CH-1364

One of the many unsung heroes of 1940. Flight Rigger John Milne served at Fowlmere & Duxford with 19 Squadron keeping their Spitfires operational.

Courtesy of Mr John Milne

George Unwin relaxes with a beer at t Vector Fine Art Marquee at Duxfo during the 60th Anniversary of the Bat of Britain in September 2000.

Courtesy of Vector Fine Art

The unveiling of the George Unwin Memorial Bench at Duxford in May 2007, former 19 Squadron veterans Ken Wilkinson and Air Chief Marshal Sir Bill Wratt

Courtesy of Vector Fine Art

ll Franklin pictured sitting in a small
cht on the River Nile during his posting
No. 84 Squadron out in Egypt in 1935.
rtesy of Mr Stan Kogel

The Wedding of Bill Franklin and Louise
Kogel in 1937.
Courtesy of Mr Stan Kogel

o. 65 'East India Company' Squadron, Rochford, August 1940. Left to right: Sgt
ll Franklin*, Sgt Harold Orchard*, Unknown, F/O John Nicholas, F/Lt Gordon
live, S/Ldr Henry Sawyer*, F/O Thomas Smart*, F/O Ronald Wigg, Sgt Colin
ewlett*, F/O Brendan Finucane*, F/O Stanley Grant and Sgt Joseph Kilner in front
Spitfire R6799. (* Killed in action)   Courtesy of Mr Stan Kogel

Bill Franklin pictured during the Battle of Britain 1940. Courtesy of Mr Stan Kogel

Louise Franklin pictured at Buckingha Palace after the award ceremony to colle her late husband's Distinguished Flyin Medal and bar in 1941. Courtesy of Mr Stan Koge

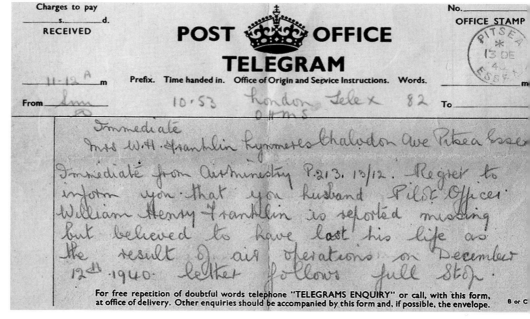

Telegram received by Louise Franklin notifying her that her husband was missir in action on 12th December 1940. Courtesy of Stan Kogel

onald Kingaby in uniform aged 14
ears during his time at King's School,
y in Cambridgeshire.

Sergeant Pilot Kingaby pictured with his 92
Squadron Spitfire in October 1940.

viation artist Geoff Nutkins depiction
Don Kingaby's combat with the
lesserschmitt 109 flown by Unteroffizier
orst Perez on 30th September 1940.
erez's engine failed and he force-landed
a field at East Dean.

The wedding of Don Kingaby to Helen
Watkinson on 7th February 1942.

Don and Helen Kingaby with baby son David at his DSO investiture held at Buckingham Palace on 22nd June 1943.
Courtesy of Kingaby Family

With 64 Squadron in October 1942 at Fairl Aerodrome. Left to right:1st P/O Curd, 2 Sgt Patterson, Don Kingaby standing, 8 S/Ldr Tony Gaze in deck chair, 9th F/I Michael Donnet behind
Courtesy of RAF Hornchurch Association.

Kingaby with fellow pilots of No. 72 Squadron during his time as squadron CO at North Weald.
Courtesy of Kingaby Family

50th Battle of Britain Anniversary Symposiu in the USA on the 3rd March 1990.L/R: Diet Hrabak, Adolf Galland, Gunther Rall, Do Kingaby and Peter Townsend.

Hornchurch's tribute to Don Kingaby.
Courtesy of Mr Jim Davies

The medal awards to W/Cdr Donald Kingab
Courtesy of Kingaby Family

There was a professional golfer at the Ferndown when George first joined in 1956, named Doug Sewell. He had been on the professional circuit, so he was a very experienced player. I have been told by many members of the golf club that Doug Sewell said, that George could play a terrific short game and could get a six handicap on his better days, he was brilliant one hundred yards from the flag. I actually asked Sewell, was George that good, and he said, 'he was the best.' He was often down in two from that distance.

He was a great supporter of the Battle of Britain Fighter Association and other groups and societies that remembered the role of the 'Few.' He was often seen at air displays around the country, especially at the Imperial War Museum at Duxford, where he would sign prints and books for the public.

Sadly, George Unwin passed away on 28th June 2006, after suffering a heart attack, two days after falling and breaking a hip, he was aged 93 years. His funeral was held on 10th July at the Bournemouth Crematorium, with a reception held afterwards for refreshments at the Ferndale Golf Club.

Today a memorial bench to him is sited at Duxford. This was paid for by kind donations from fellow pilots, friends and the public, organized by the Vector Fine Art Gallery in 2006. John Milne who served as a flight rigger with 19 Squadron in 1940 remembers him with affection:

> George Unwin as a pilot and myself as a flight rigger were both part of 'A' Flight, and I therefore saw him almost every day. He was one of the best pilots at Duxford and Fowlmere, quick and clever, almost unflappable, courteous and genial. I respected and admired him. As he had started at the bottom of the Royal Air Force, he appreciated the ordinary airmen like myself and treated us with respect, and was grateful for our efforts.

Unwin's name will always be linked and remembered as one of the most recognized sergeant pilots who fought in the Battle of Britain, a man who was straight talking and got on with the job. When future generations talk or think of No. 19 Squadron and RAF Duxford, George Unwin's name will always be remembered.

CHAPTER 5

WILLIAM 'GUNNER' FRANKLIN

William Henry Franklin was born on 2nd October 1911, the son of George Henry Franklin and Harriet, Amelia Franklin nee Parker. William entered this world delivered at the family home at No. 396 Commercial Road, Poplar in East London. His father was a general labourer who worked in the Mile End area. The family then moved to 65 Roswell Street in Bow. It was a difficult childhood and needy time being brought up in the streets and roads around East London. But there was some escape in being interested in various modes of transports of which the young William was keen.

William was educated at the Thomas Street Central School in Limehouse and was an enthusiastic pupil. After four years at the school he left with a glowing report from his headmaster Mr A.E. Bailey, who wrote a glowing testimonial stating that the curriculum that Franklin had undertaken had included mathematics, science (chemistry, physics and mechanics) art, technical drawing, wood and metal workshop practice. He then concluded that throughout the course, he had worked well and his conduct was exemplary. He was of good intellectual promise and this was happily associated with a sound moral development. He is recommended with confidence.

He left school just after his sixteenth birthday. Stan Kogel, William Franklin's brother-in-law recalls.

> He had this very great interest in mechanics and the mechanical equipment. He was very interested in transport in as much as motor cycles, motor cars of which he was very passionate and flying which was still in its infancy, but still quite exciting.
>
> When he eventually left school he was a little bit undecided and for a very short time he went and worked for a chemist, to be tutored in the practice of the profession, but this was to humdrum, it didn't excite his mind.

Franklin decided chemistry was not for him and became restless. His next decision was to join the Territorial Army with the Royal Artillery, a one years service. He enlisted as Gunner No.778531 of 337th Battery (Territorial Army) Essex F. Battalion, Royal Artillery on 31st January 1928. By July, he had been appointed as a driver, but he already had other thoughts on his mind, when he was discharged on 14th January 1929.

Just before enrolling into the Royal Air Force, Franklin was to meet someone who would change his life. While walking in Commercial Road, he went into a local confectionary shop in Salmons Lane and was served by a beautiful tall dark-haired young woman. Bill Franklin who stood at five foot six, with blond hair and blue eyes was immediately struck by the beauty of this young woman and the chemistry between them was instantaneous. The young woman was Louise Eliza Kogel. She found Franklin to be an elegant person who was very articulate. From the first time they met the two became inseparable. He was soon welcomed in to the Kogel family who lived in Ellesmere Street in a small terraced house.

The Kogel family consisted of Father Gustav who originated from a village in Saxony in Germany named Abberoda. Born in 1874 of farming stock, one of his first jobs after schooling was as a locksmith. He then left the country due to domestic reasons, then joined the navy and travelled around the world as a sailor, eventually becoming a stoker, working in the ships engine room. Sailing into an English Port, the East India Docks in London, a friend of his at that time named Dick Cakebread introduced Gustav to a family whom Cakebread lodged with while ashore. It was with this family that Gustave met and soon courted and married Mary Ann. They had eight children, four boys and four girls, Louise being the eldest; and a great deal of happiness was generated within the household.

Franklin enlisted into the Royal Air Force on 15th January 1929 to enter as a boy aircraft apprentice, No. 562984 and went to learn his trade at the Royal Air Force School at RAF Halton in Buckinghamshire.

Franklin excelled in his new career being part of No.4 Wing, so much so that the RAF offered him twelve years regular service from 2nd October 1929; he was then aged eighteen years old. While at Halton, he had entered into the small bore rifle team in which he was very successful, winning the 1930/31 trophy. It was here that he acquired the nickname of 'Gunner' harking back to his army days in the artillery.

He was then placed under training to become a fitter on aero engines in January 1930 and after completing the course was reclassified as a Leading Aircraftman on 15th January 1932 at the Fighter Aircraft Establishment with No. 58 Squadron at Worthy Down.

The squadron was then posted overseas on 18th October 1933 to Iraq, where the squadron undertook operations against tribal unrest within the country.

Franklin re-mustered as a part-time air gunner during this period and by the 15th March 1935 was posted to 84 (B) Squadron at Shaibah. By this time, he was determined that his future was that of a pilot. Four months later on 11th July, he was undergoing pilot training at No. 4 Flying Training School at Abu Sueir. Here he learnt to fly on Avro 504 and Avro Tutor biplane aircraft. After finally going solo and gaining his wings, he was promoted to sergeant on 3rd April 1936 and posted to No. 64 Squadron at Ismailia on 24th April, that same month.

The squadron was commanded by Squadron Leader P.J.R. King and flew Hawker Hart biplanes during this period, but they suffered many engine failures due to the heat and sand within the biplanes Rolls-Royce Kestrel engines. Five months later, the squadron returned home to Britain and was then based at Martlesham Heath in Suffolk from 12th September 1936. Franklin remained with 64 until 21st April 1937, when his posting came through to join No. 79 Squadron at Biggin Hill in Kent.

This squadron had been disbanded after the First World War and had only been reformed a month earlier on 22nd March, when B Flight of No. 32 Squadron was detached to form the new squadron. Franklin was one of many pilots brought in to bring the squadron up to strength. The aircraft they were given to fly was the Gloster Gladiator, the RAF's new front-line fighter.

After a brief stay of less than two months with this squadron, he received instructions to join No. 65 Squadron based at RAF Hornchurch in Essex on 1st June 1937. The squadron was commanded by Squadron Leader C.F.H Grace and was about to exchange its old Gloster Gauntlet biplanes for the new Gladiator, which Franklin had already had experience on while at Biggin Hill. William soon made friends at Hornchurch among his fellow sergeant pilots, especially Sergeant Percy Morfill whom became a good friend. Franklin and Morfill had both trained at Halton as apprentices, they both were quiet and dedicated to flying, but each had a wonderful sense of humour. Stan Kogel remembers the friendship between the two men:

> They were very close, Morfill and Franklin. Morfill was about three years younger, but the magical thing was they talked in the same language, they were very, very knowledgeable regarding aircraft production, armament and engines, right down to the last nut and bolt, conrod or piston, they knew everything about it. Bill Franklin was renowned for his dry humour and Morfill had a strong West Country accent and occasional they would have a dig at one another, but they really respected one another.

At Hornchurch, his love for rugby was renewed with games and competitions against local and armed services teams. Stan Kogel again:

> He was very much involved with the rugby there. Evidently, he was quite renowned and I can remember that many times after he came back from a game, he'd go into the bathroom with all the iodine and embrication and goodness knows what, and all the scars from playing the matches. I was quite concerned about it, and I was only a kid. When he came back after this, he would be refreshed then and talk about his exploits.

William Franklin and Louise Kogel were finally married in 1937 at the All Saint's Church, Poplar, which was rather a grand church and very impressive. Soon after, they moved to a brand new house at Elm Park, Hornchurch in Essex. It was seen as quite an achievement in those days for a young chap in his mid-twenties to buy his own home which was at No.504 Orchard Avenue (later renamed Calbourne Avenue).

During this time, Franklin who had previously been dead keen on motor cycles decided it was time to change transport and bought his first motor car. Stan Kogel:

> The first car he bought was an MG; it was a two-seat with a small single seat in the back. He had been a staunch motor cyclist since he'd been a teenager. He had owned a Rudge Ulsterman, a Norton and later a Panther with sidecar. Consequently, after the MG, he had a procession of various sports cars, a Frazier Nash that had been entered into the Brooklands circuit at one time, a Jaguar S100 which had the dropped head coupe, the Alvis, he has so many beautiful cars; he

also had a Riley and he bought for Louise, a Singer Le Mons, which was similar to the MG as a two-seater sports car. He had bought it with the intention that she was going to be instructed.

During the pre-war years the Royal Air Force had a special one-day event, named the Empire Air Day, when RAF Stations would open their gates to the public and allow them to visit certain areas around the aerodromes. The day would also include a chance for the public to take a trip in an aircraft or view the new types of aircraft that were now coming on-line within the service. Aerobatic displays provided awe inspiring sights for the visitors and perhaps a few new recruits into the RAF. Money raised through the gate admissions was given to the RAF Charity, or other worthwhile causes. Stan Kogel was always excited when he had the chance to go to such an event at Hornchurch:

> On Empire Days it was spell binding as a young boy, the variety of aeroplanes and what they did with aerobatics was incredible. They would tie two biplanes with a rope and they would take off and undertake manoeuvres and loops tied together and finally land it again. This was absolutely magic. At times I would be there, when Bill Franklin came back from his time on duty, so I would walk home with him.

Unfortunately, the days of peace were to be numbered as Nazi Germany under the leadership of its Chancellor Herr Hitler, had plans for German expansion.

By 1938, the Munich Crisis had erupted and war had only been stopped through negotiations and the handing over of land in the Sudetenland region of Czechoslovakia. Franklin along with others at Hornchurch and other British aerodromes had been put on a war footing during this period and had been brought to the brink of conflict. The aircraft had been camouflaged and gas attack and air raid exercises had become the norm.

After Chamberlain, Britain's Prime Minister had returned from Germany claiming peace, nobody believed that Germany could be trusted and so the RAF remained on active alert in case further hostilities might resume.

Fortunately for Britain the Royal Air Force had three years earlier, contracted and ordered the first batch of Hawker Hurricane fighter aeroplanes designed by Sir Sidney Camm. His aircraft was the first of the new monoplane fighter aircraft to be produced in Britain. In March 1936, a new shape was seen in the skies above Eastleigh airfield, as another revolutionary aircraft made its first flight. The Supermarine Spitfire was the brainchild of Reginald Mitchell, who had previously designed the fast seaplanes that had won the Schneider Trophy competitions for Britain. The RAF was impressed and immediately placed an order for three hundred and ten of the new fighters.

Unfortunately, on the minus side unlike the Hawker Hurricane whose construction harked back to the previous era with a wood and aluminium construction and was far easy to produce, the new Spitfire which had a complete metal airframe and skinning was far more involved production wise. This resulted in the aircraft taken longer to produce and took time to get to the RAF Squadrons. For Britain and especially Europe time was running out.

On 13th February 1939, No. 74 Squadron was the first of the Hornchurch squadrons to receive their new Spitfire fighters. They were followed by 54 Squadron then finally 65 Squadron on 21st March flown in by Flight Lieutenant A.N. Jones. Brian Kingcome who was a pilot officer with the squadron at this time recalled:

> We were extremely lucky that we were re-equipped in the March, several months before the war with Germany. When war did eventually break-out, we had quite a lot of Spitfire flying hours under our belts, which was a huge advantage.
>
> One was expecting it to be difficult, but it wasn't, the Spitfire always gave one great confidence. It really was a totally docile aircraft, and was very pilot friendly. It didn't have any vices at all and it wouldn't stall unexpectedly or do anything without you knowing first.

The pilots of 65 Squadron spent many hours honing the skills in their Spitfires that they would later need against the Germans during the air battles in 1940. Officers and sergeant pilots alike took time to practice various fighter attacks and mock dogfights with each other in the skies over Southern England, and Bill Franklin would have been no exception.

On 1st September, Germany shocked the world by invading Poland with incredible speed, employing their new Blitzkrieg tactics of sudden air attacks followed by swift advancing German panzer tank divisions and troops. Both British and French Prime Ministers sent Hitler an ultimatum to withdraw, but no reply was received. On 3rd September a state off war was declared against Germany.

In Britain, war had been expected for quite some time and many British families had already prepared by having an Anderson Shelter buried in the back garden. The Franklin and Kogel family were no exception. Franklin would visit his wife Louise whenever he was off duty and when war came, he would spend less time at home as his war duties became more demanding.

During the months following the outbreak of war, in October and November, the squadron was given the mundane job of patrolling merchant convoys bringing valuable cargos to Britain. In December through January, the winter was one of the coldest and little flying was carried out. No wonder at this time, the people of Britain called it the 'Phoney War.'

It was not till May 1940, that the Germans finally started their big push, when they evaded the defensive Maginot Line, an impregnable fortification that stretched almost across the width of France. The Germans pushed through the Ardennes Forest which was deemed impassable for tanks and outflanked the French, Belgian and British forces. In just a few weeks, the Allied armies had suffered irreversible defeats as the Germans continued their advance towards the Channel coast.

It was on 17th May that the squadron scored its first enemy victory of the war, when a Junkers Ju88 was shot down near Flushing by Flying Officer John Welford.

As the British Expeditionary Force retreated towards the port of Dunkirk with the remnants of the French and Belgium armies, preparations were being prepared for a full scale evacuation of the troops by means of naval ships large and small. Craft of all types were commandeered and made ready for the trip across the Channel to pick up the troops off the beaches and landing stages.

To provide air cover for the evacuation, the RAF fighter squadrons from aerodromes around the south-east would try and keep the Luftwaffe from bombing the troops as they made their way onto the ships arriving to pick them up.

At Hornchurch, 54, 65 and 74 Squadrons prepared themselves for the task in hand. This was to be their first real encounter with the Luftwaffe and especially the Messerschmitt 109 fighter, whose performance had already been witnessed in Spain and now France by the RAF's Hurricane pilots.

65 Squadron's first patrol over Dunkirk came on 21st May 1940, when they flew alongside 74 Squadron along the Belgian coast. 65 did not enter into any action, but 74 Squadron did, sighting two Heinkel 111 bombers near the French coast at 5.30 pm. Both aircraft were attacked and shot down. The following day at 8.30 am, 65 were again ordered to patrol, this time between Calais and Dunkirk. This proved to be another uneventful trip, apart from when the Spitfire flown by Pilot Officer Ken Hart suddenly developed engine problems. Flames began to come from the engine and he had no option but to force-land his aircraft with undercarriage up, at North Foreland. He jumped from his aircraft on landing and was unhurt, but his Spitfire was totally burnt out. He later returned to the squadron. Later that day, just after 1.00 pm 65 was sent off to patrol again between Boulogne and Calais, when at 2.00 pm, Blue Section led by Flight Lieutenant Gerald Saunders sighted a lone German aircraft. Bill Franklin was flying Spitfire N3101 as Blue 2, when they sighted a single Junkers Ju88 off Calais at 4,000 feet. His report of the engagement that day reads:

> I was on patrol with 65 Squadron flying as Blue 2. Blue Leader had dived on to an enemy aircraft, and on getting out of range had been followed by Blue 3. He closed on the enemy aircraft and was about to override him, when I closed in from behind and slightly to starboard – in a steep banking turn. As I came out of the turn and straightened out behind the enemy aircraft's tail, I fired a burst of two seconds at 400 yards, which seemed to hit the pilot, causing the enemy aircraft to stagger badly. I was now straight behind and slightly above at 300 yards. I fired a second burst of one second which silenced the starboard engine. The enemy machine now turned into a thick cloud and as he disappeared, I fired a final burst of one second at 300 yards, no damage noticed.
>
> The enemy never fired back and no movement could be seen of the guns. When last seen in cloud the starboard engine was smoking badly. It is very doubtful whether the aircraft would have got very much further.

Franklin claimed a half share on the Ju88 as a damaged. His first enemy claim of the war.

During the early evening of 24th May, the squadron was called to patrol again. Taking-off at 5.40 pm, nine Spitfires headed once more for the French coast. Having patrolled for nearly an hour with no enemy contact Blue Section became aware of a lone German reconnaissance aircraft flying inland near Calais at a height of 4,000 feet.

The Spitfires attacked the Henschel Hs.126, which on seeing the attackers dived for the ground. Both Blue 1 and Blue 3 fired several bursts at the machine; then Franklin (Blue 2) followed in firing a four second burst from 350 yards closing to 200 yards range. The enemy aircraft was then seen to crash to the ground in flames. For this action, Franklin received yet another half share in the destruction of an enemy aircraft.

As the intensity of the air fighting continued over Dunkirk, patrols began to increase to three or four patrols a day. An early morning patrol was the order of the day for 65 Squadron on Sunday 26th May when at 5.05 am, twelve aircraft led by Squadron Leader Desmond Cooke took off in company with Spitfires of No.54 Squadron from Hornchurch. At precisely 6.45 am, enemy contact was made when a large group of Messerschmitt 110s in four Vic's of twenty aircraft was seen just off Calais at 17,000 feet.

The squadron attacked causing the Me110s to break their formation. Franklin dived on to one of the enemy from three quarters starboard and delivered a two second burst from 400 yards. The German began to emit smoke from one of the engines. Franklin then closed in further and fired again from 250 yards, causing the enemy aircraft to stall and dive straight for the sea, where he saw it crash and explode into flames. The rest of the squadron had routed the remaining German aircraft who now headed inland to escape. In all 65 Squadron had claimed three Me110s destroyed with a further two claimed as probable destroyed or damaged. Sadly, there was one casualty, that of Flying Officer John Welford who was shot down by anti-aircraft fire. He managed to bale out of his stricken aircraft (P9437), but he was too low an altitude for it to deploy and he was killed. Both Hornchurch Squadron's landed back at base between 6.15 and 6.45 am. William Franklin being able to this time to confirm this claim as definitely destroyed.

After a quick bite to eat and cups of tea, the squadron was called to readiness for another patrol just over an hour and half later. Airborne at 8.18 am, they reached the French coast just off Calais to find that engagement with the Luftwaffe had already been met. Duxford based No. 19 Squadron, who had come south to operate from Hornchurch was already mixing it with Junkers Ju87 dive-bombers and their 109 escorts. Squadron Leader Cooke led the squadron into the attack, each pilot picking out a target. Franklin's combat report reads:

> On patrol near Calais, the squadron was engaged in a dogfight and I managed to engage two aircraft. One, a Me110 escaped without signs of damage, after I had put into him two short bursts. Later, I engaged an Me109 from astern and above. I fired a short burst at 300 yards and again at 250 yards causing the enemy aircraft to dive for the ground and home. I followed him inland at ground-level for twenty to thirty miles. After several short bursts at 400 yards, he gave out smoke and flames, but carried on. I delivered a final burst and the German aircraft crashed into the ground. During this time, I noticed a large amount of anti-aircraft fire.

The rest of the squadron had been heavily involved in the melee and had achieved considerable success. Pilot Officer Tommy Smart and Flying Officer Walker each claiming an Me110 destroyed, Flying Officer John Nicholas and Pilot Officer Ken Hart and Franklin, each an Me109 destroyed, Flying Officer George Proudman a Henschel 126 destroyed and one Me109 probable. A further five 109s were also claimed as probably destroyed or damaged. The only casualty was that of Ken Hart, whose Spitfire K9912 was hit by enemy fire forcing him to make an emergency landing on the Dunkirk beach. Unhurt, he returned to 'Blighty' by means of a boat.

Back at Hornchurch, the claims for German aircraft were submitted by the returning pilots from both 19 and 65 Squadrons. Amazingly, both squadrons had accounted for twenty-four enemy aircraft destroyed or probable destroyed for the loss of two RAF pilots missing and one wounded.

The next day, Monday 27th May, 65 Squadron undertook two patrols, but it was not until the second patrol during the afternoon that the squadron met any significant Luftwaffe activity and Bill Franklin adding once more to his score. Eleven Spitfires took-off from Hornchurch at 1.00 pm and after patrolling for forty-five minutes saw an enemy formation of twenty Dornier 17s and Junkers Ju88s at 8,000 feet over Calais heading towards Dunkirk.

The squadron sections moved into an attacking position and combat was met. Franklin followed his section leader Flight Lieutenant Gerald Saunders as they dived down on a small formation of Dornier 17s. Franklin attacked one of two German bombers and fired a five second burst from a closing range of 400 yards before breaking away at 100 yards. Saunders in turn fired at the same aircraft and as he did he noticed the German airmen deserting the stricken aircraft before it crashed into the sea. Franklin then observed two Ju88s out to sea, flying in line astern. He attacked the rear aircraft and saw his fire hitting home. This bomber then also crashed into the dark waters.

He claimed a Junkers Ju88 destroyed and claimed a half share on the Dornier with Flight Lieutenant Saunders.

Tuesday 28th May dawned at Hornchurch with dreary weather, rain and low cloud. The orders for the day, was that the squadrons based at Hornchurch, would fly as a Wing formation in aid to engage the large Luftwaffe fighter formations that were now operating over the Dunkirk area. No. 54 Squadron took off first followed at 8.57 am by 19 and 65 Squadrons. The nine aircraft of 65 Squadron in lead formation, but below 19 Squadron arrived over Dunkirk and on coming out of cloud sighted nine Dornier 17 bombers at 8,000 feet. The time was 9.15 am. Franklin recalls in his report:

> I sighted a Dornier 17 aircraft flying between clouds. Red Section attacked first and broke away getting lost in clouds. Blue 3 attacked port aircraft and had to force land due to glycol leak. I followed up attack on port aircraft firing a burst of six seconds from 400 yards closing to 100 yards. Later confirmation was received by French troops that on this occasion two Dorniers were seen to crash.

Blue 3 who had been forced to break away from the attack was Pilot Officer Tommy Smart in Spitfire P9435. He force-landed on a nearby beach uninjured and boarded a naval destroyer to get back home. Squadron Leader Cooke had been successful in destroying one of the German bombers, while both Franklin and Sergeant Joseph Kilner claimed a half share on the Dornier. Later that day, 65 Squadron was withdrawn from operations and sent to Kirton-in-Lindsey, Lincolnshire for a brief rest period.

No. 65 returned to resume operations from Hornchurch a few weeks later. During this period, there was a lull in the air activity from the Luftwaffe as they awaited orders from Hitler and Reichsmarshall Herman Goring for the next phase of the war, the invasion of Britain. This pause in the fighting gave the RAF a short time to replenish the aircraft and pilots they had lost during the Battle of France and over Dunkirk. This break in the fighting was only brief and soon the air-fighting resumed.

Bill Franklin's next victory over the enemy came on 25th June 1940, when 65 Squadron engaged Messerschmitt 109s over northern France. Taking off at 4.25 pm, on an offensive patrol, the nine Spitfires headed out across the Channel. At 5.00 pm, just north of Abbeville they intercepted twelve Me109s at a height of about 15,000 feet. Bill Franklin reported:

> We attacked per section. An enemy aircraft circled on to my sections tail and I immediately broke away to engage, but Blue 3 got there before me. I was then attacked by two Me109s and so turned sharply to get on the tail of one. I manoeuvred into position behind his tail and fired a short burst of fire from my guns at about 200 yards. The aircraft burst into flames and dived vertically. I was then engaged by a second enemy aircraft. I latched on to his tail, as two other Germans attacked me from the rear. I broke away and after considerable manoeuvring, had lost height to 4,000 feet.
>
> One Me109 attacked again from behind, but I was able to turn slightly and get on to his tail. I followed him down as he turned and seeing me closing on him, he half rolled. This brought the other two enemy aircraft out of position for an attack on me. I followed inside the first aircraft and fired two very short bursts at about 250 yards and witnessed the Messerschmitt dive into the ground.

Franklin broke off his attack and headed swiftly for home. On his return, he claimed the two Messerschmitts as destroyed, firing in all only 240 rounds of ammunition.

On 7th July, at 8.20 pm, B Flight of 65 Squadron was detailed to intercept German raiders picked up by the radar defence chain, approaching the coast between Dover and Folkestone. Green Section was the first to sight the enemy, Flying Officer George Proudman flying as Green 1 observed the aircraft coming out of cloud. Green Section was ordered to engage, but as they dived down to attack, Blue section noticed another formation of Messerschmitt 109s diving down to attack the Spitfires.

Franklin searched the sky for the enemy. Suddenly, Franklin sighted five Messerschmitt 109s attacking the section from astern. He informed Blue 1 (Flight Lieutenant Saunders) and the section broke away and manoeuvred to attack the German fighters. Franklin pursued one fighter as far as Calais and fired a burst of fire, which caused the German aircraft to dive and crash into the sea. He climbed away heading back towards the English coast, where he spotted several Me109s protecting some bombers.

The German aircraft were in two Vics of three and four aircraft. He climbed above and dived to attack the formation. One machine was hit in the engine and pulled away towards France through cloud. Franklin followed, firing at intervals before finally observing the enemy aircraft make a forced descent in the sea about ten miles from the English coast. The aircraft then sank.

Returning towards home, Franklin then saw what he thought to be another Me109 and attacked, but then recognised it to be a Hurricane aeroplane. He looked for the markings and saw none. He moved in closer and observed that the only markings visible, was a red dope centre and a dark blue outer circle on the wings. No markings on the fuselage were visible. He was doubtful of the aircraft, but returned to Hornchurch without firing.

The two German aircraft were confirmed and added to his score. The rest of Blue Section returned safely, but Green Section consisting of Flying Officer Proudman, Pilot Officer Brisbane and Sergeant Hayes failed to return and were listed as missing. The operations book stating: It is tough losing three of our boys like this, but such is war. A darn good show by Franklin though.

The following day, on 8th July, 65 were again in action over the English Channel, when three sections were sent out to engage the enemy. At 3.39 pm while approaching the French coast they sighted several enemy aeroplanes, Me109s. The squadron broke into sections in line astern and prepared to engage. Bill Franklin was suddenly distracted when he witnessed a bomb burst near Dover and proceeded to investigate. While he was circling around, he noticed below a Messerschmitt 109 stalking a Spitfire (Blue 1). Franklin descended down and attacked the enemy fighter giving a three second burst beginning with deflection and ending dead astern of the German. Franklin observed the aircraft's flaps badly damaged and one leg of the undercarriage come down. There was then an explosion behind the cockpit, bursting it into flames and falling down into the sea about eight miles off Dover. His victim had been an aircraft belonging to II/JG51.

Squadron Leader Sawyer who had recently joined the squadron to take over from Squadron Leader Cooke had been attacked by four Messerschmitts simultaneously, but by using aggressive evasive tactics was able to score a hit on one of the attackers, which probably crashed. Sadly Desmond Cooke who had led the patrol and taken his section through cloud was not seen again, although attempts were made to contact him over the R/T. The squadron logbook entry records: *Another nice effort by Flight Sergeant Franklin, but it is certainly sad losing the C/O in this way, it is very doubtful if anything more will be heard of him, but we hope for the best. Squadron Leader Henry Sawyer now assumes command.*

The very next day, William Franklin learned on 9th July 1940 that he had been awarded the Distinguished Flying Medal, for his outstanding flying achievements against the enemy. The citation of the award read:

<u>An Award</u>

<u>Promulgated in the London Gazette</u>

<u>dated</u>

<u>9th July 1940</u>

Air Ministry,
9th July 1940

The King has been graciously pleased to approve the under mentioned awards
In recognition of gallantry displayed in flying operations against the enemy:-

Awarded the Distinguished Flying Medal

562984 Flight Sergeant William Henry Franklin

During a period of six days in May 1940, Flight Sergeant Franklin took part in numerous offensive patrols over Northern France and on eight occasions was in combat with the enemy. He has himself shot down one Junkers and two Messerschmitt aircraft and in company with his section, he has destroyed three other enemy aircraft.

One day in June 1940, in company with his squadron, Flight Sergeant Franklin engaged fifteen to twenty Messerschmitt 109s and destroyed two. Throughout these engagements he has shown great skill, courage and determination in pressing home his attacks. On one occasion he chased an enemy aircraft more than 20 miles, almost at ground level, before destroying it.
    On 25th July 1940, the squadron was patrolling the Dover area at around 12.40 pm., when on their right they became aware of a large number of German aircraft above. Franklin flying his usual position of Blue 2 became separated from his section and climbed to 25,000 feet over Dover. Looking down he sighted five Messerschmitt 109s below over the Channel at 2,000 feet. He dove down on the enemy, but before he could get into range, the Messerschmitts dispersed in all directions. In the ensuing engagement, he pursued one towards Calais just above the water. Franklin glanced in his mirror just in time to see a second Messerschmitt diving in on him from above, he pulled his Spitfire away and the German failed to pull out and crashed into the sea, for no apparent reason. He then set course back to the English coast, claiming one Me109 destroyed without firing a single round. The German aircraft was later identified as belonging to 8/JG52.
    The next day of 26th July, 'A' Flight was ordered to operate from the forward airfield at Manston. During that morning they were able to carry out

some flying practice, but during the afternoon ay 4.30 pm, twelve aircraft of 65 Squadron was detailed to intercept raiders in the direction of Folkestone. The enemy was not sighted, but a single Dornier 17 was observed and Red Section was detached to attack it, but owing to cloud, the German was able to evade the British fighters.

Almost at the same time however, Blue Section caught sight of a Junkers Ju88. Franklin flying as Blue 2 reported:

> I was patrolling over Folkestone at approximately 12,000 feet. We were above cloud when we sighted enemy bombers in cloud. The R/T orders became confused and we dived down to attack. I saw one Ju88 diving into cloud and followed, coming out over the Channel. I again saw the enemy bomber and gave chase.
>
> While attacking the Junkers, an Me109 attacked me from the port side. I pulled away and fought the Me109, getting a short burst of about two to three seconds in at a quarter position. The enemy began to emit smoke and dived into the sea. I also then saw several aircraft over the Channel heading towards France, which I took for enemy aircraft. They disappeared towards the south. (Note: I observed a high speed launch take-off from the coast and head for the scene of the crash). The Me109 crashed into the sea about four miles off Folkestone.

The squadron returned back to Manston without further incident and later that evening flew back to Rochford airfield near Southend. The 65 Squadron Operations book reports for that day:

> We seem to be getting more action nowadays and Flight Sergeant Franklin is enjoying himself thoroughly, we hope he keeps up the good work. How about some decorations?

During August, the daily routine was to fly down early morning to Manston and operate there for most of the day, then fly back if possible at days end. On 12th August, the Luftwaffe targeted Portsmouth and nearby Isle of Wight where there was the Chain Home radar station at Ventnor. This was attacked by Ju87 dive-bombers and primarely put out of action. At 12.45 pm, while the pilots of 65 Squadron were sitting at dispersal, a formation of low-flying Dornier 17 bombers escorted by twin-engine Messerschmitt 110 fighters approached the airfield undetected and began dropping their bombs. 65 Squadron had been caught on the hop and the pilots immediately raced for their aircraft to try and get airborne. The first section managed to get into the air and then the second, but one aircraft's engine stopped due to the blast from a nearby bomb. Bill Franklin was one of those who managed to get airborne, as did Pilot Officer Dave Glaser that afternoon. He recalled the attack on the airfield:

> Jerry had come in unseen at low-level and bombs were dropping all over the place. Everybody just ran for their aircraft, opened up the throttles and went hell for leather.

A bomb dropped in front of Pilot Officer Wigg's Spitfire and this stopped the airscrew. Wigg jumped out and ran like hell for the nearest hedgerow. Sergeant Kilner had just got out of his Spitfire and was waiting for his oxygen bottle to be replaced, when his ground crew suddenly disappeared from view, this was when the bombs started to fall. He then bolted for the nearest shelter where he found his crewmen. Fortunately, we didn't loose anybody during the attack.

On the next day, Tuesday August 13th, the Luftwaffe increased their attacks by launching Adler Tag, 'Eagle Day.' This new operational phase was planned to wipe out the RAF airfields and installations and as many aircraft on the ground as well as in the air. Both Luftwaffe air fleets would operate; Luftflotte 2 commanded by Generalfeldmarschall Albert Kesselring and Luftflotte 3 under Hugo Sperrle. The weather that day began with low cloud and poor visibility, so the operation was postponed for a few hours.

Hornchurch squadrons were brought to readiness that morning, but only 74 Squadron engaged over Whitstable and destroyed four Dornier 17s. Sadly 65 lost one pilot that day, but not to enemy action. Pilot Officer Felix Gregory was killed when his Spitfire R6766 crashed during night-flying practice.

That same day William Franklin received the news that he was to be awarded for his outstanding airmanship and courage in the face of the enemy during the Dunkirk evacuation and those following months. He was also commissioned to the rank of pilot officer. The London Gazette printed the following:

An Award

Promulgated in the London Gazette

dated

13th August 1940

Air Ministry
13th August 1940

Royal Air Force

The King has been graciously pleased to approve the under-mentioned awards
In recognition of gallantry displayed in flying operations against the enemy:-

Awarded a Bar to the Distinguished Flying Medal

562984 Flight Sergeant William Henry Franklin, D.F.M

Since the 22nd May, 1940, this airman has shot down ten enemy
aircraft and assisted in destroying a further two. On two
occasions, during these engagements, he shot down two
Messerschmitt 109s in one sortie. On another occasion, after
chasing a Messerschmitt across the Channel to Calais, he
encountered seven enemy fighters, five of which he engaged,
destroying one of them. His skill, courage and determination are
of the highest order.

On 16th August, 65 Squadron was operating once again from Manston and
during late afternoon received instructions to patrol Deal, Kent at 4.17 pm.
At 4.45 pm, off Deal, they sighted a mixed formation of 160 fighters and
bombers at a height of between 16,000 to 22,000 feet. Seeing the enemy
fighters above the squadron climbed to engage. Franklin suddenly found
himself passing straight through a compact formation of twenty-four Me109s
(Franklin's combat report states the aircraft as Heinkel 113s). He was in turn
attacked by two of the Me109s firing with deflection shots. Fortunately, their
shooting was so bad that their fire all went astern of Franklin's Spitfire. From
this, he gathered that the 109s could not turn quick enough. In the ensuing
combat, he had no difficulty in getting on to the tail of one German aircraft
and firing a short burst from astern, sending it down in flames.

Due to the fighting, he had ended up over mid-Channel and after a few
minutes flying, sighted below a Dornier 17 followed by a single Me109
heading back towards France. Franklin dived down from 20,000 feet to 6,000
feet and closed in on his first target. He pressed the firing button and fired a
good burst into it from astern. The German began to blow out grey smoke
from both engines and pieces of airframe from the fuselage. He then diverted
his attention to the Messerschmitt, which had begun to dive for the Inglevert
aerodrome. Following the German fighter down, Franklin at 1,500 feet
released a five second slight deflection burst of fire from his guns, which sent
the enemy crashing into the ground near the aerodrome. Satisfied with the
outcome, Franklin set course for home. On landing, he claimed in his report
one Me109 destroyed, one He113 destroyed and one Dornier 17 damaged.

The squadron continued to claim against the German raiders and heavy
fighting continued through to the end of August, until on 28th they received
orders to withdraw to Turnhouse in Scotland for a rest period, which they
undoubtedly needed. They had lost seven pilots during the battle. Their place
was taken by No. 222 Natal Squadron who travelled down from Kirton-in-
Lindsey, Lincolnshire. After nearly six years as one of the home-based
squadrons 65 Squadron left for the final time the following day.

During the next two months, the squadron remained at Turnhouse and
took no further action during the battle. Here they spent time training up new
replacements and during October flew affiliation sorties with No. 263
Squadron who flew the Westland Whirlwind twin-engine fighter. During this
period, Bill Franklin was given leave and was able to visit his family down
south in Essex.

At the end of November, 65 received orders to return south, to operate
from the aerodrome at Tangmere. There was very little action during the first
week apart from when Pilot Officer Strang on patrol over Mayfield on 1st

December, suddenly noticed his engine burst into flames. He was forced to bale out, but landed safely.

The squadron did engage the enemy on 8th December, when Red Section led by Flight Lieutenant Gordon Olive intercepted a single Messerschmitt 110 over Portsmouth. The section went into line astern and Olive attacked firing a long burst, which sent the German diving in flames crashing into the sea. The squadron's first success since arriving at Tangmere.

During the winter afternoon of 12th December 1940, 'B' Flight led by Squadron Leader Gerald Saunders took off from Tangmere and proceeded in the direction of Selsey Bill and sighted a single Junkers Ju88. Blue Section manoeuvred into a line astern formation to attack. The Junkers replied firing from its twin cannon and then dived very steeply towards the French coast and into cloud. Sergeant Lawson managed to get close enough to the Junkers to fire off a two second burst, but in spite of this the Junkers escaped. It then was noticed that both William Franklin and Sergeant Merrick Hine were no where to be seen. It was reported that a Spitfire had been seen to break up and dive into the sea. Although the area was searched by the rest of the squadron and search and rescue was notified, no trace of either pilot or his aircraft was found. They were both presumed killed and listed as missing in action.

The squadron operations book recorded his loss:

> Pilot Officer Franklin first joined the squadron in the spring of 1937 as a sergeant pilot and was awarded the DFM and Bar for his success during intensive operational period of July to September 1940 and was promoted to pilot officer in October 1940. He had 14 enemy aircraft destroyed and _ probable to his credit. Sergeant Hine joined the squadron in August and though he accompanied the squadron on several other operational flights, this was the first time that he came under enemy fire.

Stan Kogel remembers the day when the family received the telegram notifying them of Franklin's loss:

> I was playing out on the corner of the avenue that I lived and I saw the telegram boy as they were in those days with the pillbox hat. I was just eleven years old, but I had an intuition that he was going into our bungalow and he went in and I couldn't wait. I went in and the telegram was there. Louise had been living there for a while because at that time the situation had worsened with the bombing around London. When I came into the bungalow and saw the devastation in my parents, but mainly in my sister Louise, at the shock, it was terrible.
>
> I could actually manage to read the telegram myself. My sister was like a zombie, it was horrific and it took many, many days for her to attempt to revive anything like her real self. When this happened it was very uncertain as the telegram said he was missing, so she lived in hope. After a day or two, she received a letter from his squadron's CO.

On 17th December 1940, William Franklin's widow received a letter of sympathy from 65 Squadron's commanding officer, it read:

Dear Mrs Franklin

It is with deepest regret that I find myself writing this letter informing you that your husband P/O W.H. Franklin has been reported missing, believed killed; following an engagement with enemy aircraft on the 12th December 1940.

I was leading my section and Pilot Officer Franklin was leading another, when the enemy aircraft were sighted. Everything after this happened so quickly that it is impossible to give a detailed account of what took place, but it was noticed that a Spitfire, turned away very steeply and dived towards the sea. It was not until the flight landed that it was noticed that your husband, together with a Sergeant Pilot Hine had not returned. Enquiries were immediately put in hand and other machines were sent out in endeavour to find them. But unfortunately no trace of the missing machines or pilots could be seen.

It has been my fortune to have known your husband since spring 1937, when I was his deputy flight commander and he a sergeant pilot and later I as a squadron leader and he as pilot officer, and I personally feel that I have lost a real friend. To his fellow pilots his absence has come as a stunning blow and to the squadron as a whole, the loss of this most popular, experienced and cheerful pilot is very heavily felt.

I would like to take this opportunity of expressing the sincerest sympathies of both myself and also the whole of the personnel of 65 Squadron to you in your bereavement.
If there is anything I can do, please do not hesitate to let me know.

Yours Sincerely
G.W. Saunders.

There has been some conjecture since, regarding how two Spitfire pilots, one of whom was an exceptional and experienced fighter pilot, could have been lost as a result of attacking a lone German bomber. The action did take place at high altitude in winter and it was cloudy. The German bomber had been shot at by the section led by the squadron commander Gerald Saunders before they broke away, claiming that the rear gunner had been hit. Franklin leading the second section with Sergeants Hine and Lyons continued to follow the bomber which was heading into cloud, at this point Sergeant Lyons peeled away. The two remaining Spitfires then followed the Junkers 88 into cloud and could have been shot down by the German gunner or another of the bombers aircrew on coming out of cloud. The coldness at that altitude would have been extreme and it was not uncommon for the guns or windscreen on the Spitfire to freeze up, disabling the pilot to open fire. With both scenarios taking place the German gunner could have shot them both down without return fire from his enemy. Whatever did take place that winter day, the result was the same, the loss of Bill Franklin and Sergeant Hine

His wife Louise devastated by his loss, remained loyal to his memory until her own death on 20th September 1975. She was invited to attend Buckingham Palace in 1941, to receive from King George VI the Distinguished Flying Medal with Bar. It was a proud, but sad moment for her as she received the award to her late husband.

William Henry Franklin was aged 29 years, when he was lost in action. Had he lived, he probably would have gone onto greater achievements in the Royal Air Force or civilian life. But his name is not forgotten and he is remembered on the Royal Air Force Runnymede Memorial Panel 8. At Hornchurch, a road is named after him as a fitting tribute, 'Franklin Road.' But he will always be remembered as one of the ace pilots of 1940.

CHAPTER 6

DONALD KINGABY
'THE 109 SPECIALIST'

Donald Ernest Kingaby was born on 7th January 1920 in the Borough of
Islington, London, the only child of Percival (Percy) Frederick Kingaby and
Esther Louisa (nee Hastings) Kingaby. His family moved frequently as his
father pursued a living as a Church of England minister and his early
childhood was spent in London, Suffolk, Hertfordshire, Ontario in Canada,
and finally at Histon in Cambridgeshire.

During his time in North London, living near the gates of Highbury
Stadium as a ten year old, he established a life-long love of the Arsenal
football team, especially as they entered their fabulous run of success
which continued all through the 1930s.   He would follow the
'Gunners' ups and downs throughout his life. His other sporting passion was
cricket, but it was in 1926 that another interest would be awakened, as he later
recalled:

> In the summer of 1926, when I was six years old, my mother and
> father took me, on a glorious sunny day, for a picnic in Highgate
> Woods in North London. Before long, I had inveigled father
> into accompanying me to the edge of the playing fields there for
> a game of cricket. Using a massive oak as a wicket, and father as
> bowler, fieldsman, wicket-keeper and umpire I began to practice
> my dreams of Hobbs, Sutcliffe, and Hendren, treating the
> bowling with the cruel inconsideration of extreme youth. Father
> was only saved from complete exhaustion by the tea interval,
> which mother, with a keen tactical eye for his state of health,
> called just after the score had reached a hundred for no wickets.
> During this respite, three gaily painted biplane fighters began
> cavorting, fairly low down, over the far edge of the playing fields.
> Loops, rolls and stall turns in formation by the three held me
> spellbound for some five minutes until they headed away back to
> their base, presumably Hendon. I had of course seen aeroplanes
> before, but for the most part they had droned impersonally,
> straight and level, across the sky, holding one's attention for only
> a short interval before they disappeared from sight. But the
> joyous abandon of the fighter formation was something entirely
> different, suggesting an unknown freedom, and although I was
> too young to appreciate it I am sure that then was born my
> ambition to become a pilot.

In 1934, Don Kingaby was enrolled at King's School, Ely. At first, dismayed
by the prospect of attending a boarding school, homesick and at the bottom
of his class and after missing several vital segments of education due to the

family's frequent moves, he eventually settled down to the happiest of his school days, doing well academically and playing football for the school's First XI.

During school holidays, he was kept abreast of the rising power of Hitler's Germany by his father, who had served in the Honorable Artillery Company during the First World War, and the young Kingaby's desire to join the Royal Air Force was reignited. At sixteen years of age and with no money to continue his education at Ely, he was reluctantly persuaded to look for other career options and, somewhat gloomily, chose insurance.

Upon leaving school, he went to work for the Ocean Accident and Guarantee Corporation Ltd in Cambridge, where he worked from 1936 to 1939. As the threat of Germany became stronger, and he was now old enough, he joined the RAF Volunteer Reserve and was accepted for training as a sergeant pilot in April 1939. As was the practice, all training in the Volunteer Reserve was done in spare time except for a fourteen day period each year, which employers were asked to grant to any members of their staff who were under training. During training, Kingaby noted with amusement that 'no pilot was to partake of more than one pint of beer at lunchtime' and as he was a teetotaler at that time, thought one pint would have been much more than enough! He also recalled at that time:

> I thought that in early 1939 that it was pretty obvious that there was going to be a war. I always had wanted to fly and I had no ambition to be a foot slogger, so I joined the local branch of the RAF Volunteer Reserve, where you could learn to fly in your spare time.
>
> I did about a hundred hours flying during the three and half months between the time I joined and the outbreak of war. I then spent about three months stagnating in an initial training camp at Cambridge, billeted in the colleges there. We did a lot of foot slogging before I went up to Scotland to finish my flying training.

Kingaby took to flying with great gusto and enthusiasm and accumulated 110 hours of flying time in four months, all in his spare time, in Tiger Moths and Hawker Hind aircraft. His first flight was in a Tiger Moth and after the initial fright of take-off, he felt exhilarated and exulted in the experience from that moment on. Despite receiving only an average final grade and a couple of close calls on failing altogether, he received his mobilisation papers and commenced full time training in September 1939.

After initial flying training he was sent to No. 5 Operational Training Unit at Aston Down on 10th June 1940, where he spent a seven day, ten hour conversion course and was taught how to fly a Spitfire fighter aircraft. After gaining precious flying hours on Spitfires, he received his first posting, to join No. 266 'Rhodesia' Squadron at Wittering on 24th June as a sergeant pilot.

On arrival to his new squadron, he was highly elated and bursting with the overconfidence of every newly trained pilot. He then proceeded to demonstrate all the wonderful things he could do in a Spitfire! Upon landing, he was sent immediately to the squadron commander, where he was 'verbally trimmed, pruned, and generally cut down to size' during a fifteen minute tongue lashing.

During the early weeks of August 1940, the squadron was sent south to participate in the Battle of Britain. The squadron was sent to operate out of Eastchurch as part of 11 Group and it was here on 10th August, that the aerodrome came under attack during a bombing raid. Kingaby narrowly missed death by escaping from the hut he had just slept in, which received a direct hit. He and his commanding officer, Squadron Leader Rodney Wilkinson were also instrumental in saving some Spitfires in a burning hangar.

Kingaby's first success against the enemy came two days later on 12th August 1940. No. 266 Squadron was ordered to patrol over the Solent Estuary and the south of Portsmouth. The weather was fine and cloudless with only 4/10ths cloud at 6,000 feet. Kingaby was flying as part of Green Section-B Flight, when at 12.05 pm they sighted twelve German aircraft, a mixed formation of Me110s and Junkers Ju88s. Kingaby's report of the following action states:

> I was flying as Green 3, when we sighted enemy aircraft located over the Solent. Green Section carried out a No.1 attack from astern on a Ju88. I gave it one burst of about eight seconds, my range decreasing from 200 yards to 100. The starboard engine of the aircraft caught fire. I then broke off and attacked another Ju88 from astern and saw pieces fall from the fuselage. Three other fighters then attacked and I transferred my attention to an Me110 which I chased out to sea and eventually caught about sixteen miles from the French Coast. I attacked from astern and heavy smoke poured from both its engines and it began to lose way. I had no ammunition left, so I returned to base. I had observed anti-aircraft fire over Portsmouth. There was no return fire from the Ju88 I had attacked. A single gun firing astern from the Me110 using incendiary ammunition, but was not very effective.

On his return to the airfield at Eastchurch, He relayed the information to the awaiting intelligence officer and put in a claim for three damaged aircraft, two JU88s and Me110.

On 18th August, 266 Squadron led by Flight Lieutenant Denis Armitage had led eleven of his pilots during the early part of the afternoon to patrol over the Kent coast. At about 2.15 pm, Armitage received orders from control to land and refuel at Manston aerodrome. The flight path of the drome was heavily potholed with bomb holes from previous raids, so the dispersal of aircraft on landing was made difficult and the Spitfires of 266 were therefore at risk. As the last of the aircraft landed and the pilots were stepping out of their aircraft, without warning a small force of Messerchmitt 109s came in over the field and began strafing men and machines. The pilots on the ground ran in all directions seeking cover as the airfield defences sprung into action against the German raid. Caught in the open, Kingaby threw himself to the ground. He recalled the next frightening seconds:

I had hardly walked ten yards, when there came a burst of machine gun fire. I was feeling very jumpy and looked around to see where the row was coming from. To my horror I found myself looking straight at the nose of an Me109 not three hundred yards away. To have run would have been suicide, and for some reason I did not panic. I threw myself to the ground and rolled out of the Hun's line of fire. As he passed over me I thought I would be able to get up and run, but the Heinie was not alone, he'd brought the rest of his boys with him. I had to lay on the ground, rolling back and forth while about seven of the twelve gave me a personal run over. When the last one had passed, I got up and ran like a hare for the nearest cover about a hundred yards away. I had about five yards to do before number one Heinie was back again firing at me, so I just took one terrific leap behind a mound of earth that covered a shelter. The Hun missed me and I thought I had got away scot free from the whole show. It was then I noticed that my hand was bleeding at no mean rate and realised that I had 'had' operations for the next week or so. When I got to the sick quarters and looked at my overalls I found two other bullet holes in them but was untouched myself.

I was pushed off on sick leave, and was not back on operations for another month. I found the leave a great blessing for, in four days, I had had my first combat, had my sleeping quarters blown to kingdom come within minutes of leaving them, and been strafed on the ground and wounded. My nerves were in a pretty poor state and but for this enforced rest I am sure I would not have lasted much longer.

Another pilot, New Zealander Richard Trousdale had also been caught in the open; he had still been wearing his parachute pack and had been seen kneeling down with his parachute pack facing the enemy. Their commander, Armitage later joking, said that he had looked like a Mohammedan at prayer

The German fighters made two runs at the airfield before heading back across the Channel. On the ground two Spitfires had been totally destroyed with another six damaged, but repairable. Miraculously, none of the squadron's pilots had been killed. Kingaby's finger was dressed as he observed the carnage at Manston. The squadron was withdrawn from the battle and sent to Wittering.

The squadron spent the next few weeks recovering from their losses and exchanged their Mk1 Spitfires for MkIIs and flying patrols covering Duxford. Kingaby remained with them until he was posted to No. 92 Squadron based at the 11 Group aerodrome of RAF Biggin Hill.

After spending a few days leave with his family, Kingaby travelled by train on 25th September from London and alighted at Bromley South Station and boarded the local bus to Green Leaves village. He then walked the final part of his journey to the aerodrome. On arrival, he was dumb struck at the scene of bombed buildings and debris caused by the Luftwaffe's attempts to knock out the aerodrome and its squadrons. No sooner had he taken in the devastation when he suddenly became aware of the sound of an aircraft flying overhead. The aeroplane was a German Junkers Ju88; fortunately it dropped no bombs and once over the station headed south and back for France.

Kingaby had during this time, like everybody else, jumped for cover into the nearest slit trench or shelters. Once the threat was over, he asked the way to the Sergeants' Mess and on arrival found this deserted. He waited around and eventually was shown by a flight sergeant, where he was to be billeted and to whom he would share a room. After meeting some of the other sergeant pilots and having a meal, he settled down for the night.

After a somewhat disturbed sleep caused by the local anti-aircraft gun-site firing off at intervals at night raiders, he was woken just before dawn and prepared himself for his first day with 92 Squadron.

After a quick breakfast, he was taken down to the crew room at dispersal and here he met some of the other airmen he would fly with. After changing into his flying kit and picking up his parachute, he was then under the guidance of Flight Lieutenant Brian Kingcome, now an old hand with 92 Squadron; he was shown the Spitfire he would be flying that day. After checking with his ground crew, Kingaby returned to the dispersal room and sat down with the rest of the pilots and waited for the call to action.

One sergeant of 92 Squadron was Ralph 'Titch' Havercroft, probably the smallest fighter pilot in Fighter Command at five foot three, but he would also become an ace pilot.

The weather on the 26th was not ideal, with heavy cloud. It was not until the afternoon that Green Section of 92 Squadron was called upon to patrol. No enemy formations were sighted, but they did encounter separately three German aircraft and one was claimed as probably destroyed.

The next day however, was to be quite different on 27th September, with Radar picking up large plots of enemy formations during the early morning. At 9.05 am, 92 and 72 Squadrons were ordered into the air and picked up a formation of twenty Dornier 17s with Me109 escort at 9.15 am near Sevenoaks. Led by Brian Kingome, he ordered the squadron down into a diving attack against the bombers before the German fighters joined in the affray.

A number of enemy aircraft were shot down, Kingcome claiming a Dornier destroyed and one damaged, while Sergeant Hugh Bowen-Morris and Pilot Officer Allan Wright damaged a further two and a Messerschmitt Me110 was seen to be severely damaged by Pilot Officer Trevor Wade. In return the Germans shot down two of the squadron's aircraft, Spitfire R6767 in which Sergeant Charles Sydney was killed and Spitfire X4422 flown by New Zealander Flying Officer James Paterson. His aircraft was hit and set alight by 109s over Maidstone; Paterson was unable to extricate himself from his burning aircraft and was killed when it crashed at Sparepenny Lane, Framlingham, Kent.

Following the mornings engagement, during which 92 Squadron had suffered the loss of two experienced pilots, the squadron was called into the air again at 11.45 am and for a third time. At 2.45 pm, they were scrambled once more from Biggin Hill, flying in company with No. 66 Squadron. The two Spitfire squadrons led again by Brian Kingcome, spotted a formation of Junkers Ju88s at 15,000 feet over Sevenoaks at 3.00 pm. He ordered an attack from head-on and in doing so, the enemy split it's formation. Kingaby attacked the leading enemy machine with a beam attack from starboard, firing a short two second burst. He did not have time to see the results of his attack as in the next instant he was under attack from five Messerschmitt 109s:

> As I was attacked by the 109s, I dived doing an aileron turn to evade the attack, but the 109s followed me down. I straightened out and a 109 overshot me. I got him in my sights and gave him a short burst and pieces came out of his starboard wing. Cannon fire from behind came too close to be comfortable and I went into an aileron turn dive again. When I came out the 109s had disappeared. There was no damage to my own machine.

On landing back at Biggin, he learnt that the squadron had claimed four Ju88s destroyed, but had lost another pilot killed, Sergeant Trevor Oldfield. Kingaby claimed his Me109 as only damaged. Kingaby recalls this period of hectic activity and how continuous action and tiredness did become the norm for fighter pilots to endure; and memories of waiting the call to action at dispersal:

> We had to be on from about 4.00 am in the morning to about 10 o'clock at night. There were very few spare pilots around and sleep became quite a problem at night. I felt that at Biggin particularly, they had been fighting very hard and I felt I must keep fit, but I found this rather difficult because the billet we had been placed in was only fifty yards away from a heavy ack-ack battery, which practically blew us out of bed every night. I tried taking aspirin and going down air-raid shelters for the night, the aspirins didn't work and in the shelter you could hear everything just as much. I would wake with a foul mouth in the morning and feel absolutely washed out. After about four days of this I just joined the other chaps in the bar, had a few pints of beer, after which I was able to sleep contentedly.
>
> The next morning I would arrive down at the dispersal hut in the gloom of the pre-dawn period, collect my kit, parachute and helmet and take them over to my aircraft, the one that I had been allotted. I would then hang the helmet over the control stick and check around the cockpit and make sure everything was ready for a quick getaway.
>
> Back at the dispersal hut we played cards, pontoon, poker, or read a book and played gramophone records. We had a couple of pilots who were great 'Jazz' enthusiasts, 'Titch' Havercroft and Bob Holland. We had an old piano there that they use to jive around on.
>
> There was a telephone line from the sector operations room direct to our hut and as soon as a message came through on that, the clerk would yell out scramble. Bells would begin to ring and flares would be sometimes fired and there would be a mad rush out of the door, as every pilot would do his damnedness to get to his aeroplane as quick as possible.

We would then form up as a squadron of twelve if available; then all take off in formation together. It could be a bit hazardous at times if the leader slightly misjudged his throttle handling, because usually at Biggin you had to avoid obstructions or where bomb holes had sometimes not been completely filled in.

Once we were airborne, it would vary as to the time we made contact with the enemy, depending on the type of raid and the tactics that the fighter controller back in the sector ops room was using. During September, we were mainly intercepting bombers, flying at between 17,000 to 20,000 feet heavily escorted by fighters. The controllers would try to divert us away from the bombers at first, and then bring us back into them from the sun and from above if they could, to give us the advantage.

Kingaby's next claim came on 30th September, over Lewes, Sussex while on patrol flying as Green 2, he sighted two Messerschmitt 109s at 5.00 pm at an altitude of 8,000 feet. He carried out a quarter attack on the leading aircraft and fired a four second burst from his machine guns, which immediately caused heavy black smoke to belch from the 109s engine. Suddenly, his own aircraft came under attack from the enemy aircraft. He broke off and headed for home, claiming the Me109 as a damaged.

This aircraft has since been identified as Messerschmitt 109-4 Werke No. 1190 of 4/JG26. The aircraft suffered engine failure having been attacked by Kingaby, its pilot Unteroffizier Horst Perez managed to undertake a near perfect forced-landing at Eastdean near Eastbourne at 5.30 pm. Perez was captured and the aircraft which was hardly damaged was later shipped to Canada in 1941 as a publicity tool for the 'Bundles for Britain' scheme. It finally came back to Britain in the 1960s, before finally being restored at the Imperial War Museum at Duxford, where it is now on display to the public within the Battle of Britain Hall.

Kingaby would later recall his impression of the Luftwaffe pilots and the Spitfires role in defeating them:

> I think our own pre-war trained air pilots were superior to the Germans; but the Germans had the benefit of combat experience having fought in the civil war in Spain previously; as compared with the Volunteer Reservist pilots like myself, it took us time to catch up with them and we lost a lot of chaps during that process.
>
> The Spitfire's eight machine guns were very much responsible for its success against the Luftwaffe, particularly when you realised that a lot of us had not been very well trained on shooting; a lot of us were volunteer reservists, over fifty percent in my squadron and we hadn't had much shooting practice or instruction for that matter. If you had eight guns you could spray around a bit, it helped

The squadron continued to be heavily engaged and continued to score against the Luftwaffe during the last days of September and the beginning of October. The German's tactics changed during that month as fewer large bomber formations appeared during daylight hours in exchange for greater attacks by high-flying Messerschmitt 109 fighter sweeps, some aircraft carrying a single bomb load. Kingaby remembers the change of tempo as his squadron had to deal with more fighters than bombers:

> In October, the Huns gave up nearly all their bomber raids by daylight and put in fighters carrying bombs. We had to go in straight towards them and they were pretty fast. The Me109s were about equal to the Spitfire for speed, they were slightly better off at top altitude, they could get a little higher than us, but on the other hand we could turn in a much smaller circle than them, which gave us a greater advantage when it came to combat.

Don Kingaby's next claim did not come until 12th October 1940, when during that afternoon, the squadron was alerted to large enemy fighter formations entering over the Kent countryside. His report of that action details the following:

> I took off as Yellow 3 at 4.00 pm and near Rochester sighted fifty Me109s at 24,000 feet. We attacked at 4.25 pm. An Me109 flew broadside across and about fifty feet below the squadron. He crossed my sights and I gave him a full deflection shot at about 70 yards range. I fired a three to four second burst and saw smoke and glycol pour from him. He went into a shallow dive and Sergeant Fokes (Blue 1) saw him continue the dive in a battered condition.
>   I broke off the attack immediately, I saw he was in a bad condition and attacked another 109 from astern, giving him a short burst at about 150 yards range. He began to dive slightly, but I broke off the attack as there was another plane behind me. It was Sergeant Ellis (Blue 3), he followed the 109 down and saw it crash and explode five miles south-east of Rochester. I presume I killed the pilot as I did not see any result of my fire.

These two aircraft were claimed as one confirmed and one probably destroyed.
   Pilot Officer Trevor Wade and Flight Lieutenant Kingcome also claimed one Me109 destroyed. The squadron suffered one fatality, that of twenty-one year old Pilot Officer Aberconway John Sefton Pattison who was shot down over Hawkinge in Spitfire X4591.
   Three days later on 15th October, 92 Squadron was called into combat twice that morning against enemy fighter sweeps withdrawing from sorties over London. Kingaby with ten fellow airmen took off from Biggin at 8.45 am and were given instructions to meet up in the air over the aerodrome with No.66 Squadron. The two squadrons were then vectored on to the enemy, who were now heading south towards the Channel. The squadrons caught up

with the Me109s and a massive dogfight ensued. During this combat, Kingaby managed to chase and fire several short bursts into one of the enemy machines over mid-Channel, sending it plunging into the murky water below.

Fellow Sergeant Ronnie Fokes also had success with one Me109 and a lone Heinkel 111 bomber destroyed.

Kingaby was able to claim a quarter share of a Messerschmitt 110, which was caught by the squadron east of Tonbridge Wells, Kent on 20th October. The German aircraft was intercepted at height, on a reconnaissance mission by 92 Squadron in company with No.222 Natal Squadron. The Me110C-5 coded L2+MR (2228) dived to low level in hope of avoiding the RAF fighters, but was shot down. The aircraft belonged to 7(F)/LG2, it force-landed and burnt out at Bockingfield, Hormonsden at 12.50 pm. Oberleutnant Lemmerich was captured, Unteroffizier Eberling was killed.

During the battle the comradeship and courage of the pilots was never in question, but the status between the officer ranks and the NCOs has since been debated as sometimes less than cordial. What were Don Kingaby's thoughts about the class divide?

> On duty, the officers' in 92 Squadron treated us as themselves and I think we all appreciated this, and we did our best not to abuse the privilege that they afforded us in doing that. Off duty, we quite often would meet up with them in a local pub, later on that was, because during the Battle of Britain of course our licensing laws shut the pubs before we could get out to them.

He developed close friendships in the Sergeant's Mess, and nine of them kept together for about nine months, a miraculous time span in those days. Of the nine, two died and two became prisoners of war, but Kingaby remained close friends all his life with Jed Cheminault, Ralph "Tich" Havercroft, Hugh Bowen-Morris and Walter "Johnnie" Johnston. During this time, no longer a teetotaler, he and his friends had many good times at the Jail pub and at the Bromley Country Club.

The squadron was called to readiness early morning on the 24th October 1940, with the pilots climbing into their aircraft and taxiing to take-off at 9.20 am. Airborne at 9.25 am to patrol over Maidstone, Kent at 15,000 feet. Kingaby was flying in Red Section.

While acting as weaver, he spotted an aircraft going east, flying just above the clouds at 6,000 feet. Kingaby decided to go down and investigate. He kept between the sun and the aircraft and found it to be a Dornier 17 bomber at 7,000 feet. He continued to fly on a parallel course to the German and kept in the sun. Kingaby then positioned himself for a beam attack. At 10.20 am, he dived out of the sun, opening fire from a range of 200 yards. The German's port engine then began to throw out heavy black smoke as he observed his incendiary bullets going into the cockpit area.

He continued his attack, turning to fire from the quarter beam and breaking off at fifty yards range, Kingaby presumed he must have hit the pilot, when the Dornier dropped its port wing and went into an almost vertical dive.

He spiralled his Spitfire down through the clouds and came out over the sea. A moments search revealed a large green patch on the water where the German had ended its dive twenty miles east of Deal. Kingaby climbed his aircraft back up above the clouds to look for any further aircraft, but could find none and therefore set course for home. The Dornier was credited as destroyed.

The next day, 25th October at 12.50 pm, the squadron was ordered to patrol over Rochford in Essex. Here they were joined by No. 222 Natal Squadron from Hornchurch. They were both vectored when large numbers of Messerschmitt 109s were plotted coming in over Kent, south-east of Maidstone at altitudes ranging from 20,000 to 28,000 feet. At 1.30 pm, the Me109s were sighted, some seventy fighters flying at a lower height of 8,000 feet. The Spitfires went in to attack. Kingaby chased a 109 for several minutes and opened fire at 200 yards range from dead astern. He fired two short bursts of two seconds causing radiator glycol to pour from the German. The enemy aircraft then dived into the clouds and Kingaby followed. Coming out of the clouds, he found he had crossed the French Coast. There was no sign of the Messerschmitt, so he returned to base claiming the enemy as damaged.

Kingaby's luck and ability was to continue six days later, when he claimed another German fighter on 1st November. He recalls:

> I took off with 92 Squadron as Green 3 at 1.25 pm. We were patrolling the mouth of the Thames, when we sighted the enemy aircraft at about 5,000 feet, attacking ships in the estuary. We dived down from 20,000 feet. I was engaged by two Me109s (Yellow nosed) which tried to do a beam attack on me. I avoided them by going into a steep turn and got on the tail of the second 109. I gave it a medium burst from about 150 yards range. Flames came from its engine and it went into a steep dive into the water. The pilot did not bale out and there was no sign of life around the spot where he went in.

In a wartime radio interview, Kingaby talked of his successes, especially of the day when he was to shoot down four of the enemy:

> The reason I've got so many Messerchmitts maybe is because it was just my luck to have run into more of these enemy machines than of any other type. The day I shot four of them down was when they were coming in over the Channel in droves. We don't see them like that at present, just odd ones and two's, dodging about in the cloud.
>
> On 15th November 1940, our squadron of Spitfires was sent out in the morning and intercepted a large formation of 109s coming in over the Channel. There were fifty of them. When our leader, a Canadian, gave the order to attack, I got onto the tail of four 109s at about 17,000 feet and attacked the outside one. After I had given him two short bursts of fire, he dived and crashed near Gravesend. When I looked around again the sky was full of Messerschmitts, scattering in all directions. We chased

them back to France and returned to our station for lunch. It seemed to me to be a pretty good mornings' work. In the afternoon, we were sent up again and told there were some 109s off Selsey Bill. We saw them when we were at about 20,000 feet.

There were about forty of them about 500 feet above us. As they outnumbered us at about three to one, I suppose they thought they were on to a good thing. But in all events, they started to dive on us. We evaded their first attack and then turned on them. I picked on three, who had now made their way back towards France. One was straggling a bit behind. I concentrated my fire on him and he went down in flames. The other two Messerschmittts had not seen me come up, so I closed up behind the leader and gave him a burst. As I did so the other 109 came up on my tail, but I held on to the fellow I had got. He must have been carrying a bomb, for after another burst from my guns he blew up before the one behind could protect him. There was nothing left of him in the sky that you could recognise as an aircraft, just a flash and a puff of smoke and bits of debris hurtling down all over the place. I must give that third Jerry pilot his due. He could have got away, but he stayed to fight. But the Spitfire's eight machine guns were too much for him and after a couple of turns; he went down in flames, then I turned, found the squadron and returned home.

Following his amazing success on the 15th, he claimed another victory on 1st December, shooting down another Me109, fifteen miles south of Dungeness. On 6th December 1940, the London Gazette printed the medal awards. Donald Kingaby's well earned award of the Distinguished Flying Medal was listed and stated the following:

L.G. 6/12/40 Kingaby, Donald, Ernest. 745707 Sergeant, No.92 Sqn. (Immediate)

On 15th November 1940, the squadron encountered about 40 Me109s over Selsey Bill. Sergeant Kingaby singled out a vic of three and, closing in, shot No.3 down in flames. He then attacked No.1 which, after a short burst, exploded in mid-air. No.2 had by this time got on his tail, so he went into a steep turn and, after three turns got in a quarter attack at 50 yards range and shot it down. He also shot down one Me109 earlier on the same day. This pilot has always displayed great tenacity and energy and has himself destroyed seven Me109s, one Dornier 17, one Me110 and a further four enemy aircraft probably destroyed or damaged.

Remarks by Air Officer Commanding:

On 15th November 1940, in particular, this gallant young Sergeant Pilot scored a magnificent success, personally destroying four enemy aircraft. He has shown great tenacity and

has destroyed nine enemy aircraft and probably destroyed or
damaged a further four. I strongly recommended him for an
immediate award of the Distinguished Flying Medal.

Kingaby continued to fly operationally throughout December, but did not
score further that year. The squadron had further success in claiming six more
enemy aircraft destroyed in three separate sorties, but as winter and bad
weather drew in the air activity was less frequent with few enemy aircraft
venturing over the Channel.

The winter was particularly bad with heavy snow and this continued into
January, and most aircraft were grounded. However, those in high position
within Fighter Command were now preparing to resume the fight against the
Nazis. Plans were put into effect to take the fight back across into Northern
France and Belgium with Fighter Sweeps and small bombing raids with fighter
escorts. The Spitfire and Hurricanes would escort Blenheim light-bombers to
targets such as Luftwaffe airfields, installations, munitions in the hope that not
only would they destroy the target, but also encourage the German fighters up
to engage in combat.

The first of these sweeps took place on Friday 10th January 1941, when six
Blenheim aircraft of No. 114 Squadron set off to attack the Foret de Guines
airfield in north-west France. They were escorted by three Hurricane
squadrons from North Weald and three Spitfire squadrons from Hornchurch.
No. 92 Squadron accompanied by No. 66 and 74 Squadrons had the job of
patrolling the Channel area, as the sweep crossed over into France, but were
not involved in any action. This was the start of offensive operations, which
would carry on and build continuously until final victory against the enemy
was completed.

At 11.11 am on 14th February 1941, Don Kingaby accompanied by
another squadron pilot took off on a convoy patrol from Manston. Flying
below cloud base at 9,000 feet they picked up the convoy north of Margate,
when over the R/T they were given instructions to join 66 Squadron at 5,000
feet over Ramsgate. Kingaby joined up over mid-Channel, but lost the aircraft
of 66 Squadron as they went up through cloud. Kingaby's No.2 had to return
to base owing to losing radio contact. As he neared the French coast at 12,000
feet, above cloud he sighted again the aircraft of 66 Squadron, but was almost
immediately attacked from astern by an enemy fighter. He pulled around his
aircraft very hard, causing him to almost blackout. In the process, he managed
to get in a short burst of fire from his machine-guns from the beam and
continued with a quarter attack firing a three second burst. The German
machine rolled over onto its back and dived down. Kingaby followed through
cloud and was in time to see the Messerschmitt crash and explode as it hit the
ground, approximately three miles from Cap Gris Nez.

It was while having an evening off and attending a dance at the Bromley
Country club that, in the spring of 1941, Don Kingaby met the beautiful
Helen Watkinson of Bromley. Helen, the daughter of Arthur Edward and
Helen Maud (nee Wyborn) Watkinson, was born the 5th October 1920. She
and her elder brother, Gerald, were raised in Bromley, with their mother
working full time, and their father Arthur, a draper's window dresser well
known in the area for his artistic flair. He had experienced gas poisoning

during World War I, and suffered frail health, although he lived until the age of seventy. Helen, at that time aged twenty, worked as a secretary at Robinson & Cleaver, a draper's firm from Belfast, which was located on Regents Street in London. Both siblings inherited their father's artistic talents, and Gerry eventually became an artist and art teacher.

Back at Biggin Hill, the fighter sweeps increased and so did his score. On 16th May, Kingaby claimed another two Messerschmitt 109's, one damaged over Dungeness, the other destroyed five miles off Calais. He was nicknamed the '109 Specialist.'

The squadron was involved with a Circus operation on 23rd June, to escort bombers over Bethune. They arrived over the target at the same time as the bombers, but no hostile aircraft were encountered. Whilst diving down towards the French coast on their return leg of the mission, they suddenly sighted Me109s about ten miles inland from Le Touquet. Kingaby chased after one of the enemy fighters down to five thousand feet, but lost him, when he thought he was under attack himself. About two minutes later He sighted another 109 flying inland at five hundred feet and he dived towards this. He carried out a beam attack, but must have spotted the Spitfire, as before Kingaby could open fire, the German executed a very steep turn and spun into the ground and exploded south-east of Boulogne.

Having witnessed the German slam into the ground, without him having to fire a single shot was a bit of a shock. He then turned his aircraft and caught up with the returning bombers, claiming the 109 on his return to Biggin.

At 11.50 am on the morning of 2nd July, 92 were detailed to take part in Circus 29 Operation. Kingaby was flying as Yellow 3, that day and soon after take off had to take over lead from his leader due to mechanical problems. The rest of the squadron then headed for Lille. His report of the operation reads:

> We went to Lille at 17,000 feet without hindrance from enemy fighters or ack-ack, we did a circuit over the town where we noted anti-aircraft firing at the bombers. On our way back from Lille, enemy fighters were several times reported in that vicinity. But we were not molested. As the coast drew near things began to liven up and Garrick leader (call-sign for 92 Squadron) gave the order to attack some 109s. I could not see the aircraft however, and so I maintained my height with Yellow 2 at 15,000 feet. I then crossed the French coast about six miles east of Gravelines.
>
> Suddenly two aircraft which I mistook to be Hurricanes dived down in front of us and then I realised that they were Me109F's. It was then too late to follow them down.
>
> This was really a blessing in disguise for the next moment two more 109F's came diving down in front of us. Obviously the first two had been bait for us, while the second pair was supposed to shoot us up. I whipped into a turn and delivered an attack from the port quarter above. I had no tracer in my guns and so I laid off about four rings deflection and let them run through a five second burst from my cannon and machine guns.
>
> I did not wait to see what happened to them as I had a strong suspicion that there were another two coming down after us. I

pulled up hard and climbed up to regain height in time to see two more 109s turning toward the French coast. Beneath me was the pleasant sight of first, a parachute and then two large splashes in the water, where the two 109s had gone in. Sergeant Carpenter and others confirmed this. I then made my way home through a thick haze to Manston and there with Yellow 2, we refueled.

On the following day, good news arrived that he had been awarded a Bar to his DFM with the citation,

'This airman pilot has continued to prove himself a very able section leader, who fights with coolness and courage. He has now destroyed at least 14 enemy aircraft and damaged others.'

On their next Circus operation, No.67, on 7th July they were part of the escort wing to rendezvous with six Blenheims and close support at Manston.

Crossing the French coast at Gravelines they experienced light Flak about five miles inland. Two Messerschmitt 109F's passed under the squadron and Kingaby led Blue Section down to attack. He fired a three second burst with his cannon and machine guns at five hundred yards range and saw several high explosive shells hit the fuselage of the 109 on the right. He immediately turned and climbed to rejoin the squadron and on looking back over his shoulder saw the enemy machine going down out of control with black smoke pouring from it.

As they approached the target area of St Omer with the bombers, they noticed there were many 109s in the vicinity, flying in pairs, but none of these attacked the bombers. Just after they had turned for home, two enemy fighters made a quarter attack on Kingaby's aircraft from starboard. He turned towards them and saw their tracer bullets pass underneath him. The Germans then turned inland and fled. Two minutes later, he noticed two further Me109s passing in front at a range of six hundred yards. He opened fire with both cannon and guns and hit the first aircraft several times. The German then swung round in a turn and did a head-on attack on his Spitfire, missing a collision by only a matter of feet, when he broke away. Kingaby did not see him again. As he crossed back across the coast at Gravelines, he attacked another German fighter which then dived inland. He did not see any results from his fire and made his way back home. He claimed for one Me109 probable and one damaged.

In early August, on the 7th he claimed two further enemy aircraft, as reported in his combat report for that day:

I took off with Garrick Squadron as Blue 3 at 5.20 pm on a fighter sweep. We crossed the French coast at Boulogne at 25,000 feet with two other squadrons above and behind us. Garrick Leader sighted a bunch of 109s to starboard and ordered the top cover squadron to jump them. They could not see them however, so our leader turned and dived on them. Blue 1 chased the enemy aircraft which dived inland and I followed him. We had our backs to the sun and one enemy machine dived down behind us and fired a short burst. I was forced to turn and lost Blue 1, but could not see the German who was firing at us. I then saw four Me109s turning in behind me over Boulogne at 15,000 feet. I climbed into the sun and they lost me. I then made an attack on them from behind, but miss-timed it and they dived through the cloud over Hardalot, but could not find them again.

I then stayed under cloud base and saw two further 109s climbing up at Le Touquet at about 3,000 feet. I stalked them and dived down on the left hand aircraft when they were at 6-7,000 feet. I fired at two second burst at a range of 150 yards. The enemy aircraft wobbled violently and gradually turned over and went down with glycol and black smoke pouring from him. I last saw him going straight down at about 2,000 feet.

After I had delivered this attack I climbed right up again, just underneath the cloud base. The other German aircraft was going round in a steep turn to the left, evidently looking for me. I dived down on him and delivered an attack from the port quarter above, giving him a two second burst. The fight then developed into a turning competition and I had too much speed and could not get inside his turn. I pulled my nose up and skidded violently and brought my speed down and then began to out turn him. I gave him a couple of short bursts from my machine guns at about seventy yards and saw several bullet strikes on the wings and fuselage. His aircraft stopped turning and straightened out and was going into a half roll, when I fired a further two second burst from astern. He gradually turned over and dived straight into the ground about five miles south of Le Touquet.

The Spitfire aircraft Kingaby had flown that day was W3320, which was a presentation aircraft named 'The Darlington Spitfire.' This aircraft had been bought with the £5,082 contributed by the citizens of the town of Darlington in County Durham; during the towns War Weapons Week of National Savings Campaign held in 1940. The aircraft was one of four hundred and fifty ordered on 22nd March 1940, constructed at Vickers-Armstrong. Built initially as Spitfire Mark Is, they were finally completed as Mark VBs. with 20 millimetre cannon and machine guns. The Mark Vs were basically a Spitfire Mark I/II aircraft with the fuselage longerons strengthened to take a more powerful engine. They were powered by the Rolls-Royce Merlin 45 which was combat rated at 1,470 horsepower, giving 440 hp more, than that of the Merlin III, which powered the Spifire Mark I. This gave the aircraft a top speed of 374 mph at 13,000 feet. The service ceiling was 37,000 feet and the maximum range was 470 miles. The aircraft's presentation name was painted below the cockpit on the starboard side. From the factory it was sent to No. 9 Maintenance Unit on 12th June 1941 and one month later it was flown to No.92 Squadron; they were the first RAF Squadron to be given the new Mark VBs.

W3320's first operational flight had been on 20th July 1941, when Don Kingaby flew the Spitfire over the Channel during an early evening sweep. The sortie lasted one and half hours during which the squadron was told to look for enemy shipping, but nothing was sighted.

One week into September, Squadron Leader Jamie Rankin became Wing Commander at Biggin Hill and Flight Lieutenant Milne DFC was promoted to Squadron Leader and made CO of 92 Squadron. The anniversary of the unit's stay at Biggin Hill on 8th September was the excuse for a big rip-roaring party.

On 25th September, 92 Squadron was moved from Biggin Hill to the airfield at Gravesend. The airfield was situated two-miles south of the River Thames on the Kent side and was first opened in June 1932 as a small civil airport. During the Battle of Britain, it had been the satellite airfield for Biggin Hill in 11 Group.

Kingaby was again at the controls of W3320 on 1st October 1941, when the Biggin Hill Wing was ordered on a Channel offensive sweep that morning. Taking off at 11.30 hours, he was flying the position of Blue.1. When nearing Cap Gris Nez, he and his No.2 sighted what they thought to be Messerschmitt 109s, below cloud base at 13,000 feet. They decided to investigate, but were unable to catch them up. Suddenly, they were jumped by four 109s, which dived out of a cloud causing both the Spitfires to pull up into cloud above to avoid the enemy fighters. Kingaby then became detached from his No.2, but waited under the cloud base until he saw four 109s approaching from inland on his port quarter from about half a mile away. He then pulled back up into cloud and turned the aircraft left and came down and found the Messerschmitts diving into a gaggle of Spitfires.

Kingaby sized the moment and attacked one Me109 which showed its underside in plain view at between forty to fifty yards range. Kingaby pressed his firing button and gave a one second burst from his cannon and machine guns, which sent the German down with glycol pouring from both radiators. He then turned his Spitfire and flew inland over France for about ten miles, still hugging cloud base.

He resorted to try the same trick again, when he sighted another formation of eight Me109s coming towards him, this time from the front port quarter. Climbing up through cloud, he turned, dived and came out about fifty yards to the right and one hundred yards behind the German fighters. He chose the last enemy machine and opened fire from quarter astern firing a four second burst. As he did pieces from the aircraft began to fall away and glycol began to stream back. The 109 then dived and broke into separate parts as it went. The tail parted company from the rest of the fuselage and followed it down to earth. Kingaby fired at another of the 109s, this time with only machine guns; but he had to beat a hasty retreat back into cloud, when the remaining Messerschmitts turned to attack. He continued his return back across the Channel staying in cloud and landed back at Gravesend.

92 Squadron was instructed two days later to act as escort for RAF bombers during Circus operation 105. 'Garrick' Squadron took off from Biggin Hill on 3rd October at 1.38 pm, and met up with the bombers over Clacton on the east coast of Essex; they then proceeded to the target at Ostend in

Belgium. Once over the target, they encountered a fair amount of flak from the German ground defences and observed a large fire which was started by the bombing. Kingaby at that time had his own predicament to deal with, when his radio and reflector gun-site both failed due to an electrical problem.

He decided in this situation, the best thing was to head off home, but shortly after leaving the target, he noticed eight enemy 109s behind his own squadron about three hundred yards astern. He decided to try and warn his fellow pilots, but remembered his radio was useless and so decided to turn around into the Messerschmitts. He had not however, bargained for the speed of the 109s, which in a matter of seconds had closed in on one of the Spitfires and shot it down. Kingaby was then immediately confronted with six of the German aircraft and suddenly his cockpit began to fill with glycol fluid. His first thought was that he had been badly hit.

Unable to contact any of the squadron, he tried to draw the rest of the 109s away, while making for the English coast before his Merlin engine seized due to lack of coolant. He put his aircraft into a snaking dive at full throttle as three 109s began firing at him, with another four following him down. His manoeuvre proved successful and he managed to shake off seven of the enemy fighters, except one. The enemy fighter behind managed to overhaul Kingaby's damaged aircraft and he now had a fight on his hands.

Kingaby pulled his aircraft over into a steep left turn as the 109 opened fire with a deflection shot of one hundred and fifty yards. After completing two turns, he began to out turn the German, who did not like it and broke away, pulling up in a half roll as he did.

The German changed his mind, rolled back again and then headed back towards France. Kingaby by this time had got on to the German fighters tail at about one hundred yards range at 1,000 feet. The chase continued at a height of 500 feet, as Kingaby opened fire, giving a two to three second burst. Although his reflector gun-site was out of action, his aircraft had been fitted with a bead site and he was able to get a rough sighting. As the shells hit home on the enemy fighter a big puff of black smoke issued forth and it dived down straight in to the murky waters below.

On landing back at Manston aerodrome, Kingaby pulled himself exhausted from the cockpit of his Spitfire and discovered to his surprise that not one enemy bullet had hit his aircraft. The glycol in his cockpit had come from the windscreen anti-freeze device, which had gone wrong and not fortunately from the main coolant tank. It had been a lucky escape for him considering the circumstances.

One month later on 11th November 1941, saw an unprecedented second bar to the DFM awarded to Don Kingaby, a feat never before or since achieved by any other pilot, and this is now recorded in the Guinness Book of Records. A newspaper citation read: *'This airman leads his section and occasionally the flight with great skill and courage. He has participated in 36 operational sorties, during which he has destroyed 17, probably destroyed 6, and damaged a further 7 enemy aircraft. Flight Sergeant Kingaby has at all times displayed the greatest determination and sound judgement, combined with a high standard of operational efficiency.'* It was, however, the comments written in his log book by commanding officer, Flight Lieutenant J.H. Sanderson, that meant more to him:

'Kingaby has proved himself one of the most brilliant fighter pilots of this war. His keenness to engage the enemy and his courage and resource in action are of the highest order.'

That same month, he was promoted with a commission to the rank of pilot officer on 15th November and was also posted away from operational duties to No. 58 Operational Training Unit at Grangemouth as an instructor to pass on his experience to new pilots.

On the romantic side, Don and Helen soon became attracted to each other and married on a snowy day, on the 7th February 1942 at St. Johns Church in Bromley; at the same time, date and place as Helen's parents had married twenty-four years before. As Don had neglected to book a hotel in London and could not then get reservations, they spent their wedding night at the Bell Inn in Bromley. The next night, however, he made up for it by a night at the Waldorf and they spent the rest of their honeymoon in London, catching every movie they could, including *'Gone with the Wind'*.

In March, he was put back on operations and spent one month with No.111 Squadron based at Debden in Essex. Their commander was Squadron Leader Peter Wickham DFC.

Kingaby's stay was only brief and in April, he was posted to No. 64 Squadron based at RAF Hornchurch. No. 64 was commanded by Squadron Leader Wilfred Duncan-Smith another excellent fighter pilot, who was extremely successful and a good leader of men.

Kingaby's first claim with his new squadron came on 2nd June 1942, when the Hornchurch Wing consisting of No. 64, 122 and 313, was detailed to act as close escort to six Hurricane-bombers on Circus Operation 181 that early morning. They crossed the French coast at Le Crotoy and proceeded up the Somme Estuary and had flown about five miles inland, when a number of Focke-Wulf 190s approached them from head-on. Kingaby opened fire giving a one second burst as one of the German machines approached. He saw a strike on the fuselage of the enemy aircraft and for a few seconds a stream of black smoke came from it. He fired again, but did not see any further hits. On his return to Hornchurch, he claimed the enemy aircraft as damaged.

On 30th July 1942, Kingaby was to record history as being the first pilot to shoot down an enemy aircraft using the new Spitfire Mk.IX. No.64 Squadron at RAF Hornchurcxh had been the first unit to be equipped with the new aircraft, becoming operational only two days earlier on 28th July. The squadron was undertaking a sweep, flying as top cover at 25,000 feet in a Diversionary Wing to St Omer. Ten miles off Dieppe, during the late afternoon, at 6.00 pm they sighted aircraft below. Kingaby's report of the following action records:

I sighted approximately 12 FW190s 2000 feet below us at 12,000 feet just off Boulogne, proceeding towards the French Coast. We dived down on them and I attacked a FW 190 from astern and below, giving a very short burst of about a half second from 300 yards.

I was forced to break away as I was crowded out by other Spitfires. I broke down and right and caught another FW as he commenced to dive away. At 14,000 feet approximately I gave a burst of cannon and machine guns at 400 yards range hitting the enemy aircraft along the fuselage. Pieces fell off and the aircraft continued in a straight dive nearly vertical. I followed the enemy aircraft down to 5,000 feet over Boulogne and saw him hit the deck outside the town of Boulogne and explode and burn up. I returned to base at zero feet.

On his return, he was congratulated by the rest of the squadron, but was also greeted with the news that he was to be posted within twenty-four hours to the Middle East. Fortunately, news came through later that evening that it had been cancelled thankfully.

George Mason who was flying with 64 Squadron remembers the arrival of the new Spitfire MkIXs.

My first flight in the Spitfire IX was on the 12th July, when flying it I reached 40,000 feet, which was fantastic. The squadron then deployed to Martlesham Heath for air to air firing practice and to work up. My first operation on Mk IXs was a rodeo on the 28th July, but we had no action. The first action was on the 30th July. My flight commander, 'Tommy' Thomas and I had to turn back before the engagement because our drop tanks were not working.

Don Kingaby got an FW190 and the squadron accounted for three others destroyed and one damaged. We had experienced quite a lot of trouble with our drop tanks at that time; one pilot actually ditched when his engine failed to pick up after changing from main to drop tanks. The Mk IX made all the difference in the world. For the first time we were on the tactical offensive. Up to then both the Messerschmitt 109 and the FW190 were always above and could choose their moment to attack, but now we could be on top. This joyous freedom was short-lived however, because the United States Army Air Force B17s began operations and being the only squadron that could fly high and fast enough, we were mainly used as close escort and confined to 25,000 feet. However, even then, we could always climb out of trouble if need be. Later when more squadrons got the Mk. IX, we had more freedom of action and the fun began again.

It was a beautiful fine day on 17th August 1942, when the Hornchurch Wing took off to rendezvous and act as close escort with twelve B17 Flying Fortresses on Circus 204 on a bombing raid to Rouen. This was the first bombing operation by the Americans with the RAF fighters as support. Rendezvous was made over Beachy Head with 401 Squadron, 2,000 feet above 611 and 402 Squadrons, and above them all Spitfire MkIXs.

64 Squadron turned right over the target observing all the bombs bursting in the target area. The formation was not attacked by enemy fighters until they were within ten miles of the French coast and from there to about fifteen

miles out into the Channel, things began to heat up, when forty Focke Wulf
190s attacked. Kingaby reported:

> About ten miles from the French coast coming from Rouen, I
> was flying 1,000 feet above the Fortresses, who were at 23,000
> feet. I was on their starboard and on the down sun side, looking
> chiefly into the sun, watching out for a beam attack. Suddenly I
> noticed about twelve FW190s coming down in a beam attack on
> the bombers, to my surprise, from down sun side.
>   I turned to starboard and I attacked an enemy aircraft from
> head on with Blue 2. All the Germans broke away and one went
> up in a stall turn about 1,000 feet over the bombers with white
> smoke or petrol pouring from him. Blue 2 saw him going down
> in a vertical dive, still with stuff pouring from him, but I was
> unable to wait and see him crash.

This aircraft was claimed as damaged. One pilot who recalls Don Kingaby
during this time was George Mason:

> We called him 'Kingo' He was always laughing, always smoking,
> but essentially a sympathetic kindly man, except to the enemy!
> Quick as a flash in the air and a wonderful shot, but he always
> looked after his chaps. I remember him most for his cry of 'climb
> boys, climb' over the R/T whenever the enemy was sighted. His
> flight or squadron always seemed to be about a thousand feet
> above everyone else – except when diving to attack, when he was
> a thousand feet lower. One amusing story I recall was when ace
> pilot Charlton 'Wag' Haw had just been awarded the
> Distinguished Flying Cross and was walking with Kingo. Haw
> suddenly jokingly said 'Well how does it feel to be walking out
> in the company of a chap with a DFC? An immediate roar of
> laughter ensued including Kingaby.

On 19th August 1942, 'Operation Jubilee' was launched against the harbour
town of Dieppe. The raid consisted of landing British and Canadian troops in
a large force of 6,000 men to attack and destroy local defences, power stations
and aerodrome installations near the town. To cover the ground forces during
the attack and withdrawal, air cover was provided by the RAF's fighters and
bombers and some American B17s.

The Hornchurch Wing provided cover that day and flew from early
morning onwards.

At 9.35 am, 64 Squadron took off on their first mission of the day, to escort
twenty-four B17 bombers of the 97th Bombardment Group to their target,
the aerodrome of Abbeville/Drucat. The Fortresses were based at Polebrook
and Grafton Underwood.

The mission was named Circus No. 205 and accompanying 64 Squadron
was 402 from Kenley, No. 411 based at Lympe and 611 Squadron from
Redhill. The operation was succesful and the bulk of the bombs fell on the
German aerodrome. All returned safely.

At 11.50 am, the squadron was sent off again, this time to cover the shipping that was bringing back the troops from Dieppe. On the ground, things were going from bad to worse at Dieppe, with Allied soldiers taking heavy casualties now that the Germans were bringing in more troops into the area to repel the attack. The order to withdraw the British and Canadian troops was given at 11.00 am. As 64 Squadron carried out a sweep over Dieppe, they encountered some Dornier 17s and attacked them, as George Mason recalls:

> 'Kingo' Kingaby spotted some Dorniers about 15,000 feet below. We dived on them, but a voice over the radio warned us they were friendly, so we broke away in disarray, but not before Don Kingaby, who knew a Dornier when he saw one, sent it crashing down. We never did establish whose voice it was, but it was an expensive call.

The squadron carried out its third sortie later that day and during this sweep, their squadron commander Squadron Leader Duncan-Smith was shot down, he baled out and was rescued from the sea by a naval vessel. Kingaby was forced to return early from this flight after suffering engine trouble. The rest of the squadron returned and landed at 4.15 hours. The Hornchurch total for that day was ten destroyed, one probable and fourteen damaged for the loss of three pilots and four aircraft.

Later that month, he was posted as a flight commander to No. 122 'Bombay' Squadron also based at Hornchurch.

On the 20th January 1943, the wing was led by Kingaby flying with 122 Squadron. They climbed from base on course to Calais, but did not exceed 12,000 ft owing to cloud conditions. They swept over St Omer and came out at Gravelines quite without incident. When halfway back across the Channel, Kingaby saw six Focke Wulf 190s in the Calais area, he then turned the squadron to attack. At this, the Germans dived into cloud immediately and were lost sight of. The squadron then returned to base landing at 5.15 pm. 64 squadron took off again and were over Cap Gris Nez, and managed to jump some enemy aircraft. The result of which was they destroyed one Me109 and damaged a further two. Kingaby claimed one of the Messerschmitt 109Fs destroyed his 20th victim and a message of congratulations on the days work was sent from the air officer commanding to the squadron.

Kingaby was to have further success the next day at 3.09 pm on the 21st, in spite of unfavourable cloud conditions Spitfires of 64 Squadron took off again on Rodeo 156. Climbing to Cap Gris Nez above cloud to 25,000 feet they patrolled the area for some 20 minutes the operations room then informed them of German aircraft were up from St Omer and heading north towards them. Five minutes later, Kingaby saw eight FW190s flying in loose pairs at 21,000 ft between two cloud layers he took the squadron above a slight cloud and then, leaving the squadron on top at cover he dived down on the unsuspecting enemy. His report of the engagement states:

> I went down on a FW190 and opened fire at 400 yards astern, with cannon and machine gun fire, closing very fast, until I had

to break away to avoid hitting the enemy aircraft. I saw hits all over the fuselage and then a sheet of flame, but had to break away to stop colliding with him. Flight Lieutenant Haw, Squadron Leader Kain and others saw the enemy machine spinning down in flames I claim this as destroyed.

Approximately three minutes later, Kingaby claimed his second victim over Gravelines at 3.53 pm:

I climbed back up, heading north, and I judged that I was near Gravelines above 10/10ths cloud at 23,000 feet, when I saw one FW190 about 1,000 feet below. I went down fast and delivered an attack from port quarter. I hit the enemy machine in the petrol tank and white smoke poured out and then a second later, black smoke from just above the wing root. I had to break away as I was overshooting, but the German took no evasive action and just went down into cloud before I could get another squirt. I claim this FW 190 as damaged, with the request that the category may be stepped up to a probable, if evidence allows this.

After landing, he submitted his two claims, as one destroyed and one damaged. Another outstanding day.

1943 had been as exciting year for him and Helen. He received the Distinguished Service Order award on 24th February and their son David Hugh was born on 15th March, named after their good friends David Lloyd, who was killed in action during the war, and Hugh Bowen-Morris. Both Helen and baby David attended his DSO investiture at Buckingham Palace on 22nd June1943.

As his tour expired in May, he spent a year on a staff appointment at Fighter Command Headquarters, Bentley Priory. He briefly returned to operations during June 1944, when D-Day was launched and the Allied forces stepped ashore at Normandy on 6th June. At that time, he was attached to 501 Squadron and it was while with them, that he claimed his final aircraft victory of the war, a half share in a Messerschmitt 109, shot down in the Cazelle area. There then followed a posting at the Advanced Gunnery School in Catfoss where he worked under his former Wing Leader 'Sailor' Malan. By the end of the war he had been further decorated with an American DFC and Belgian Croix de Guerre.

His family was not to get off totally scot free during the war, however, and he nearly lost his wife and son on 7th July 1944, when a Doodlebug bomb hit the house next door and demolished everything but the front wall of their house. Helen and David had taken refuge under the shelter table and Helen, pregnant with their second child, remembers looking out in shock at the open fields beyond and staring at amazement at some milk bottles that remained intact.

A few months later, their second son Stephen Michael was born on 21st November 1944, but Kingaby was not allowed leave at this time and in January 1945, he was posted abroad to India for eighteen months. Nor was he granted leave a few months later when Stephen tragically died of crib death on 20th March 1945. Helen, devastated, did not see Don again until 1946, and had to endure alone not only the loss of her baby but the trauma of the stringent inquest that followed. She still grieves to this day that Don never knew his second son.

Following his demobilisation in July 1946, Don rejoined the RAF in November and accepted a posting on the military staff, assigned to Air Chief Marshal Sir Guy Garrod, at the RAF Delegation to the United Nations in New York. In March 1947, he sailed on the S.S. Acquitania to New York, where he worked in an office in the Empire State Building. Helen followed in April, also on the Acquitania, and they settled into a home on Long Island, where their daughter, Patricia "Tish" Katherine was born on 24th September. His posting up the following spring, they sailed home on the SS Mauritania in May — graciously sharing the ship with celebrated movie star, Rita Hayworth!

From February 1949 to April 1952, Kingaby served as officer commanding No. 72 squadron at Odiham and North Weald; during which time he led his Vampire aerobatic team who were the first to roll seven aircraft in line abreast. His team performed for and received commendation from Princess Elizabeth. While at North Weald, Don and Helen's second daughter, Susan Margaret, was born on 15th January 1951, and in 1952, he was awarded the Air Force Cross.

His final years of service were as Wing Commander, 139 Wing, at RAF Celle in Germany and Cologne. His son David followed in his footsteps by attending boarding school at King's School Ely during these years, while Helen and their two daughters lived with him in Germany. On 29th September 1958, he retired from the Royal Air Force under an offer of early retirement due to the bottleneck of men awaiting promotion to senior rank and also due to the decision to disband fighter squadrons. He retained the rank of wing commander

In civilian life, the whole family returned to London, staying with his aunt, Mollie Harding, in Palmers Green until they were able to find a home of their own. They eventually settled into the Grange Park area and he tried a stint running a sub-post office in London, but shortly afterward took a job with the Air Ministry which then became his only employment until his children had completed their schooling. At that time, persuaded by a close friend who was General Manager at Cinerama, he took a job with that company and learned the movie industry.

His success in his new career led to a position as International Prints Manager, managing distribution of movies throughout Europe for the company that handled Universal operations. This job was challenging and exciting and used his full potential and he greatly enjoyed working there until 1983, when it was discovered during a checkup for routine knee surgery that he had two aneurisms in his head which required immediate major surgery. The surgery and those that followed led to his full retirement.

In 1965, the family had suffered more blows when his elder son David died in a car accident on 9th July, aged 22. Within three days, Helen's father Arthur also died, succumbing to emphysema. In 1969, Tish married a United States Air Force sergeant and moved to the United States, and in 1971, his daughter Susan suffered the loss of her prospective fiancée who died while training to be a pilot, and eventually sought solace in different places and faces by moving to the United States to be with her sister. Through no specific life plan, both daughters remained in the States as they started their own families, and in 1985, Don and Helen made the decision to emigrate also, settling in Westfield, Massachusetts, to be closer to their children and grandchildren, Tish's daughter Gillian and Susan's children Jennifer and Keith David.

In the spring of 1990, Don Kingaby was invited by Virginia Bader, cousin to the famed Douglas Bader, to participate in a symposium featuring three British RAF pilots, including Sir Hugh Dundas and Peter Townsend, and three German Luftwaffe pilots. Don and Helen travelled to several American cities where all the pilots were well feted and received gratifying approbation of their achievements from their audiences, and the whole group was immensely pleased to have an afternoon visiting with General Doolittle. As the 50th anniversary of the Battle of Britain and its brilliant plans for celebration drew near, he and his wife looked forward eagerly to travelling home to participate in the ceremonies, but in an ironic step of fate this was not to be.

One month before the anniversary, he suffered a stroke. In late October, he had recovered enough to return home, but in November he suffered a second stroke which left him completely paralyzed and non responsive. Told that he would pass away within a matter of days his family waited and hoped for recovery. Tough and determined to the end, Don Kingaby hung on for seven weeks, finally passing away from pneumonia on New Year's Eve, 1990.

His wife and daughters brought his ashes home to England and a family plot in Bromley, a memorial service was held for him at St George's Memorial Chapel at Biggin Hill on 21st September 1991. Twelve of 'The Few' remaining pilots attended this service, including Johnnie Johnson, Brian Kingcome, Tony Bartley and Paddy Barthropp, and at a reception at the White Hart in Brasted which followed, many sincere toasts were raised in memory of Don Kingaby, a gallant and courageous hero of the Battle of Britain.

His wife Helen still lives in Massachusetts, and shares a home with daughter Susan and her family. Although afflicted with Parkinson's disease, her lifelong spirit and courage – every bit as valiant as her husband's, continues to shine through and is an inspiration to her family. At Hornchurch, where Don Kingaby flew from and scored so many of his victories, a road now bears tribute to one of the greatest fighter aces of the Second World War.

APPENDICES

APPENDIX A

Enemy Aircraft Claims of Frederick Higginson

1940

17th May	Do17	Hurricane I	N2440	SE Douai	56 Sqn
"	He111	"	"	10m E.Cambrai	"
18th May	Me110	"	"	10m S.Vitry	"
29th May	Me109E	"	N2662	N.Dunkirk	"
15th July	Do17	"	N2440	10m E.Harwich-Channel	"
12th Aug	Do17 Damaged	"	"	10m N.Margate	"
16th Aug	Do17	"	P3547	S. Whitstable	"
18th Aug	Do17	"	P3473	W. Burnham on Crouch	"
25th Aug	Me110 Probable	"	V7532	near Colchester	"
26th Aug	Me110	"	"	off Herne Bay	"
31st Aug	Me109E	"	V6625	Colchester-Chelmsford	"
14th Sep	Do17	"	P3702 'W'	Bournemouth	"
27th Sep	Me110 Damaged	"	N2386 'U'	"	"
30th Sep	2 Me110s	"	P3702 'W'	10m S. Portland	"

Total : 12 destroyed, 1 probable, 2 damaged.

APPENDIX B

Enemy Aircraft Claims of Peter Morfill

1940

Date	Aircraft		Type		Location	Sqn
11th May	Me110		Hurricane I		near Tourteron	501 Sqn
					between Aisne & Meuse	"
12th May	He111		"		10m SW St. Hubert	"
29th Jul	2 Ju87s	Damaged	"	P3397	5-10m E.Dover	"
"	Me109E		"	"	"	"
12th Aug	Me110		"		The Downs	"
24th Aug	Me109E	Damaged	"	P3397		"
30th Aug	He111		"	"	Dungeness	"
2nd Sep	Do17	Damaged	"	"	Maidstone-Ashford area	"
11th Sep	1/6 Do17		"	"	Thames Estuary	"
15th Sep	Do17		"	P5193	Ramsgate	"

Total : 6 and 1 shared destroyed, 4 damaged

APPENDIX C

Enemy Aircraft Claims of Frederick Barker & Edward Thorn

1940

28th May	3	Me109Es	Defiant I		10m N. Dunkirk	264 Sqn
29th May	Ju87		"		off Dunkirk	"
"		Me110	"		"	"
"	1/3	He111	"		"	"
"		Ju87	"		"	"
31st May	He111		"		"	"
"	2	He111s Damaged	"		"	"
24th Aug		Ju88	"		Ramsgate	"
26th Aug	2	Do17s	"	L7005	Manston	"
"		Me109E	"	"	"	"

1941

9/10th Apr	He111 (a)	"		Brooklands

Total : 12 and 1 shared destroyed, 2 damaged.

(a) He111 Gi + DN of 5/KG55, crashed in flames at Burbridge, near Godalming.

APPENDIX D

Enemy Aircraft Claims of George Unwin

1940

Date	Claim	Aircraft	Serial	Location	Squadron
27th May	Hs126	Spitfire I	K9856	Dunkirk	19 Sqn
28th May	Me109E	"	K9799	"	"
1st Jun	Me110	"	K9856	NE Dunkirk	"
"	Me110 Unconfirmed	"	"	"	"
"	He111 Unconfirmed	"	K9853	Dunkirk	"
16th Aug	Me110	"	R6776	E.Clacton	"
"	Me110 Probable	"	"	"	"
3rd Sep	Me110	"	"	SW Colchester	"
7th Sep 2	Me109Es	"	P9546	Ramsgate-Thames Estuary	"
11th Sep	He111 Probable	"		Gravesend	"
"	Do17 Damaged	"		"	"
15th Sep	3 Me109Es	"	X4179	London-South East	"
18th Sep	Me110	"	"	E. Kent	"
27th Sep	Me109E	"	X4425	Thames Estuary	"
5th Nov	Me109E	"	P7425	Dover	"
15th Nov	1/6th Me110	"	P7427	Thames Estuary	"
28th Nov	Me109E	"	P7425	20m S.E. Southend	"

Total : 13 and 2 shared destroyed, 2 unconfirmed destroyed, 2 probables, 1 damaged.

APPENDIX E

Enemy Aircraft Claims of William Franklin

1940

22nd May	1/2 Ju88 Damaged	Spitfire I	N3101	off Calais	65 Sqn
24th May	1/2 Hs126	"	N3104	Calais area	"
26th May	Me110	"	N3164	off Calais	"
"	Me109E	"	"	Calais	"
27th May	1/2 Do17	"		N. Dunkirk	"
"	1/2 Ju88	"		Calais area	"
28th May	1/2 Do17	"	N3164	Dunkirk area	"
25th Jun	2 Me109Es	"		N. Abbeville	"
7th Jul	2 Me109Es	"		Dover-Folkestone area	"
8th Jul	Me109E (a)	"		8m off Dover	"
25th Jul	Me109E (b)	"		off Dover	"
26th Jul	Me109E	"		off Folkestone	"
5th Aug	Me109E Damaged	"		10m S. Dover	"
"	Me109E (c)	"		"	"
16th Aug	Me109E	"		Off Deal	"
"	'He113' (d)	"		"	"
"	Do17 Damaged	"		"	"

Total : 13 and 3 shared destroyed, 2 and 1 shared damaged.

(a) Me109 of II JG51,(b) Me109 of 8/JG52;(c) Me109 of JG54, Lt. Reinhard Seiler baled out; (d) Claim against an Me109E.

APPENDIX F

Enemy Aircraft Claims of Donald Kingaby

1940

Date		Claim	Aircraft	Location	Sqn
12th Aug	2	Ju88s Damaged	Spitfire I	Solent-/Portsmouth.	266 Sqn
"		Me110 Damaged	"	"	"
27th Sep		Me109E Damaged	"	Biggin Hill area	92 Sqn
30th Sep		Me109E Damaged	"	Lewes	"
12th Oct		Me109E Probable	"	Rochester area	"
"		Me109E	"	5m SE Rochester	"
15th Oct		Me109E	"	Mid-Channel	"
20th Oct	1/6	Me110	"	E. Tonbridge Wells	"
24th Oct		Do17	"	20m E. Deal	"
25th Oct		Me109E Damaged	"	Channel	"
1st Nov		Me109E	"	Thames Estuary	"
15th Nov		Me109E	"	E. Gravesend	"
"	2	Me109Es	"	Selsey Bill area	"
"		Me109E Probable	"	"	"
1st Dec		Me109E "		15m S.Dungeness	"

1941

Date		Claim	Aircraft		Location	
14th Feb		Me109	Spitfire Vb X4225		Mid-Channel	"
16th May		Me109 Damaged	"	R6882	Dungeness area	"
"		Me109	"	"	5m off Calais	"
23rd Jun		Me109	"	R8532	S.E. Boulogne	"
2nd Jul	2	Me109Fs	"	W3249	off Gravelines	"
3rd Jul		Me109E Probable	"	"	off St. Omer	"
7th Aug		Me109 Probable	"	W3320	St. Omer area	"
"		Me109F Damaged	"	"	"	"
9th Aug		Me109F	"	"	Boulogne	"
"		Me109F Probable	"	"	"	"
1st Oct		Me109F Probable	"	"	Gris Nez area	"
"		Me109F	"	"	"	"
3rd Oct		Me109F	"	"	10m off Ostend	"

Enemy Aircraft Claims of Donald Kingaby (contiuned)

1942

2nd Jun	FW190 Damaged	Spitfire Vb	BM347	Le Crotoy	64 Sqn
30thJul	FW190	Spitfire IX	BR600	5m Boulogne	"
17th Aug	FW190 Damaged	"		10m off Dieppe	"
19th Aug	Do217	"	BR592	10-12m S. of Dieppe	"

1943

20th Jan	Me109F	"	BS405	Guines area	122 Sqn
21st Jan	FW190	"	"	10m S. Calais	"
"	FW190 Damaged	"	"	Gravelines	"
8th Mar	FW190	"	EN473	Cleves-Pont d'Ailly	"

1944

30th Jun	_	Me109	Spitfire Vb	DE-K	Cazelle area	att 501 Sqn

Total : 21 and 2 shared destroyed, 6 probables, 11 damaged.

APPENDIX G

Letter from Squadron Commander Norman Ryder
of No.56 Squadron sending his sympathy to Taffy Higginson's wife,
after he was shot down over France.

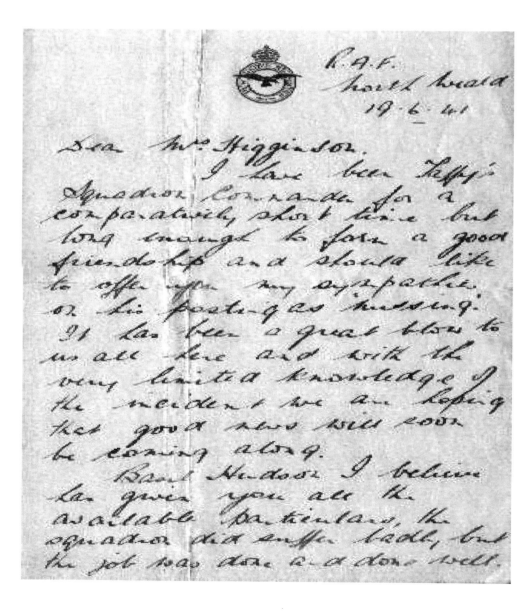

APPENDIX G (continued)

APPENDIX H

Letter from the Air Council to Mrs. Shan Higginson,
informing her that her husband is missing in action.

Dept. Q.J.

P.359762/41/P.4,Casualties.

2/ June, 1941.

Madam,

I am commanded by the Air Council to express to you their great regret on learning that your husband, Acting Flight Lieutenant Frederick William Higginson, D.F.M., Royal Air Force, is missing as the result of air operations on 17th June, 1941.

The only information so far available is that your husband's aircraft is believed to have crashed in Northern France after being damaged by enemy action.

I am to explain that this does not necessarily mean that he is killed or wounded and that if he is a prisoner of war he should be able to communicate with you in due course. Meanwhile enquiries will be made through the International Red Cross Society and as soon as any definite news is received, you will be at once informed.

In the event of any information regarding your husband being received by you from any source it would be appreciated if you would kindly communicate it immediately to the Air Ministry.

The Air Council desire me to convey to you their sincere sympathy with you in your present anxiety.

I am, Madam,

Your obedient Servant,

L.G.S.Reynolds

Mrs. F.W. Higginson,
"Kernicaj",
Bettws,
Ammanford,

APPENDIX I

Letter from the Air Ministry stating that all payment of service
to Taffy Higginson will suspended while he is missing,
and that a temporary allowance is available to his wife.

Stroud 740

TELEPHONE:

Exm. ....

Any communications on the
subject of this letter should
be addressed to :
THE
UNDER SECRETARY
OF STATE
and the following number
quoted :—

A. 227989/41/Accts. 15A.

AIR MINISTRY,

LONDON, W.C2.

STROUD, GLOS.,

27th June, 1941.

Madam,

        I am directed to refer, with
regret, to the casualty report relating
to your husband, Flight Lieutenant
F.W. Higginson, D.F.M., of which you have
been advised, and to state that in
consequence, payment of his Royal Air
Force emoluments has been suspended.

        A temporary allowance is,
however, normally payable to the wife of
an officer who is reported missing, and
if you wish to claim such an allowance,
I am to request that the enclosed form
may be completed and returned to this
Department, in order that such temporary
allowance as may be admissible under the
regulations may be paid to you as soon
as possible.

        I am, Madam,
        Your obedient Servant,

        for Director of Accounts.

F.W. Higginson,
"Wernisa",
Bettws,
Ammanford, Carmarthen.

APPENDIX J

A letter to Shan Higginson informing her of her husband's safety
and well being and a French rail ticket used by 'Taffy' Higginson during
his travels in France while evading capture.

FRIENDS SERVICE COUNCIL

Friends House, Euston Road, London, N.W.1.　　　　*Telephone: Euston 3601*

Temporary Address : c/o OLD JORDANS HOSTEL, Nr BEACONSFIELD, BUCKS.

12th August 1941

Mrs Higginson,
Harptree House,
Balderton,
Newark, Notts.

Dear Friend,

　　　　We have just received the following wire from
our office in Marseilles:-

PLEASE ADVISE HIGGINSON HARPTREE HOUSE BALDERTON NEWARK NOTTS
THAT FRED BASIL BENNETT IS WELL　- QUAKERS

We do not know more than this, so send the message as it stands.

　　　　　　　　　　Yours sincerely,

for FRED J. TRITTON,
Assistant General Secretary.

APPENDIX K

Letter from the Caterpillar Club notifying the Adjutant of 56 Squadron at Matlask of the award to 'Taffy' Higginson of the Caterpillar Brooch.

LESLIE L. IRVIN
F.R.AE.S., F.R.I.S.A.
HONORARY SEC.
EUROPEAN BRANCH

c/o IRVING AIR CHUTE
OF GREAT BRITAIN LTD.
ICKNIELD WAY
LETCHWORTH, HERTS

CATERPILLAR CLUB

September 27, 1943.

Your Ref:
56S/103/1/Org.

The Adjutant,
No. 56 (Punjab) Squadron,
R.A.F. Station,
MATLASKE.
Norfolk.

Dear Sir,

Further to my letter of September 18, we have now received S/Ldr. Higginson's Caterpillar, and I have pleasure in sending it to you herewith.

Shall be glad if you will present it to S/Ldr. Higginson with our compliments and the hope that it brings him Good Luck.

Yours sincerely,

For: Leslie L. Irvin.

MEL.
Encl. Pin.

APPENDIX L

Telegram from Air Ministry to Louise Franklin notifying her that her
husband is missing in action on 12th December 1940.

APPENDIX M

Fighter Command Sergeant Pilots awarded the Distinguished Flying Medal
for their actions against the enemy during 1940

Name	Squadron	Date of award
Geoffrey Allard	85	31st May 1940
George Atkinson	151	7th March 1941
Cyril Babbage	602	25th October 1940
Frederick Barker	264	14th June 1940
John Bentley Beard	249	22nd October 1940
Frederick Berry	1	20th August 1940
Michael Boddington	234	26th November 1940
Leslie Butterfield	213	14th June 1940
Frank Carey	43	21st February 1940
Charles Casbolt	80	December 1940
Horatio Chandler	610	22nd October 1940
John Craig	111	6th September 1940
Arthur Clowes	1	20th August 1940
James Culmer	25	24th December 1940
Alfred Cumbe	141	18th March 1941
William Dymond	111	6th September 1940
Paul Farnes	501	22th October 1940
Ronald Fokes	92	15th November 1940
William Franklin	65	9th July 1940
Josef Frantisek	303	1st October 1940
Basil Friendship	3	31st May 1940
Glyn Griffiths	17	26th November 1940
Laurence Hayden	264	11th February 1941
Herbert Hallowes	43	6th September 1940
Ronald Hamlyn	610	13th September 1940
Alan Harker	234	22nd October 1940
Frederick Higginson	56	30th July 1940
Harold Howes	85	25th October 1940
Jozef Jeka	238	19th February 1941
Bernard Jennings	19	4th April 1941
Frederick King	264	14th June 1940
Donald Kingaby	92	6th December 1940
James Lacey	501	23rd August 1940
Reginald Llewellyn	213	22nd October 1940
Andrew McDowell	602	8th October 1940
Donald McKay	501	7th January 1941
Percy Morfill	501	22nd October 1940

APPENDIX M (continued)

Name	Squadron	Date of award
Gareth Nowell	87	May 1940
James Phillips	54	June 1940
William Rolls	72	8th November 1940
William Skinner	74	21st December 1940
George Smythe	56	30th August 1940
Joseph Soper	1	May 1940
Arthur Steward	17	17th December 1940
Harry Steere	19	25th June 1940
Edward Thorn	264	14th June 1940
George Unwin	19	1st October 1940
Thomas Wallace	111	25th October 1940
Basil Whall	602	24th September 1940
Alfred Whitby	79	28th June 1940
John White	72	24th December 1940
Clifford Whitehead	56	30th August 1940
Eric Wright	605	26th November 1940

BIBLIOGRAPHY

The following books are recommended by the author as essential background reading for those interested in the RAF campaigns of 1940-1945

Aces High, Christopher Shores & Clive Williams, Grub Street, 1994
Battle of Britain Then & Now Mk.V, Winston Ramsey, After the Battle 1980
Fighter Squadrons in the Battle of Britain, Anthony Robinson,
   Arms & Armour 1987
Fighter Squadrons of the RAF, John Rawlings, MacDonald & Co 1969
Hornchurch Scramble, Richard C. Smith, Grub Street, 2000
Hornchurch Offensive, Richard C. Smith, Grub Street, 2001
Hornchurch Eagles, Richard C. Smith, Grub Street, 2002
The Air Battle of Dunkirk, Norman Franks, Grub Street, 2000
Smoke Trails in the sky, Tony Bartley, Kimber 1984
Spitfire into Battle, G/Capt W. Duncan Smith, John Murrey Ltd 1981
Spitfire Squadron, Dilip Sarkar, Air Research Publications, 1990
Greyhounds in the slips, unpublished manuscript by Donald Kingaby

Documents, Station and Squadron Operations Books etc, consulted at the National Archive, Kew, London.

No. 19 Squadron	Operations Book	Air 27/252
	Combat Reports	Air 50/10
No. 56 Squadron	Operations Book	Air 27/528
	Combat Reports	Air 50/22
No. 64 Squadron	Operations Book	Air 27/590
	Combat Reports	Air 50/24
No. 65 Squadron	Operations Book	Air 27/593
	Combat Reports	Air 50/25
No. 92 Squadron	Operations Book	Air 27/743
	Combat Reports	Air 50/40
No. 122 Squadron	Operations Book	Air 27/915
	Combat Reports	Air 50/46
No. 264 Squadron	Operations Book	Air 27/1553
	Combat Reports	Air 50/104
No. 266 Squadron	Operations Book	Air 27/1558
	Combat Reports	Air 50/105
No. 501 Squadron	Operations Book	Air 27/1949
	Combat Reports	Air 50/162
No. 613 Squadron	Operations Book	Air 27/2117

Imperial War Museum Sound Archive, Lambeth, London.

Frederick Higginson interview   No. 15111/5
George Unwin interview   No. 11544/3
Donald Kingaby interview   No. 02276/E

INDEX

PERSONNEL

Aldridge, P/O, 39
Alizera, A. 28
Armitage, D. F/Lt, 109, 110
Ash, F/Lt, 57

Babington, P. S/Ldr, 61
Bader, D. F/O, 65, 66, 74, 77, 81, 130
Bader, V. 130
Bailey, A.E. 89
Baker, B. Sgt, 57
Baker, R.D. Sgt, 10, 11
Ball, A, 3
Ball, E. F/O, 67
Baldwin, J.E.A. AVM, 61
Banham, A. F/Lt, 56, 57
Barker, Frederick Sgt, 47- 60
Barnet, G. 24
Barrett, AVM, 36
Bartley, T. 130
Barthropp, P. 130
Barwell, E. P/O, 49, 53
Bicknell, L. F/Lt, 30, 31
Bowen-Morris, H. Sgt, 111, 115, 128
Brisbane, P/O, 98
Brinsden, F. Sgt, 69, 74
Broadhurst, H. F/Lt, 2, 26, 27, 62
Burgoyne, E. P/O, 80
Burnwell, Sgt, 34

Cakebread, R. 90
Camm, Sidney, 92
Campbell- Colquhoun, F/Lt, 55
Carnaby, W.F. P/O, 57
Carpentier, A. 21
Chamberlain, N. PM, 4, 32, 63, 92
Chapman, V.R. Sgt, 57
Cheminault, J. 115
Clouston, W. F/Lt, 66, 69, 79
Clube, M. S/Ldr, 33
Cole, P, 21, 22
Constable-Maxwell, M. P/O, 10, 17, 18
Coghlan, J.H. F/Lt, 10, 11
Cooke, D. S/Ldr, 95, 97, 98
Cooke, N. F/Lt, 49, 53
Cornwall, Edna, 62

Cox, D. Sgt, 80
Cozens, H. S/Ldr, 63
Cross, K. 'Bing', 2
Cunningham, W. P/O, 74

Daffron, R.C. Sgt, 34
Daisley, L.C.W. Sgt, 51
Davies, Sgt, 33
Dickinson, L.R. 61
Dickinson, M. 61
Dickinson, T. 61
Dixon, F. Sgt, 37
Donaldson, E. S/Ldr, 12
Dowding, Sir H. ACM, 72, 81
Down, P. P/O, 6, 7, 16
Dryden, K.C. P/O, 10
Duckenfield, L.B. P/O, 34, 38
Dundas, H. S/Ldr, 26, 130

Edwards, R. F/Lt, 19, 20
Elliot, J. Sgt, 10, 11
Ellery, C.C. P/O, 57

Ereminsky, L. P/O, 10, 11
Fairbrother, LAC, 53
Fidler, A. LAC, 53
Fisher, F/O, 10
Flash, 64
Folkes, R. Sgt, 113
Fox, P. Sgt, 20
Franklin, 89-106
Franklin, G.H. 89
Franklin H.A. 89
Franklin, W. Sgt, 30
Fulford, Sgt, 83, 84

Galland, A. 57
Garrod, G. A.M, 129
Garrow, I. 23
Garvin, G.D. S/Ldr, 57
Gash, F. Sgt, 59
Gibson, J. F/O, 38, 40
Glaser, D. P/O, 100
Glowacki, Sgt, 39
Goring, Herman, 97
Grace, C. F. H. S/Ldr, 30, 91
Gracie, E. F/Lt, 13, 16

Graham, L.W. P/O, 14
Green, W. Sgt, 38, 39, 46
Griffiths, C. F/Lt, 35

Hackett, K.A. F/O, 85
Hackwood, G. P/O, 58
Haine, L. P/O, 71, 84
Hairs, P. P/O, 35
Hancock, P. P/O, 35
Hardy, S. S/Ldr, 47
Hart, K. P/O, 94, 96
Hatfield, J.E. P/O, 49, 51
Havercroft, R. Sgt, 111, 112, 115
Haw, C. F/Lt, 126, 128
Hawkins, B. F/Lt, 24, 23
Hayes, S. Sgt, 30, 98
Hewitt, D. P/O, 37
Hickman, G.L. P/O, 53
Higdon, Sgt, 24
Higginson, 'Taffy' F, 1-28
Higginson, F, 1
Higginson, P, 4
Hine, M. Sgt, 103, 104
Hitler, Adolf, 5, 31, 63, 65, 92, 93, 97
Hogan, H. S/Ldr, 36, 37, 38, 40, 42
Hope-Boyd, A, 30
Howard-Williams, P. P/O, 73, 74
Horne, F/Lt, 3
Hradil, F. P/O, 83
Hughes, D. F/O, 59
Hulse, C.L. P/O, 34
Hulton-Harrop, P/O, 5, 6
Hunter, P. S/Ldr, 48, 49, 50, 51, 52, 53

Irwin, C.A. Sgt, 68

Jenkins, S, 3, 4
Jennings, B. Sgt, 69, 71, 74, 83
Johnson, C.E. P/O, 57
Johnson J.E. G/Capt, 130
Johnson, LAC, 49, 53
Johnson, W. 113
Jones, A.N. F/Lt, 93
Jones, P/O, 55
Jones, E.J. LAC, 51
Joubert, C. P/O, 13

Kain, S/Ldr, 128
Kay, D. P/O, 51
Kenner, P.L. P/O, 57
Kent, J. P/O, 62
Kesselring, A. 101
Kilner, J. Sgt, 97, 101

King, F. LAC, 49, 50, 51, 54
King George VI, 43, 45, 105
King, P.J.R. S/Ldr, 90
Kingaby, Donald, 107-130
Kingaby, E.L. 107
Kingaby, P.F. 107
Kingaby, David, 128
Kingaby, Patricia, 129
Kingaby, Susan, 129
Kingcome, B. P/O, 93, 111, 114, 130
Knowles, E.V. S/Ldr, 10
Kogel, 93
Kogel, G. 90
Kogel, L. 89, 91
Kogel, S. 89, 91, 92, 103

Lacey, J. Sgt, 34, 37, 38, 41, 43
Lane, B. F/Lt, 68, 70, 71, 74, 76, 83
Launder, A.J. Sgt, 57
Lawrence, T.E. 2
Lawson, V. F/Lt, 78, 83
Leacocks, S/Ldr, 3
Lee, K. P/O, 34, 38
Lee, R.H. F/Lt, 10
Leigh-Mallory, T. AVM, 50, 54, 74, 81, 82
Lippert, A. Cpl, 49, 53
Lloyd, David, 128
Lyons, Sgt, 104
Lyne, M. P/O, 68
Lukaszewicz, K. P/O, 38

Mackenzie, K. W/Cdr, 45
Malan, A.G. 'Sailor' 30
Malfoy, C.E. F/O, 34
Manton, S/Ldr, 18
Marston, K. F/O, 19
Mason, G, F/O, 125, 126, 127
Maxwell, Walter, Sgt, 57
Milne, J. 73, 87
Milne, F/Lt, 120
Mitchell R.J. 32, 92
McCudden, J. Capt, 3
McLeod, A/ P/O, 51
McKay, D. Sgt, 34, 38
McPherson, S, 27
Mounsdon, P/O, 18
Morfill, A, 29
Morfill, E, 29
Morfill, Percy, 'Peter' 29-46, 91
Morfill, Nan, 29
Myrda, Father, 25

Nebarra, Sgt, 24
Nicholas, J. F/O, 95
Nouvean, L, 23, 25
Nouveau, R, 23

O'Connell, A. F/O, 58
O'Leary, P. 23, 24, 25
O'Malley, D.K.C. F/O, 57
Oldfield, T. Sgt, 110
Olive, G. F/Lt, 102

Page, G. P/O, 9, 13
Park, K, AVM, 81, 82
Paterson, J. F/O, 111
Pattison, A.J.S. P/O, 114
Payne, A.D. Sgt, 34
Perez, Horst, 113
Percy, A.C.J, F/O, 34
Petain, Marshal, 24
Petre, J. F/O, 66, 68
Philips, N. Sgt, 30
Pickering, A. Sgt, 41, 42
Pickup, D. F/O. 34
Pinfold, H.M. S/Ldr, 18, 20
Pinkham, P. S/Ldr, 69, 75
Potter, J. Sgt, 70, 74
Price, D. 42
Proudman, G. P/O, 30, 31, 96, 97, 98

Qinnie, Sgt, 49
Queen Elizabeth, Queen Mother, 45

Rankin, J. S/Ldr, 122
Ramsey, B. Vice Admiral, 10, 66
Rasmussen, L.A.W. Sgt, 57
Ray, R. Sgt, 19
Revill, LAC, 51
Robinson, Janet, 45
Robinson, Sgt, 17
Roden, Sgt, 74
Rodocanochi, G. Dr, 23
Rohde, W. Cpl, 35
Rose, T. P/O, 5, 6, 8
Rose-Price, A. P/O, 42

Sartin, Winifred, 29
Sanderson, J.H. F/Lt, 121
Saunders, G. F/O, 30, 32, 94, 96, 97, 103
Sawyer, H. S/Ldr, 98
Sewell, D. 87
Scott, H. P/O, 51
Sinclair, G. F/O, 68, 71
Slatter, L.H. S/Ldr, 61

Smalley, Sgt, 49
Smart, T. P/O, 96
Duncan-Smith, W. S/Ldr, 124, 127
Smythe, G. Sgt, 10, 19
Soden, I. P/O, 6, 7, 8
Sperrle, H. 101
Spreadborough, F/Sgt, 9
Steere, H. Sgt, 62, 66, 71, 78, 84
Stephenson, G. S/Ldr, 67, 68
Stephenson, I. P/O, 57
Stokes, R. P/O, 53
Straight, W, 24
Strang, P/O, 101
Sutton, B. P/O, 6, 8, 13
Sydney, C. Sgt, 111
Sylvester, P/O, 37
Syson, E. P/O, 8

Tew, P. Sgt, 30
Thorn, E. Sgt, 47, 48, 50, 54
Thomas, P/O, 49
Townsend, P. G/Capt, 130
Trenchard, Eva, 25
Trousdale, R. F/O, 110
Tuck, R.S, 30, 31
Turner, R.C. LAC, 49, 54, 57

Unwin, Brian, 61, 64, 86
Unwin, George, 61 - 88
Unwin, G.H, 61

Van de Hove d' Erstenrijck, A. P/O, 42

Wade, T. P/O, 111, 114
Walker, F/O, 96
Watkinson, A.E. 118
Watkinson, H. M, 118
Watkinson, Helen, 118
Watson, P. P/O, 67
Westmacott, I. F/O, 9, 18
Weaver, P. F/O, 9, 17, 18
Welford, J. F/O, 93, 95
Whitfield, Sgt, 34
Whitehead, K. Sgt, 6, 8, 16, 17, 18
Whitehouse, P/O, 49, 51
Whitehouse, A. Sgt, 41
Whitley, P/O, 49, 53, 54, 57
Wickham, P. S/Ldr, 124
Wilkinson R. S/Ldr, 109
Wigg, P/O, 101
Williams, E.S. F/Lt. 34
Williams, W.D. P/O, 20
Wright, A. P/O, 111

Wyatt, E, 1

Young, M. P/O, 49, 50, 53

Zenker, P/O, 39

GENERAL – PLACE NAMES

Abberoda, 89
Abbeville, 11, 21, 85, 97, 126
Acton, 26
Adler Tag (Eagle Day), 13, 101
Air Ministry, 26, 27, 45
Aiene, 34
Angure, 35
Amiens, 11, 12, 27, 66, 85
Andover, 37
Antwerp, 27
Ardennes, 33, 92
Ashford, 15, 42, 80

Banbury, 61
Banyuls-sur-mer, 24
Battlesbridge, 75
Battle of Barking Creek, 5
Battle of Britain, 4, 12, 26, 37, 54, 64, 72, 74, 81, 82, 87, 109, 115, 122, 130
Battle of Britain Fighter Association, 87
Battle of the River Plate, 65
Bazenville, 27
Belgium, 6, 33, 34, 50, 66, 69, 71, 118, 122
Betheniville, 33, 34, 35
Betws, 2
Big Wing, 75, 81
Bishop Wandsworth School, 29
Blackenburg, 6
Blitzkrieg, 33, 35, 66, 93
Bloodhound, 28
Bolton-on-Dearne, 61
Boos, 35
Boulogne, 9, 77, 94, 119, 120, 121, 124, 125
Bournmouth, 18
Bracknell, RAF Staff College, 27
Brentwood, 60, 64
British Expeditionary Force, 10, 35, 36, 66, 93
Bristol, 19, 79
Bristol Aircraft Company, 28
Bromley, 110, 115, 124, 130
Brooklands, 59, 91
Brough, 2
Brussels, 7, 8, 27

Buckingham Palace, 43
Burnham-on-Crouch, 15, 16

Calais, 10, 67, 95, 96, 98, 99, 102, 119, 127
Camberley, Army Staff College, 27
Cambrai, 7
Cambridgeshire, 2, 61
Canet Plage, 25
Canterbury, 15, 77, 80, 82
Cap Gris Nez, 57, 118, 122, 127
Carmathen, 3
Carmanthenshire, 1
Castle Bromwich, 31
Castle Camps, 27
Caterham, 42
Channel Islands, 36
Chatham, 14, 32, 42
Chelmsford, 17, 18
Cherbourg, 12, 36
Chichester, 33, 45
Chilham, 42
Coach & Horses Inn, 29
Colchester, 16, 17, 18
Commercial Road, 89
Cranwell, RAF, 30
Croix de Guerre, 37
Czechoslovakia, 31, 63, 92

Daily Mirror, 6
D-Day, 27, 85, 128
Deal, 40, 68
Dieppe, 11, 124, 126, 127
Dinard, 36
Distinguished Flying Cross, 18, 26, 124
Distinguished Flying Medal, 13, 26, 43, 45, 54, 58, 50, 79, 80, 84, 98, 99, 101, 105, 117, 118, 126
Distinguished Service Order, 8, 86, 128
Doncaster, 61
Dorset, 19
Douai, 7, 27
Dover, 12, 37, 56, 77, 82, 83, 97, 98, 99
Dulcross, 60
Dungeness, 41, 82, 117, 119
Dunkirk, 9, 10, 11, 12, 35, 50, 51, 54, 58, 65, 66, 72, 93

East Grinstead, 14
Eastleigh, 92
Egypt, 60
Eindhoven, 27
Elm Park, 91
Ellesmere Street, 90

Eltham, 40
Empire Air Day, 30, 31, 92
Essex, 3, 5

Faversham, 57
Ferndown Golf Club, 86, 87
Fighter Command, 3, 6, 19, 54, 68, 78
First World War, 3, 47, 73, 80, 108
Fleet Air Arm, 29
Flushing, 6
Folkestone, 37
Foret de Guines, 21, 118
Fort de la Revere, 24
France, 5, 6, 19, 23, 32, 33, 36, 44, 50, 65,
    66

Germany, 4, 31, 32, 33, 65
Glamorgan, 1
Gibralter, 26
Guinea Pig Club, 14
Gorseinon, 1, 2
Gosport, 29
Gowerton School, 1
Graf Spee, 65
Gravelines, 68, 119, 120, 127, 128
Guernsey, 46

Hague, 49
Hamble, 29
Hampshire, 29
Hardalot, 121
Harwich, 12, 74
Hendon Pageant, 39, 62
Hereford, 27
Herne Bay, 17, 56, 57
Hickleton, 61
Holland, 6, 33, 49, 50, 66
Home Defence Exercises, 63
Honorable Artillery Company, 108

Imperial War Museum, 87, 113
Isle of Sheppey, 79
Isle of Wight, 19, 100

Jersey, 36

King's School, Ely, 107

Le Havre, 11
Le Mons, 35, 36
Lille, 21, 22, 117
Limehouse, 88
London, 44, 72, 78, 79, 83

London Gazette, 13, 54, 58, 99, 101
London Irish Rifle Regiment, 14
Luftwaffe, 10
Luton, 17

Maginot Line, 93
Maidstone, 42, 80, 111, 115, 116
Malaya, 86
Margate, 13
Marseilles, 23, 24
Meuse, 34, 35
Middle East, 27
Mile End, 89
Monte Carlo, 25
Montevideo, 65
Munich, 4, 5, 31, 32, 63, 92

NAAFI, 35
Napiers, 26
Newark, 5
Nice, 24, 25
Nieuport, 71
Normandy, 85
Norrant Fontes, 8, 9
North Sea, 5, 6
Nottinghamshire, 5

Opel, 4
Ostend, 6, 9, 122
Oxford

Panzer, 33, 35, 66, 93
Paris, 22
Parnell Aircraft Factory, 19
Pas de Calais, 24, 78
Pembrokeshire, 28
Perpignan, 24, 25
Phoney War, 6, 33, 65
Poland, 32, 64, 93
Portland, 20
Portsmouth, 47, 100, 103
Poplar, 89, 91
Pwllhelli, 47

Ramsgate, 13, 38, 42
Rezayat, 28
Rheims, 33, 34
Roehampton, 34
Rolls Royce, 47, 90
Rosines, 85
Rouen, 11, 85
Royal Air Force, 5, 10, 11, 27, 28, 32, 63
RAFVR, 47, 108

RAF Auxiliary, 86
Royal Artillery, 89
Royal Marine, 29
Ryarsh, 39

St Andre, 27
St. Clare's, 28
St Helier, 36
St. Hippolyre-du-Fort, 24
St. Hubert, 34
St. Omer, 10, 120, 124, 127
St. Malo, 36
St. Martin-le-Beau, 22
Salisbury, 29
Saudi Arabia, 2
Schneider Trophy, 32, 92
Scotland, 60, 102, 108
Scottish Tea House, 25
Sedan, 34, 66
Singapore, 86
Somerset, 1
Somme, 11
Southampton, 36
Southend, 17, 31, 41
Special Operations Executive, 26
Stowmaries, 75
Sudetenland, 31, 92
Swansea, 1, 2

Territorial Army, 89
Toureton, 34
Training Command, 27
Third Reich, 5

Vector Fine Art, 87
Ventnor, 100
Victoria Hospital, 14
Vitry en Artois, 6, 7, 8, 9
Vouziers, 34

Wales, 5, 28, 47, 60
Wath-on-Dearne, 61
West Harpgate, 1
West Kingsdown, 39
Whitstable, 14, 17, 101
Wimbledon, 28
Woolwich, 40

Ypres, 69

Zeebrugge, 6

AIRCRAFT

Taylorcraft Auster, 27
Hawker Audax, 29
Avro 504, 61, 89
Avro Anson, 27, 45
Avro Tutor, 29, 89

Boulton Paul Defiant, 47, 48, 59
Bristol Blenheims, 118, 120
Bristol Bombay, 34
Bristol Brigand, 86
Bristol Bulldog, 29, 62

De-Havilland Mosquito, 60, 85
De-Havilland Tiger Moth, 62, 108
De-Havilland Vampire, 45
Dornier Do17, 7, 8, 13, 34, 38, 43
Dornier Do215, 7
Dragon Rapide, 6

Fiesler Storch, 27
Focke-Wulf 180, 124, 126, 127

Gloster Gauntlet, 2, 30, 62, 91
Gloster Gladiator, 3, 4, 30, 89

Hawker Demon, 47
Hawker Fury, 29
Hawker Hart, 29, 90
North American Harvard, 45
Hawker Hurricane, 4, 10, 26, 32, 92
Hawker Typhoon, 26
Heinkel He111, 7, 10, 11, 60, 71
Henschel He126, 7, 69, 95, 96

Junkers Ju87 'Stuka', 10, 37, 38, 52, 68, 95
Junkers Ju88, 11, 18, 38, 55, 93, 94, 96, 99,
    100, 103, 104, 109, 111

Messerschmitt 109, 8, 11, 18, 21, 32, 67
Messerschmitt 110, 8, 10, 15, 16, 17, 19, 20,
    70
Miles Magister, 26, 40, 48
Miles Master, 45

Supermarine Spitfire, 27, 32, 33, 62, 63, 64,
    79, 108, 109, 110, 111, 113, 114, 116
    125, 127

Vickers Virginia, 2

Westland Helicopters, 28

Westland Lysander, 7
Westland Whirlwind, 102

Zeppelin, 3, 73

RAF AIRFIELDS, CAMPS & HEADQUARTERS

Angle, 60

Bentley Priory HQ, 126
Biggin Hill, 3, 33, 37, 41, 42, 59, 75, 82, 90,
    91, 110, 111, 112, 113, 114, 119, 122
Bircham Newton, 3
Boscombe Down, 3, 18, 19, 20
Bradwell, 26

Charmy Down, 44
Colerne, 44
Coltishall, 65, 74
Croydon, 4, 36, 43

Debden, 124
Digby, 9
Dunsfold, 85
Duxford, 2, 32, 48, 49, 61, 62, 63, 64, 65,
    66, 75, 77, 78, 79, 81, 82, 87, 110, 113

Eastchurch, 55, 109
Exeter, 26

Filton, 44
Fowlmere, 73, 74, 77, 80, 81

Gravesend, 6, 37, 39, 40, 41, 42, 76, 116,
    122

Hatfield, 26
Halton, 1, 2, 26, 29, 30, 47, 90, 91
Hawkinge, 18, 37, 39, 41
Hornchurch, 5, 17, 29, 31, 41, 54, 55, 57,
    62, 66, 69, 70, 76, 91-98, 101, 105
Horsham St. Faith, 49, 65, 66
Hunsden, 26

Kenley, 42, 59, 126
Kirkam, 86
Kirton-in-Lindsey, 54, 57, 97, 102

Lasham, 84, 85
Leaconfield, 85

Luton, 57
Lympe, 126

Matlask, 26
Manston, 6, 10, 11, 12, 15, 38, 50, 51, 53,
    55, 60, 98, 99, 101, 109, 110, 118, 120,
    123
Martlesham Heath, 6, 12, 48, 49, 89
Middle Wallop, 19, 37

Northolt, 26
North Weald, 3, 4, 5, 6, 9, 10, 11, 12, 14, 15,
    16, 17, 20, 62, 75, 77, 82, 118, 129

Odiham, 129

Redhill, 27
Rochford, 12, 14, 15, 17, 57, 100
Ruislip, 61

Sealand, 2
Stanmore, 47
Sutton Bridge, 3, 32, 47

Tangmere, 12, 26, 33, 34, 36, 45, 102, 103
Tengah, 86
Thorney Island, 27, 86
Turnhouse, 102

Uxbridge, 61, 65

Warmwell, 19, 20, 37
Wittering, 108, 110
Worthy Down, 1, 2, 90

Yatesbury, 36

SQUADRONS

No.1, 35
No.7, 2
No.17, 36
No.19, 1, 2, 61, 63, 66, 67, 69, 70, 79, 82,
87, 95
No.32, 33, 41, 60, 90
No.41, 70, 71
No.43, 42
No.56, 3, 5, 6, 10, 15, 19, 20, 26, 27, 51
No.54, 30, 69, 94, 95, 96
No.58, 89
No.64, 90, 124, 125, 126, 127
No.65, 29, 30, 31, 33, 65, 91, 93, 94, 95, 96,

97, 98, 100, 101, 102, 104
No.66, 3, 49, 79, 111, 114, 118
No.72, 111, 129
No.74, 5, 30, 33, 76, 93, 94, 101, 118
No.79, 90
No.83 Group Communications Squadron, 27
No.84, 86, 90
No.92, 67, 110, 111, 114, 115, 116, 117, 118, 119, 121, 122
No.103, 33
No.111, 7, 53, 63, 124
No.114, 118
No.122, 124, 127
No.151, 10, 11, 51
No.152, 20
No.169, 60
No.213, 52
No.222, 65, 66, 70, 71, 74, 102, 115, 116
No.229, 7
No.242, 65, 74, 77
No.249, 18, 20
No.253, 7, 42
No.264, 47
No.266, 108, 109
No.302, 77
No.310, 77, 82
No.313, 124
No.401, 125
No.402, 125, 126
No.411, 126
No.501, 33-44
No.613, 84
No.605, 43
No.607, 7
No.609, 52, 53
No.611, 76, 77, 79, 125, 126
No.616, 26, 69, 70, 71

SECTORS & FLYING TRAINING SCHOOLS

E&RFTS, Woodley, 61
No.3 E&RFTS, 29
No.2 FTS, Cranwell
No.2 FTS, Montrose, 84
No.3 FTS, Hullavington, 44
No.4 FTS, Abu Sueir, 89
No.5 OTU, Aston Down, 108
No.6 FTS, Neveravon, 29
No.11 FTS, Wittering, 61
No.12 AFTU, Grantham, 84
No.16 EFT, Derby, 84
No.58 OTU, Grangemouth, 44, 124
No.60 OTU, High Ercall, 84
No.61 OTU, Heston, 44
Central Flying School, Upavon, 44, 65
Central Flying School, Norton, Rhodesia, 45
Central Flying School, Little Rissington, 45
Central Gunnery School, Catfoss, 85, 128
White Waltham, 32
No.10 Group, 18
No.11 Group, 27, 42, 54, 70, 74, 75, 77, 78, 80, 81, 82, 109, 110, 122
No.12 Group, 50, 54, 74, 75, 78, 86
No.23 Group, 86
No.28 Group, 27
No.63 Group, 45
No.139 Wing, RAF Celle, Germany, 129